ROUTLEDGE LIBRARY EDITIONS:
LIBRARY AND INFORMATION SCIENCE

I0028040

Volume 71

PUBLISHING IN JOURNALS
ON THE FAMILY

PUBLISHING IN JOURNALS ON THE FAMILY

A Survey and Guide for Scholars, Practitioners, and Students

Edited by
ROMA S. HANKS, LINDA MATOCHA AND
MARVIN B. SUSSMAN

Routledge
Taylor & Francis Group

LONDON AND NEW YORK

First published in 1992 by The Haworth Press, Inc.

This edition first published in 2020
by Routledge
2 Park Square, Milton Park, Abingdon, Oxon OX14 4RN

and by Routledge
52 Vanderbilt Avenue, New York, NY 10017

Routledge is an imprint of the Taylor & Francis Group, an informa business

© 1992 The Haworth Press, Inc.

British Library Cataloguing in Publication Data
A catalogue record for this book is available from the British Library

ISBN: 978-0-367-34616-4 (Set)
ISBN: 978-0-429-34352-0 (Set) (ebk)
ISBN: 978-0-367-42684-2 (Volume 71) (hbk)
ISBN: 978-0-367-42685-9 (Volume 71) (pbk)
ISBN: 978-0-367-85443-0 (Volume 71) (ebk)

Publisher's Note
The publisher has gone to great lengths to ensure the quality of this reprint but points out that some imperfections in the original copies may be apparent.

Disclaimer
The publisher has made every effort to trace copyright holders and would welcome correspondence from those they have been unable to trace.

Publishing in Journals on the Family: A Survey and Guide for Scholars, Practitioners, and Students

Roma S. Hanks
Linda Matocha
Marvin B. Sussman
Editors

The Haworth Press, Inc.
New York • London

Publishing in Journals on the Family: A Survey and Guide for Scholars, Practitioners, and Students has also been published as *Marriage & Family Review*, Volume 17, Numbers 3/4 1992.

The Haworth Press, Inc., 10 Alice Street, Binghamton, NY 13904-1580 USA

Library of Congress Cataloging-in-Publication Data

Publishing in journals on the family : a survey and guide for scholars, practitioners, and students / Roma S. Hanks, Linda Matocha, Marvin B. Sussman, editors.
    p. cm.
    "Has also been published as Marriage & family review, volume 17, numbers 3/4, 1992" — T.p. verso.
    Includes bibliographical references.
    ISBN 1-56024-256-6 (acid free paper)
    1. Family — Authorship — Marketing. 2. Marriage — Authorship — Marketing. 3. Family — Periodicals — Directories. 4. Marriage — Periodicals — Directories. I. Hanks, Roma S. II. Matocha, Linda. III. Sussman, Marvin B.
HQ518.P83 1992
016.3068 — dc20
                                                92-11452
                                                  CIP

Publishing in Journals on the Family: A Survey and Guide for Scholars, Practitioners, and Students

CONTENTS

EDITORIAL NOTE

The data on journals reported in this volume were obtained from returns of questionnaires sent in Winter, 1991 to approximately 400 editors representing journals abstracted in the Family Resources Database and supplemented by information obtained from other sources.

Publishing:
In Search of a Home

Marvin B. Sussman
Roma S. Hanks

The major aim of this publication is to increase the possible options of scholars in their search for a home for their scholarly writings. What follows is an up-to-date listing of journals whose editors have indicated the possibilities of publishing articles prepared by marriage and family scholars. Before we present multiple sources of publication, there are a number of issues we would like to discuss. These phenomena, currently being debated in academic circles, include: "publish or perish," peer review, and citation as criteria for career evaluation.

The editors of this guide recognize that the "publish or perish" motif continues to be a strong indicator for career advancement and receiving esteem in academia. While this predominance is somewhat discomforting, given other available criteria to evaluate quality performance such as teaching, participation and presentation at professional meetings, receipt of prizes and awards, we accept its reality and are suggesting that publishing can be fun if one is aware of various possibilities and publication sources.

In addition to publishing from a sense of joy rather than pain, there is the matter of the match—the appropriate fit between the aim and subject matter of a written article with the basic mission of a particular publication. The reality is that the journal editor quests for authors and their products as much as the author yearns to see her or his name in print and

Marvin B. Sussman, Ph.D., is UNIDEL Professor of Human Behavior Emeritus at the College of Human Resources, University of Delaware, and a member of the Core faculty of the Union Graduate School. Roma S. Hanks, Ph.D., is Assistant Professor, Department of Sociology and Anthropology, University of South Alabama, Mobile, AL.

subsequent listing in the World's information computerized networks. The mix of the journal's interest as established by the editors and their boards with the basic interests of authors fits the concept of superordinate goals. Superordinate goals emerged as a concept based on research concerned with group formation, and interaction, and the consequences for the persistence of in- and out-groups in American society. When groups, and in this case individuals as authors and journals as organizations, begin to share a common goal but do not have the means to achieve it by themselves, they tend to work together in an aura of complementarity, thus achieving an objective that both want desperately.

Given the danger of being repetitious, the paradigm just suggested exemplifies the need of a publisher for an author and an author for a publisher, in this instance a quality published journal article. Many examples can be given in other fields where the concept of superordinate goals operates in similar fashion. The largest amount of money given for research proposals is a result of the match between the granting agencies' mission statement and the applicants presentation of interests fitted with the goals of the grantor. In this situation, both need one another and the success of one means the success of the other.

Our position is that there is wisdom in searching for the appropriate match between a journal and the context of one's writing. We recognize that in many professional and academic fields, prestige ratings are accorded to different journals. We do not deny this reality nor recommend that submission to such journals, usually sponsored by the professional association of the discipline, be completely ignored. Even in *Marriage and Family Review* the article one submits should fit the current interests of the editors. It is a well known fact that editors tend to shape a journal in consonance with their basic interests; the areas they would like to see developed and expanded; as well as the emphasis on theory, research, or historical analysis. If one has an article of high quality which fits the journal's image as cast by the editor, then we encourage submission. In our judgement, your article will be among the 85-90% rejected, with few exceptions for impeccable analysis and reporting of research or mind-boggling theoretical breakthroughs unless your subject matter falls within the parameters of the editor's current thinking.

Quantity along with quality of publications is another perceived criterion of excellence and consequential progression in one's career. A recent article in the *Chronicle of Higher Education* reported that the nearly 500,000 full-time faculty members in America produced a million refereed articles, and 300,000 books, chapters, and monographs over a two-year period (Mooney, 1991). Therefore, it behooves the scholar to take advantage of numerous journals which may be interested in publishing one's work. Not only would you fit the model of superordinate goals described previously, but you will be involved in a pattern of reciprocal socialization and nurturance which could lead to improvement of one's own work and the stature of the journal. It is logical that if the articles submitted for consideration and publication are outstanding in quality because of the knowledge being added to the body of information in the field, this very act and resultant publication raises the ratings of the journal. Fine work fitted to the mission of the journal in which it is published benefits the author, the journal, and the profession.

Editors of journals not published by professional organizations, are likely to spend more time and energy with prospective authors because the rates of submission are for less than those journals sponsored by professional organizations and other societies. The journals which are listed in this collection represent a range of publication sponsors and audiences. These journals may use a peer review process or an invitational mechanism which involves working with each author to produce an article on a particular topic.

Robert Fulghem wrote the sequel to *All I Really Need to Know I Learned in Kindergarten* because he had a question to answer: "Why would anyone lie down on a burning bed?" The scientific research community consumes volumes of articles which are generated without benefit of such essential roots of inquiry. How much of what becomes the basis for graduate training and intellectual stimulation flows from more practical motives such as achieving promotion, advancing professionally, or displacing competitors by successfully challenging their theoretical and methodological soundness.

Pessimistically, research publication has been assessed as:

> . . . a tendency for people to want sophisticated statistical analyses. It is as though the statistical tail is wagging the dog and the complexity of the statistical analysis makes more difference than the relevance of the ideas. It's kind of sad. One of the results is that there is a larger proportion of mindless, statistically precise research articles that are best described as trivial pursuit. (Burr, 1991, personal communication)

and the peer review process described as a clear indicator of:

> ... how science is answerable to political power—perhaps even more than to truth. (Jasonoff, 1991:168)

Opponents of peer review support their arguments with data that show bias against the publication of articles which present simple solutions, a trend toward complication rather than clarification of essential research questions (Grassmann et al., 1986). A newly released account of the social processes of peer review in the American scientific community places peer review within its current social context and suggests alternatives with the purpose of increasing creativity while sustaining excellence.

Publishing an article which has been reviewed by peers still remains the hallmark of excellence and academicians whose work is up for review usually have to indicate whether or not their publications were peer reviewed. This process has been made into an injunction as powerful as one of the Ten Commandments. Many scholars have floundered or never found the Olympian heights of creditation and promotion because of insufficient peer reviewed articles on her or his vita. This phenomenon, if it is not insane, is neurotic and is founded on a premise not conducive to creativity and growth in the field or in tune with the reality of the process of professional development.

Most editors do some type of reviewing using knowledgeable peers although they may not call it peer review. So-called peer review often involves sending out an article to a reader known to be either for or against theory and empirical work of the article and receiving comments which enable the editor to accept the article for publication, accept pending revisions, or reject. The point is that a very small number of individuals are involved in peer reviewing—sometimes one or at most two persons including or excluding the editor in that group. Thus, this peer review process is unlike a true review in which 6-9 people might be reviewing, as is the case when a proposal is submitted to the National Science Foundation. The consequences of using such multiple reviewers can provide sound bases for approval or disapproval. Well-founded explanations of rejection and needed revision can only improve the next submission.

There is much to be said positively regarding the importance and status of doing invited articles. The invitation to do an article which fits a proposed thematic issue of a journal or even an invitation to submit an article to a general issue conceivably has equal or greater stature than one which is peer reviewed. The rationale for this statement is that the editor of the journal has already assessed the quality of the work of the invitee and makes the invitation with the expectation that the work will likely be published, although not guaranteed unless the writing is of highest quality. Even in these instances of invitations to publish, the editor arranges for these submissions to be critically evaluated, not primarily with the frame of reference to accept or reject, but to improve the submitted article. Technically, this is not peer review, but is such in actuality. The result is a quality article from a known source where a publication has been carefully reviewed with a resultant improved final version. One example outside the field of journals is the publication of handbooks in different substantive social and behavioral science areas. Here the authors have been selected for their contributions or potential givings to the field. One can be assured that these articles are reviewed by many individuals before they appear in print.

Using citations as a process to evaluate the research of members of academic departments in Great Britain has caused an uproar equal to or greater than the one which accompanied the Boston Tea Party in Boston Harbor in 1772 (Anderson, 1991:638). The outcry is that such counts will be used to assess a department's worthiness to receive block grants for research, monies which are distributed to individual investigators. Critics of the proposal, prepared by Peter Collins for the Royal Society's Science and Policy Studies Unit, indicate how unscientific and potentially negative consequences for good science if the measure is widely adopted. Observing the American experience objectors indicate that individuals seeking to improve their citation count will reference colleagues, associates, friends, teachers, and mentors. Citation cartels and circles found in the United States, not empirically validated, may spread to Britain if citation for assessing individual and departmental research quality is adopted. The opposition posture is best expressed by one British academic with the following exclamation, "Citation analysis . . . is influenced to the point of being both misleading and interestingly absurd." Absurd or not, it is part of the American academic scene and fits the philosophy and model of "publish or perish."

All the above leads to the final notion that publishing need not be a harrowing or conforming experience. If one gets out of the mode of producing the classical paper, rationally well-articulated, and so innovative that it will not be mistaken for old wine in new bottles, then one can write from the heart and publish in a variety of journals, short and pithy articles as well as basic theory and empirical reports. To proceed, one has to do the creative writing and do the match. This is where the present collection, the most up-to-date in the field, will be of great assistance. GO FOR IT!

REFERENCES

Anderson, A., Citations. Peer review and indicators of esteem. *Science* (May 3, 1991). Vol 252, 638.

Burr, W.R. (April, 1991). Personal communication.

Grassmann, W.K., Armstrong, J.S., Ayres, H.F., Barnett, A., & Kolesar, P.J. (1986). Is the fact that the emperor wears no clothes a subject worthy of publication? *Interfaces*, 16(2), 43-46.

Jasanoff, S. (1991). Reviewing peer review: Ideal versus reality. (Book review). *American Scientist*. 79(2), 168.

Mooney, C.J. (May 22, 1991). In 2 years, a million refereed articles, 300,000 books, chapters, monographs. *The Chronicle of Higher Education*, 37(36), A17.

APPENDIX

INFORMATION INCLUDED FOR EACH JOURNAL

JOURNAL TITLE: The correct, current title of the journal.

MANUSCRIPT ADDRESS: The correct address for submitting manuscripts.

TYPE OF ARTICLES: The type of articles (research, review, theoretical, etc.) which the present editor indicates he or she will usually accept for publication.

MAJOR CONTENT AREAS: The broad topics which are of prime interest to the journal, as indicated by the journal's present editor.

TOPICS PREFERRED: A list of topics which the present editor indicates he or she currently prefers to publish,

NUMBER OF MANUSCRIPT COPIES: The number of copies of a manuscript required of the editor for review purposes.

REVIEW PERIOD: The editor's estimate of the average time interval between the time a manuscript is received and the time the author is notified whether it has been accepted or rejected. It must be noted that these are averages, and any given paper may require more or less review time.

PUBLICATION LAG TIME: The editor's estimate of the usual interval between the time an article is accepted for publication and the actual time it is published.

EARLY PUBLICATION OPTION: Whether the journal will publish an article sooner than is normal lag time. There is normally an early publication charge for this service, and the advantages gained fluctuate considerably from year to year. The editor should be contacted if additional and current information on this option is desired.

ACCEPTANCE RATE: The editor's estimate of the approximate percentage of manuscripts accepted for publication.

STYLE REQUIREMENTS: The style requirements followed by the journal.

STYLE SHEET: Whether the editor will send a copy of the journal's complete style requirements to prospective authors.

SUBSCRIPTION ADDRESS: Correct address for ordering subscriptions.

ANNUAL SUBSCRIPTION RATE: Cost of individual and institutional subscriptions. It should be noted that some journals also have special rates for students, association members, etc. Since complete information on special financial arrangements could not be included for each journal, it would be advisable before ordering to check recent issues or to write to the subscription address for complete information on frequency, special supplements, availability of an annual index, etc.

CIRCULATION: The size of the journal's circulation.

FREQUENCY: The number of time per year the journal is published.

ALPHABETICAL
LISTING
OF JOURNALS

GENERAL INFORMATION

JOURNAL TITLE: **ACTIVITIES, ADAPTATION AND AGING**

MANUSCRIPT ADDRESS: **Phyllis M. Foster, Editor**
6549 S. Lincoln St.
Littleton, CO 80121

TYPE OF ARTICLES: **Research; reviews; theoretical; case studies; commentaries; book reviews**
MAJOR CONTENT AREAS: **Activities with geriatric populations and their adaptations; day care programming; retirement living; long term care; senior centers**
TOPICS PREFERRED:

REVIEW PERIOD: **3-5 mo**   EARLY PUB OPTION: **No**
PUBLICATION LAG TIME: **>6 mo**

ACCEPT WITHOUT REVISION: **45%**   REJECTION RATE: **10%**
ACCEPT WITH REVISION: **45%**

THEMATIC ISSUES USED: **Yes**

CIRCULATION

NUMBER: FREQUENCY: **Quarterly**

URRENT RATES (INDIVIDUAL): **$32**
(INSTITUTIONAL): **$75**   (ASSOCIATE/STUDENT):

NNUAL INDEX AVAILABILITY: **No**   COST:
SPECIAL SUPPLEMENTS: COST:
SUBSCRIPTION ADDRESS: **The Haworth Press, Inc.**
10 Alice St.
Binghamton, NY 13904-1580

STYLE/SUBMISSION REQUIREMENTS

STYLE: **APA**   STYLE SHEET: **No**
REVIEW CHARGE: **No**   COST:
NUMBER OF COPIES: **3 + diskette**   PAGE LIMIT: **20**
ESPONSE TO QUERY LETTERS: **Yes**

GENERAL INFORMATION

JOURNAL TITLE: **ADMINISTRATION IN SOCIAL WORK**

MANUSCRIPT ADDRESS: **Dr. Simon Slavin**
City University of New York
Hunter College School of Social Work
129 East 79'th Street
N.Y., NY 10021

TYPE OF ARTICLES: **Research and practice in management of the social services, and related social policy**

MAJOR CONTENT AREAS: **Issues and perspectives on organization and management**

TOPICS PREFERRED:

REVIEW PERIOD: **3-4 mo**　　EARLY PUB OPTION: **Yes**
PUBLICATION LAG TIME: **6-9 mo**

ACCEPT WITHOUT REVISION:　　　　REJECTION RATE: **50%**
ACCEPT WITH REVISION:

THEMATIC ISSUES USED: **Efficiency in social administration**
Leaderships
Effectiveness

CIRCULATION

NUMBER: **2000**　　　　FREQUENCY: **Quarterly**

CURRENT RATES (INDIVIDUAL): **$40**
(INSTITUTIONAL): **$85**　　(ASSOCIATE/STUDENT):

ANNUAL INDEX AVAILABILITY:　　　　COST:
SPECIAL SUPPLEMENTS:　　　　COST:
SUBSCRIPTION ADDRESS: **The Haworth Press, Inc.**
10 Alice St.
Binghamton, NY 13904-1580

STYLE/SUBMISSION REQUIREMENTS

STYLE: **APA**　　　STYLE SHEET:
REVIEW CHARGE:　　　　COST:
NUMBER OF COPIES: **1 + diskette**　　PAGE LIMIT: **15-18**
RESPONSE TO QUERY LETTERS:

GENERAL INFORMATION

JOURNAL TITLE: **ADOLESCENCE**

MANUSCRIPT ADDRESS: **3089-C Clairemont Dr.**
Suite 383
San Diego, CA 92117

TYPE OF ARTICLES: **Research; reviews; theoretical; case studies; commentaries**

MAJOR CONTENT AREAS: **Adolescence; alcohol and drug use; counseling; education; crime and delinquincy; deviant behavior; sex roles; human development; family**

TOPICS PREFERRED: **issues; sexuality; communication; physiological, psychological, psychiatric, sociological, and educational aspects**

REVIEW PERIOD: **<2 mo**   EARLY PUB OPTION: **Yes**
PUBLICATION LAG TIME: **>6 mo**

ACCEPT WITHOUT REVISION: **10%**   REJECTION RATE: **60%**
ACCEPT WITH REVISION: **30%**

THEMATIC ISSUES USED: **No**

CIRCULATION

NUMBER: **3500**   FREQUENCY: **Quarterly**

CURRENT RATES (INDIVIDUAL): **$51**
(INSTITUTIONAL): **$64**   (ASSOCIATE/STUDENT):

ANNUAL INDEX AVAILABILITY: **Yes**   COST: **Free**
SPECIAL SUPPLEMENTS: **No**   COST:
SUBSCRIPTION ADDRESS: **Libra Publishers**
3089-C Clairemont
Suite 383
San Diego, CA 92117

STYLE/SUBMISSION REQUIREMENTS

STYLE: **APA**   STYLE SHEET: **No**
REVIEW CHARGE: **No**   COST:
NUMBER OF COPIES: **3**   PAGE LIMIT: **None**
RESPONSE TO QUERY LETTERS: **Yes**

GENERAL INFORMATION

JOURNAL TITLE: **ADULT RESIDENTIAL CARE JOURNAL**

MANUSCRIPT ADDRESS: **John M. McCoin, Ph.D., Editor
310-B Kiowa St.
Leavenworth, KA 66048**

TYPE OF ARTICLES: **Research; reviews; theoretical; case studies; commentaries; book reviews; anonymous submissions**

MAJOR CONTENT AREAS: **Non-institutional community-based residential care for adults-primarily those with prolonged mental illness, mental retardation**

TOPICS PREFERRED: **Do not accept papers dealing with nursing homes; do accept topics dealing with surrogate family care for adults; incorporating non-relatives**

REVIEW PERIOD: **3-5 mo**   EARLY PUB OPTION: **No**

PUBLICATION LAG TIME: **>6 mo**

ACCEPT WITHOUT REVISION: **0%**   REJECTION RATE: **30%**

ACCEPT WITH REVISION: **70%**

THEMATIC ISSUES USED: **Yes**

CIRCULATION

NUMBER: **136**   FREQUENCY: **Quarterly**

CURRENT RATES (INDIVIDUAL): **$35**

(INSTITUTIONAL): **$90**   (ASSOCIATE/STUDENT): **N/A**

ANNUAL INDEX AVAILABILITY: **Yes**   COST: **$77/100**

SPECIAL SUPPLEMENTS: **No**   COST:

SUBSCRIPTION ADDRESS: **Human Sciences Press, Inc.
233 Spring St.
New York, NY 10013-1578**

STYLE/SUBMISSION REQUIREMENTS

STYLE: **APA**   STYLE SHEET: **Yes**

REVIEW CHARGE: **No**   COST:

NUMBER OF COPIES: **Orig + 2**   PAGE LIMIT: **20**

RESPONSE TO QUERY LETTERS: **Yes**

GENERAL INFORMATION

JOURNAL TITLE: **ALCOHOLISM TREATMENT QUARTERLY**

MANUSCRIPT ADDRESS: **Thomas F. McGovern Ed.D., Editor**
Southwest Institute for Addictive Diseases
Dept of Psychiatry
Texas Tech University Health Sciences Center
P.O. Box 5864
Lubbock, Tx 79417

TYPE OF ARTICLES: **Research; reviews; theoretical; case studies;**
commentaries; book reviews

MAJOR CONTENT AREAS: **Treatment issues in alcoholism; clinical focus**
across interdisciplinary lines

TOPICS PREFERRED: **Wide range of topics drawn from many**
disciplines which address alcohol issues
including family issues

REVIEW PERIOD: **3-5 mo**   EARLY PUB OPTION: **Yes**
PUBLICATION LAG TIME: **>6 mo**

ACCEPT WITHOUT REVISION: **15%**   REJECTION RATE: **20%**
ACCEPT WITH REVISION: **65%**

THEMATIC ISSUES USED: **Yes**

CIRCULATION

NUMBER: FREQUENCY: **Quarterly**

CURRENT RATES (INDIVIDUAL): **$35**
(INSTITUTIONAL): **$75**   (ASSOCIATE/STUDENT):

ANNUAL INDEX AVAILABILITY: **No**   COST:
SPECIAL SUPPLEMENTS: **No**   COST:
SUBSCRIPTION ADDRESS: **The Haworth Press, Inc.**
10 Alice St.
Binghamton, NY 13904-1580

STYLE/SUBMISSION REQUIREMENTS

STYLE: **APA**   STYLE SHEET: **Yes**
REVIEW CHARGE: **No**   COST:
NUMBER OF COPIES: **3 + diskette**   PAGE LIMIT: **15-25**
RESPONSE TO QUERY LETTERS: **Yes**

GENERAL INFORMATION

JOURNAL TITLE: **AMERICAN BEHAVIORAL SCIENTIST**

MANUSCRIPT ADDRESS:

TYPE OF ARTICLES:

MAJOR CONTENT AREAS:

TOPICS PREFERRED:

REVIEW PERIOD: EARLY PUB OPTION:
PUBLICATION LAG TIME:

ACCEPT WITHOUT REVISION: REJECTION RATE:
ACCEPT WITH REVISION:

THEMATIC ISSUES USED:

CIRCULATION

NUMBER: FREQUENCY: **6 X yr**

CURRENT RATES (INDIVIDUAL): **$39**
(INSTITUTIONAL): **$120**   (ASSOCIATE/STUDENT):

ANNUAL INDEX AVAILABILITY: COST:
SPECIAL SUPPLEMENTS: COST:
SUBSCRIPTION ADDRESS: **Sage Publications, Inc.**
2455 Feller Rd.
Newbury Park, CA 91320

STYLE/SUBMISSION REQUIREMENTS

STYLE: STYLE SHEET:
REVIEW CHARGE: COST:
NUMBER OF COPIES: PAGE LIMIT:
RESPONSE TO QUERY LETTERS:

GENERAL INFORMATION

JOURNAL TITLE: **AMERICAN JOURNAL OF COMMUNITY PSYCHOLOGY**

MANUSCRIPT ADDRESS: **Professor Julian Rappaport**
Dept. of Psychology
603 E. Danial Street
Champaign, IL 61820

TYPE OF ARTICLES: **Empirical & research:**
Theoretical papers

MAJOR CONTENT AREAS:
TOPICS PREFERRED: **Underrepresented populations, social policy, innovative programs & methodologies: studies which foster interrelationships between law, ecological, enrivonment & community psychology.**

REVIEW PERIOD: EARLY PUB OPTION:
PUBLICATION LAG TIME:

ACCEPT WITHOUT REVISION: REJECTION RATE:
ACCEPT WITH REVISION:

THEMATIC ISSUES USED:

CIRCULATION

NUMBER: FREQUENCY: **Bimonthly**

CURRENT RATES (INDIVIDUAL): **$60**
(INSTITUTIONAL): **$250**   (ASSOCIATE/STUDENT):

ANNUAL INDEX AVAILABILITY: COST:
SPECIAL SUPPLEMENTS: COST:
SUBSCRIPTION ADDRESS: **Plenum Publishing Corp.**
233 Spring Street
New York, NY 10013

STYLE/SUBMISSION REQUIREMENTS

STYLE: **APA**   STYLE SHEET:
REVIEW CHARGE: COST:
NUMBER OF COPIES: **3**   PAGE LIMIT:
RESPONSE TO QUERY LETTERS:

GENERAL INFORMATION

JOURNAL TITLE: **AMERICAN JOURNAL OF EDUCATION**

MANUSCRIPT ADDRESS: **American Journal of Education**
5835 Kimbark Ave.
Chicago, IL 60637

TYPE OF ARTICLES: **Research reports; theoretical statements;**
philosophical arguments; critical synthesis of an
area of educational inquiry; integrations of
educational scholarship, policy, and practice

MAJOR CONTENT AREAS: **Original inquiry in education; evaluation and**
synthesis of educational scholarship; scholarly
commentary on educational practice

TOPICS PREFERRED: **Any topic which bridges and integrates the**
intellectual, methodological, and substantive
diversity of educational scholarship and
stimulates a vigorous dialogue between
educational scholars and practitioners including
matters of policy and governance

REVIEW PERIOD: EARLY PUB OPTION:
PUBLICATION LAG TIME:
ACCEPT WITHOUT REVISION: REJECTION RATE:
ACCEPT WITH REVISION:
THEMATIC ISSUES USED:

CIRCULATION

NUMBER: FREQUENCY: **4 X yr**

CURRENT RATES (INDIVIDUAL): **$23**
(INSTITUTIONAL): **$41**   (ASSOCIATE/STUDENT): **$19**
ANNUAL INDEX AVAILABILITY: COST:
SPECIAL SUPPLEMENTS: COST:
SUBSCRIPTION ADDRESS: **University of Chicago Press**
5720 S. Woodlawn Ave.
Chicago, IL 60637

STYLE/SUBMISSION REQUIREMENTS

STYLE: **NOT APA**   STYLE SHEET: **Yes**
REVIEW CHARGE: COST:
NUMBER OF COPIES: **4**   PAGE LIMIT:
RESPONSE TO QUERY LETTERS:

GENERAL INFORMATION

JOURNAL TITLE: **AMERICAN JOURNAL FAMILY THERAPY**

MANUSCRIPT ADDRESS: **Dr. Richard Sauber, Editor**
American Journal of Family Therapy
Suite 115, 1050 NW 15th St.
Boca Raton, FL 33432

TYPE OF ARTICLES: **Research; reviews; theoretical; case studies;**
book reviews; commentaries
MAJOR CONTENT AREAS: **Family, marriage, sex**

TOPICS PREFERRED:

REVIEW PERIOD: **<2 mo**   EARLY PUB OPTION: **Yes**
PUBLICATION LAG TIME: **>6 mo**

ACCEPT WITHOUT REVISION: **10%**   REJECTION RATE: **65%**
ACCEPT WITH REVISION: **25%**

THEMATIC ISSUES USED: **Yes**

CIRCULATION

NUMBER: **3100**   FREQUENCY: **Quarterly**

CURRENT RATES (INDIVIDUAL): **$18**
(INSTITUTIONAL): **$36**   (ASSOCIATE/STUDENT):

ANNUAL INDEX AVAILABILITY: **Yes**   COST:
SPECIAL SUPPLEMENTS: COST:
SUBSCRIPTION ADDRESS: **Brunner/Mazel Publishers**
19 Union Square West
New York, NY 10003

STYLE/SUBMISSION REQUIREMENTS

STYLE: **APA**   STYLE SHEET: **No**
REVIEW CHARGE: **No**   COST:
NUMBER OF COPIES: **3**   PAGE LIMIT: **20**
RESPONSE TO QUERY LETTERS: **Yes**

GENERAL INFORMATION

JOURNAL TITLE: **AMERICAN JOURNAL OF PSYCHIATRY**

MANUSCRIPT ADDRESS: **John C. Nemiah, M.D., Editor**

TYPE OF ARTICLES:

MAJOR CONTENT AREAS:

TOPICS PREFERRED:

REVIEW PERIOD: EARLY PUB OPTION:
PUBLICATION LAG TIME:

ACCEPT WITHOUT REVISION: REJECTION RATE:
ACCEPT WITH REVISION:

THEMATIC ISSUES USED:

CIRCULATION

NUMBER: FREQUENCY: **Monthly**

CURRENT RATES (INDIVIDUAL): **$36**
(INSTITUTIONAL):   (ASSOCIATE/STUDENT):

ANNUAL INDEX AVAILABILITY: COST:
SPECIAL SUPPLEMENTS: COST:
SUBSCRIPTION ADDRESS: **APA- Circulation Dept.**
1400 K Street, N.W.
Washington, D.C. 20005

STYLE/SUBMISSION REQUIREMENTS

STYLE: STYLE SHEET:
REVIEW CHARGE: COST:
NUMBER OF COPIES: PAGE LIMIT:
RESPONSE TO QUERY LETTERS:

GENERAL INFORMATION

JOURNAL TITLE: **AMERICAN JOURNAL OF PSYCHOANALYSIS**

MANUSCRIPT ADDRESS: **Mano Rendon, M.D., Editor**
American Journal of Psychoanalysis
329 East 62nd Street
New York, NY 10021

TYPE OF ARTICLES:

MAJOR CONTENT AREAS: **Work in psychoanalysis and related fields**

TOPICS PREFERRED:

REVIEW PERIOD: EARLY PUB OPTION:
PUBLICATION LAG TIME:

ACCEPT WITHOUT REVISION: REJECTION RATE:
ACCEPT WITH REVISION:

THEMATIC ISSUES USED:

CIRCULATION

NUMBER: FREQUENCY:

CURRENT RATES (INDIVIDUAL):
(INSTITUTIONAL):   (ASSOCIATE/STUDENT):

ANNUAL INDEX AVAILABILITY: COST:
SPECIAL SUPPLEMENTS: COST:
SUBSCRIPTION ADDRESS:

STYLE/SUBMISSION REQUIREMENTS

STYLE: **Index Medicus**   STYLE SHEET:
REVIEW CHARGE: COST:
NUMBER OF COPIES: **1 orig; 3 copies**   PAGE LIMIT:
RESPONSE TO QUERY LETTERS:

GENERAL INFORMATION

JOURNAL TITLE: **AMERICAN JOURNAL OF PUBLIC HEALTH**

MANUSCRIPT ADDRESS: **Jane E. Sisk, Ph.D., Editor**
1015 Fifteenth St. NW
Washington, DC 20005

TYPE OF ARTICLES: **Research; reviews; commentaries**

MAJOR CONTENT AREAS: **Public health (45-50 disciplines)**

TOPICS PREFERRED: **Public health (all disciplines)**

REVIEW PERIOD: **3-5 mo**   EARLY PUB OPTION: **No**
PUBLICATION LAG TIME: **6 mo**

ACCEPT WITHOUT REVISION: **0%**   REJECTION RATE: **80%**
ACCEPT WITH REVISION: **20%**

THEMATIC ISSUES USED: **Yes**

CIRCULATION

NUMBER: **35,000**   FREQUENCY: **Monthly**

CURRENT RATES (INDIVIDUAL): **$85**
(INSTITUTIONAL):   (ASSOCIATE/STUDENT):

ANNUAL INDEX AVAILABILITY: **Yes**   COST: **None**
SPECIAL SUPPLEMENTS: **Yes**   COST: **None**
SUBSCRIPTION ADDRESS: **Same as above**

STYLE/SUBMISSION REQUIREMENTS

STYLE: STYLE SHEET: **Yes**
REVIEW CHARGE: **No**   COST:
NUMBER OF COPIES: **5**   PAGE LIMIT: **5000 words**
RESPONSE TO QUERY LETTERS: **Yes**

GENERAL INFORMATION

JOURNAL TITLE: **AMERICAN JOURNAL OF SOCIOLOGY**

MANUSCRIPT ADDRESS: **American Journal of Sociology**
1130 E. 59th St.
Chicago, IL 60637

TYPE OF ARTICLES: **Research; theoretical; case studies; reviews; commentaries; book reviews**
MAJOR CONTENT AREAS: **Sociology in general; theory, methods, and history, as well as perspectives from other social sciences**
TOPICS PREFERRED: **Any**

REVIEW PERIOD: **3-5 mo**   EARLY PUB OPTION: **No**
PUBLICATION LAG TIME: **>6 mo**

ACCEPT WITHOUT REVISION: REJECTION RATE:
ACCEPT WITH REVISION:

THEMATIC ISSUES USED: **Yes**

CIRCULATION

NUMBER: FREQUENCY: **6 X yr**

CURRENT RATES (INDIVIDUAL): **$35**
(INSTITUTIONAL): **$70**   (ASSOCIATE/STUDENT): **$25**

ANNUAL INDEX AVAILABILITY: **No**   COST:
SPECIAL SUPPLEMENTS: **Yes**   COST:
SUBSCRIPTION ADDRESS: **University of Chicago Press**
P.O. Box 37005
Chicago, IL 60637

STYLE/SUBMISSION REQUIREMENTS

STYLE: **Chicago**   STYLE SHEET:
REVIEW CHARGE: **$15**   COST:
NUMBER OF COPIES: **4**   PAGE LIMIT:
RESPONSE TO QUERY LETTERS: **In limited cases**

GENERAL INFORMATION

JOURNAL TITLE: **AMERICAN PSYCHOLOGIST**

MANUSCRIPT ADDRESS: **Raymond D. Fowler
1200 17th St., N.W.
Washington, D.C. 20036**

TYPE OF ARTICLES: **Current issues in psychology
Empirical, practical, theoretical**

MAJOR CONTENT AREAS:

TOPICS PREFERRED:

REVIEW PERIOD: EARLY PUB OPTION:
PUBLICATION LAG TIME:

ACCEPT WITHOUT REVISION: REJECTION RATE:
ACCEPT WITH REVISION:

THEMATIC ISSUES USED:

CIRCULATION

NUMBER: FREQUENCY:

CURRENT RATES (INDIVIDUAL): **$100**
(INSTITUTIONAL): **$200**   (ASSOCIATE/STUDENT):

ANNUAL INDEX AVAILABILITY: COST:
SPECIAL SUPPLEMENTS: COST:
SUBSCRIPTION ADDRESS:

STYLE/SUBMISSION REQUIREMENTS

STYLE: **APA**   STYLE SHEET:
REVIEW CHARGE: COST:
NUMBER OF COPIES: **5**   PAGE LIMIT:
RESPONSE TO QUERY LETTERS:

GENERAL INFORMATION

JOURNAL TITLE: **ANTHROPOLOGICAL QUARTERLY**

MANUSCRIPT ADDRESS: **Editor, Anthropological Quarterly**
Department of Anthropology
Catholic University
Washington, DC 20064

TYPE OF ARTICLES: **Research; reviews; theoretical; case studies; book reviews**

MAJOR CONTENT AREAS: **Social/cultural anthropology**

TOPICS PREFERRED: **Any related to the above**

REVIEW PERIOD: **3-5 mo**   EARLY PUB OPTION: **No**
PUBLICATION LAG TIME: **>6 mo**

ACCEPT WITHOUT REVISION: **0%**   REJECTION RATE: **66%**
ACCEPT WITH REVISION: **33%**

THEMATIC ISSUES USED: **Yes**

CIRCULATION

NUMBER: **900**   FREQUENCY: **Quarterly**

CURRENT RATES (INDIVIDUAL): **$24**
(INSTITUTIONAL): **$30**   (ASSOCIATE/STUDENT):

ANNUAL INDEX AVAILABILITY: **Yes**   COST: **None**
SPECIAL SUPPLEMENTS: **No**   COST:
SUBSCRIPTION ADDRESS: **Business Office, AQ**
Catholic University
620 Michigan Ave., NE
Washington, DC 20064

STYLE/SUBMISSION REQUIREMENTS

STYLE: **Chicago**   STYLE SHEET: **No**
REVIEW CHARGE: **No**   COST:
NUMBER OF COPIES: **3**   PAGE LIMIT: **14-15**
RESPONSE TO QUERY LETTERS: **No**

GENERAL INFORMATION

JOURNAL TITLE: **APPLIED ECONOMICS**

MANUSCRIPT ADDRESS: **Professor M. Peston**
Dept. of Economics
Queen Mary & Westfield College
Mile End Road
London E1 4NS, U.K.

TYPE OF ARTICLES:

MAJOR CONTENT AREAS: **Contributions which make use of the methods of mathematics, statistics & operations research**

TOPICS PREFERRED:

REVIEW PERIOD: EARLY PUB OPTION:
PUBLICATION LAG TIME:

ACCEPT WITHOUT REVISION: REJECTION RATE:
ACCEPT WITH REVISION:

THEMATIC ISSUES USED:

CIRCULATION

NUMBER: FREQUENCY: **Monthly**

CURRENT RATES (INDIVIDUAL):
(INSTITUTIONAL): **$730**   (ASSOCIATE/STUDENT):

ANNUAL INDEX AVAILABILITY: COST:
SPECIAL SUPPLEMENTS: COST:
SUBSCRIPTION ADDRESS: **Periodicals Dept.**
International Thompson
Publishing Services Ltd.
North Way, Andover,
Hampshire SP10 5BE, U.K.

STYLE/SUBMISSION REQUIREMENTS

STYLE: **Harvard**   STYLE SHEET:
REVIEW CHARGE: COST:
NUMBER OF COPIES: **3**   PAGE LIMIT:
RESPONSE TO QUERY LETTERS:

GENERAL INFORMATION

JOURNAL TITLE: **ARCHIVES OF SEXUAL BEHAVIOR**

MANUSCRIPT ADDRESS: **Richard Green, M.D., J.D.**
UCLA Neuropsychiatric Institute
760 Westwood Plaza
Los Angeles, CA 90024-1759

TYPE OF ARTICLES:

MAJOR CONTENT AREAS:

TOPICS PREFERRED:

REVIEW PERIOD: EARLY PUB OPTION:
PUBLICATION LAG TIME:

ACCEPT WITHOUT REVISION: REJECTION RATE:
ACCEPT WITH REVISION:

THEMATIC ISSUES USED:

CIRCULATION

NUMBER: FREQUENCY:

CURRENT RATES (INDIVIDUAL): **$65**
(INSTITUTIONAL): **$275**   (ASSOCIATE/STUDENT):

ANNUAL INDEX AVAILABILITY: COST:
SPECIAL SUPPLEMENTS: COST:
SUBSCRIPTION ADDRESS: **Plenum Publishing Corp.**
233 Spring St.
New York, NY 10013

STYLE/SUBMISSION REQUIREMENTS

STYLE: **Style Manual**   STYLE SHEET:
REVIEW CHARGE: **for bio jornls**   COST:
NUMBER OF COPIES: **4**   PAGE LIMIT:
RESPONSE TO QUERY LETTERS:

GENERAL INFORMATION

JOURNAL TITLE: **AUSTRALIAN JOURNAL OF PUBLIC HEALTH**

MANUSCRIPT ADDRESS: **Department of Public Health A27 University of Sydney NSW 2006 Australia**

TYPE OF ARTICLES: **Research; review; theoretical; commentaries; book reviews; software reviews**
MAJOR CONTENT AREAS: **Public health: epidemiology; demography; health services; health promotion; health-related social issues; environmental hlt**
TOPICS PREFERRED: **As above**

REVIEW PERIOD: **3-5 mo**   EARLY PUB OPTION: **No**
PUBLICATION LAG TIME: **3-5 mo**

ACCEPT WITHOUT REVISION: **10%**   REJECTION RATE: **40%**
ACCEPT WITH REVISION: **50%**

THEMATIC ISSUES USED: **No**

CIRCULATION

NUMBER: **1600**   FREQUENCY: **Quarterly**

CURRENT RATES (INDIVIDUAL): **$A60**
(INSTITUTIONAL): **$A150**   (ASSOCIATE/STUDENT):

ANNUAL INDEX AVAILABILITY: **Yes**   COST: **None**
SPECIAL SUPPLEMENTS: **No**   COST:
SUBSCRIPTION ADDRESS: **Public Health Association of Australia GPO Box 2204 Canberra Act 2601 Australia**

STYLE/SUBMISSION REQUIREMENTS

STYLE: **Vancouver**   STYLE SHEET: **Yes**
REVIEW CHARGE: **No**   COST:
NUMBER OF COPIES: **3**   PAGE LIMIT:
RESPONSE TO QUERY LETTERS: **Yes**

GENERAL INFORMATION

JOURNAL TITLE: **BEHAVIORAL MEDICINE**

MANUSCRIPT ADDRESS: **Heldref Publications**
4000 Albemarle St., NW
Washington, DC 20016

TYPE OF ARTICLES: **Research; case studies; occasional review**
articles; evaluation studies; book reviews
MAJOR CONTENT AREAS: **Interactions of behavior and health; factors such**
as personality type stress, and social support on
physical health
TOPICS PREFERRED: **Stress management; animal studies with clear**
human implications

REVIEW PERIOD: **3-5 mo**   EARLY PUB OPTION: **No**
PUBLICATION LAG TIME: **3-5 mo**

ACCEPT WITHOUT REVISION: **10%**   REJECTION RATE: **75%**
ACCEPT WITH REVISION: **15%**

THEMATIC ISSUES USED: **No**

CIRCULATION

NUMBER: **3000**   FREQUENCY: **Quarterly**

CURRENT RATES (INDIVIDUAL): **$36**
(INSTITUTIONAL): **$65**   (ASSOCIATE/STUDENT):

ANNUAL INDEX AVAILABILITY: **Yes**   COST:
SPECIAL SUPPLEMENTS: **No**   COST:
SUBSCRIPTION ADDRESS: **4000 Albemarle St., NW**
Washington, DC 20016

STYLE/SUBMISSION REQUIREMENTS

STYLE: **AMA**   STYLE SHEET: **No**
REVIEW CHARGE: **No**   COST:
NUMBER OF COPIES: **3**   PAGE LIMIT: **15-25**
RESPONSE TO QUERY LETTERS: **Yes**

GENERAL INFORMATION

JOURNAL TITLE: **BEHAVIOR RESEARCH, METHODS, INSTRUMENTS & COMPUTERS**

MANUSCRIPT ADDRESS: **N. John Castellan Jr.**
Department of Psychology
Bloomington, IN 47405

TYPE OF ARTICLES: **Methods, techniques, instrumentation, and computer applications in research in experimental psychology**

MAJOR CONTENT AREAS:

TOPICS PREFERRED:

REVIEW PERIOD: EARLY PUB OPTION:
PUBLICATION LAG TIME:

ACCEPT WITHOUT REVISION: REJECTION RATE:
ACCEPT WITH REVISION:

THEMATIC ISSUES USED:

CIRCULATION

NUMBER: FREQUENCY: **Bimonthly**

CURRENT RATES (INDIVIDUAL): **$38**
(INSTITUTIONAL): **$85**   (ASSOCIATE/STUDENT):

ANNUAL INDEX AVAILABILITY: COST:
SPECIAL SUPPLEMENTS: COST:
SUBSCRIPTION ADDRESS: **Psychonomic Society, Inc.**
1710 Fairview Road
Austin, TX 78704

STYLE/SUBMISSION REQUIREMENTS

STYLE: **APA**   STYLE SHEET:
REVIEW CHARGE: COST:
NUMBER OF COPIES: **4**   PAGE LIMIT:
RESPONSE TO QUERY LETTERS:

GENERAL INFORMATION

JOURNAL TITLE: **BRITISH JOURNAL OF CLINICAL PSYCHOLOGY**

MANUSCRIPT ADDRESS:

TYPE OF ARTICLES: **Original empirical research; theory; reviews; brief reports**

MAJOR CONTENT AREAS: **Neuropsychology; mental handicap; role of the clinical psychologist; concerns of clinical psychology**

TOPICS PREFERRED: **Description; aetiology; assessment and amelioration of psychological disorders**

REVIEW PERIOD: EARLY PUB OPTION:
PUBLICATION LAG TIME:

ACCEPT WITHOUT REVISION: REJECTION RATE:
ACCEPT WITH REVISION:

THEMATIC ISSUES USED:

CIRCULATION

NUMBER: FREQUENCY: **4 X yr**

CURRENT RATES (INDIVIDUAL):
(INSTITUTIONAL): **$142**   (ASSOCIATE/STUDENT):

ANNUAL INDEX AVAILABILITY: COST:
SPECIAL SUPPLEMENTS: COST:
SUBSCRIPTION ADDRESS: **British Psychological Society
St. Andrews House
48 Princess Road East
Leicister LE1 7DR, U.K.**

STYLE/SUBMISSION REQUIREMENTS

STYLE: **BPS**   STYLE SHEET:
REVIEW CHARGE: COST:
NUMBER OF COPIES: PAGE LIMIT: **5000 words**
RESPONSE TO QUERY LETTERS:

GENERAL INFORMATION

JOURNAL TITLE: **BRITISH JOURNAL OF CRIMINOLOGY**

MANUSCRIPT ADDRESS: **Editor**
British Journal of Criminology
Faculty of Law, Univ of Sheffield
Crookesmoor Bldg.
Conduit Rd.
Sheffield S10 1FL, U.K.

TYPE OF ARTICLES: **Reports on empirical work; reviews; original articles**

MAJOR CONTENT AREAS: **Criminology, very generally construed (criminal justice, sociology of deviance, articles on crime from philosophical, psychological, historical, legal perspectives)**

TOPICS PREFERRED:

REVIEW PERIOD: **17 wk**   EARLY PUB OPTION:
PUBLICATION LAG TIME: **5 mo**

ACCEPT WITHOUT REVISION: REJECTION RATE:
ACCEPT WITH REVISION:

THEMATIC ISSUES USED:

CIRCULATION

NUMBER: **2000**   FREQUENCY: **4 X yr**

CURRENT RATES (INDIVIDUAL): **$53**
(INSTITUTIONAL): **$84**   (ASSOCIATE/STUDENT):

ANNUAL INDEX AVAILABILITY: COST:
SPECIAL SUPPLEMENTS: COST:
SUBSCRIPTION ADDRESS: **Oxford University Press**
Pinkhill House, Southfield Road
Eynsham, Oxford OX81JJ, U.K.

STYLE/SUBMISSION REQUIREMENTS

STYLE: **Harvard**   STYLE SHEET: **Yes**
REVIEW CHARGE: COST:
NUMBER OF COPIES: **3**   PAGE LIMIT:
RESPONSE TO QUERY LETTERS:

GENERAL INFORMATION

JOURNAL TITLE: **BRITISH JOURNAL OF PSYCHIATRY**

MANUSCRIPT ADDRESS: **17 Belgrave Square**
London SWIX 8PG, U.K.

TYPE OF ARTICLES: **Research; reviews; theoretical; case studies**

MAJOR CONTENT AREAS: **Psychiatry; mental health; clinical psychology**

TOPICS PREFERRED: **Studies with clinical relevance**

REVIEW PERIOD: **3-5 mo**   EARLY PUB OPTION: **No**
PUBLICATION LAG TIME: **>6 mo**

ACCEPT WITHOUT REVISION: **5%**   REJECTION RATE: **70%**
ACCEPT WITH REVISION: **20%**

THEMATIC ISSUES USED: **Yes**

CIRCULATION

NUMBER: **12,900**   FREQUENCY: **Monthly**

CURRENT RATES (INDIVIDUAL): **$162**
(INSTITUTIONAL): **$265**   (ASSOCIATE/STUDENT):

ANNUAL INDEX AVAILABILITY: **Yes**   COST: **Free**
SPECIAL SUPPLEMENTS: **Yes**   COST: **Free**
SUBSCRIPTION ADDRESS: **Subs Dept.**
The Royal Society of Medicine
1 Wimpole St.
London WIM 8AE, U.K.

STYLE/SUBMISSION REQUIREMENTS

STYLE: **Specific**   STYLE SHEET: **No**
REVIEW CHARGE: **No**   COST:
NUMBER OF COPIES: **3**   PAGE LIMIT: **None**
RESPONSE TO QUERY LETTERS:

GENERAL INFORMATION

JOURNAL TITLE: **BRITISH JOURNAL OF SOCIAL PSYCHOLOGY**

MANUSCRIPT ADDRESS: **The British Journal of Social Psychology
13A Church Lane
E. Finchley
London N2 8DX, U.K.**

TYPE OF ARTICLES: **Research; reviews; theoretical; case studies; commentaries; book reviews upon request**

MAJOR CONTENT AREAS: **Attitudes and attitude change; person perception and social cognition; social interactions; ingroup relations**

TOPICS PREFERRED:

REVIEW PERIOD: **3–5 mo**   EARLY PUB OPTION: **No**
PUBLICATION LAG TIME: **>6 mo**

ACCEPT WITHOUT REVISION: **0%**   REJECTION RATE: **70%**
ACCEPT WITH REVISION: **30%**

THEMATIC ISSUES USED: **Yes**

CIRCULATION

NUMBER: FREQUENCY: **Quarterly**

CURRENT RATES (INDIVIDUAL):
(INSTITUTIONAL): **$142**   (ASSOCIATE/STUDENT):

ANNUAL INDEX AVAILABILITY: COST:
SPECIAL SUPPLEMENTS: **No**   COST:
SUBSCRIPTION ADDRESS: **As above**

STYLE/SUBMISSION REQUIREMENTS

STYLE: **APA/BPSS**   STYLE SHEET: **No**
REVIEW CHARGE: **No**   COST:
NUMBER OF COPIES: **4**   PAGE LIMIT: **<5000 words**
RESPONSE TO QUERY LETTERS: **Yes**

GENERAL INFORMATION

JOURNAL TITLE: **BRITISH JOURNAL OF SOCIOLOGY**

MANUSCRIPT ADDRESS: **Editor**
The British Journal of Sociology
London School of Economics and Political
Science
Houghton Street
Aldwych
London WC2A 2AE, U.K.

TYPE OF ARTICLES:

MAJOR CONTENT AREAS:

TOPICS PREFERRED:

REVIEW PERIOD: EARLY PUB OPTION:
PUBLICATION LAG TIME:

ACCEPT WITHOUT REVISION: REJECTION RATE: **75%**
ACCEPT WITH REVISION:

THEMATIC ISSUES USED: **Occasionally**

CIRCULATION

NUMBER: FREQUENCY: **Quarterly**

CURRENT RATES (INDIVIDUAL):
(INSTITUTIONAL):   (ASSOCIATE/STUDENT):

ANNUAL INDEX AVAILABILITY: COST:
SPECIAL SUPPLEMENTS: COST:
SUBSCRIPTION ADDRESS: **See above**

STYLE/SUBMISSION REQUIREMENTS

STYLE: **JS**   STYLE SHEET: **In each issue**
REVIEW CHARGE: COST:
NUMBER OF COPIES: **3**   PAGE LIMIT: **7500 words**
RESPONSE TO QUERY LETTERS: **Immediate**

GENERAL INFORMATION

JOURNAL TITLE: **CANADIAN JOURNAL OF PSYCHOLOGY**

MANUSCRIPT ADDRESS: **Dr. Gordon Winocur, Editor**
Dept. of Psychology
Trent University
Peterborough, ON K9J 7B8, Canada

TYPE OF ARTICLES: **a) Substantial papers on integrated series of studies that reflect a major research program, b) Theoretical reviews, c) Short articles on single experiements.**

MAJOR CONTENT AREAS: General experimental psychology

TOPICS PREFERRED:

REVIEW PERIOD: EARLY PUB OPTION:
PUBLICATION LAG TIME:

ACCEPT WITHOUT REVISION: REJECTION RATE:
ACCEPT WITH REVISION:

THEMATIC ISSUES USED:

CIRCULATION

NUMBER: FREQUENCY: **Quarterly**

CURRENT RATES (INDIVIDUAL):
(INSTITUTIONAL): **$70**   (ASSOCIATE/STUDENT):

ANNUAL INDEX AVAILABILITY: COST:
SPECIAL SUPPLEMENTS: COST:
SUBSCRIPTION ADDRESS: **Canadian Psychological Assoc.**
Vincent Road
Old Chelsea, Quebec JOX 2NO,
Canada

STYLE/SUBMISSION REQUIREMENTS

STYLE: **APA**   STYLE SHEET:
REVIEW CHARGE: COST:
NUMBER OF COPIES: **4**   PAGE LIMIT: **2500 words for short articles**

RESPONSE TO QUERY LETTERS:

GENERAL INFORMATION

JOURNAL TITLE: **CANADIAN JOURNAL OF PUBLIC HEALTH**

MANUSCRIPT ADDRESS: **Editor**
1565 Carling Ave., Suite 400
Ottawa, Canada K128R1

TYPE OF ARTICLES:

MAJOR CONTENT AREAS: **All aspects of public health & preventative**
medicine

TOPICS PREFERRED:

REVIEW PERIOD: EARLY PUB OPTION:
PUBLICATION LAG TIME:

ACCEPT WITHOUT REVISION: REJECTION RATE:
ACCEPT WITH REVISION:

THEMATIC ISSUES USED: **Yes**

CIRCULATION

NUMBER: FREQUENCY: **6 X yr**

CURRENT RATES (INDIVIDUAL):
(INSTITUTIONAL): **$60**   (ASSOCIATE/STUDENT): **Free**

ANNUAL INDEX AVAILABILITY: COST:
SPECIAL SUPPLEMENTS: COST:
SUBSCRIPTION ADDRESS: **M.O.M. Printing**
300 Parkdale Ave.
Ottawa, Ontario K1Y 1G2,
Canada

STYLE/SUBMISSION REQUIREMENTS

STYLE: STYLE SHEET:
REVIEW CHARGE: COST:
NUMBER OF COPIES: **3**   PAGE LIMIT:
RESPONSE TO QUERY LETTERS:

GENERAL INFORMATION

JOURNAL TITLE: **CHILD ABUSE & NEGLECT**

MANUSCRIPT ADDRESS: **Richard D. Krugman, M.D.**
Editor-in-Chief
Child Abuse and Neglect
Kempe National Center
1205 Oneida St.
Denver, CO 80220

TYPE OF ARTICLES: **Original; theoretical; empirical contributions;**
brief communications; case commentary; review
articles; letters to the editor; announcements or
notices.

MAJOR CONTENT AREAS: **All aspects of child abuse and neglect with**
special emphasis on prevention and treatment;
family interaction

TOPICS PREFERRED:

REVIEW PERIOD: EARLY PUB OPTION:
PUBLICATION LAG TIME:

ACCEPT WITHOUT REVISION: REJECTION RATE:
ACCEPT WITH REVISION:

THEMATIC ISSUES USED:

CIRCULATION

NUMBER: FREQUENCY: **Quarterly**

CURRENT RATES (INDIVIDUAL): **$63**
(INSTITUTIONAL): **$260**   (ASSOCIATE/STUDENT):

ANNUAL INDEX AVAILABILITY: COST:
SPECIAL SUPPLEMENTS: COST:
SUBSCRIPTION ADDRESS: **Pergamon Press, Inc.**
Fairview Park
Elmsford, NY 10523

STYLE/SUBMISSION REQUIREMENTS

STYLE: **APA**   STYLE SHEET:
REVIEW CHARGE: COST:
NUMBER OF COPIES: **4**   PAGE LIMIT:
RESPONSE TO QUERY LETTERS:

GENERAL INFORMATION

JOURNAL TITLE: **CHILD AND ADOLESCENT SOCIAL WORK JOURNAL**

MANUSCRIPT ADDRESS: **Dr. Florence Lieberman, Editor**
315 Wyndcliff Rd.
Scarsdale, NY 10583

TYPE OF ARTICLES: **Research; theoretical; case studies; policy issues**

MAJOR CONTENT AREAS: **Anything of importance to the welfare of children, adolescents, and their families**

TOPICS PREFERRED: **Clinical practice**

REVIEW PERIOD: **3-5 mo**   EARLY PUB OPTION: **No**
PUBLICATION LAG TIME: **>6 mo**

ACCEPT WITHOUT REVISION: **30%**   REJECTION RATE: **40%**
ACCEPT WITH REVISION: **30%**

THEMATIC ISSUES USED: **Yes**

CIRCULATION

NUMBER: FREQUENCY:

CURRENT RATES (INDIVIDUAL):
(INSTITUTIONAL):   (ASSOCIATE/STUDENT):

ANNUAL INDEX AVAILABILITY: COST:
SPECIAL SUPPLEMENTS: COST:
SUBSCRIPTION ADDRESS:

STYLE/SUBMISSION REQUIREMENTS

STYLE: STYLE SHEET:
REVIEW CHARGE: COST:
NUMBER OF COPIES: PAGE LIMIT:
RESPONSE TO QUERY LETTERS:

GENERAL INFORMATION

JOURNAL TITLE: **CHILD DEVELOPMENT**

MANUSCRIPT ADDRESS: **Susan C. Somerville, Editor**
Child Development
Dept of Psychology
Arizona State University
Tempe, AZ 85287-1104

TYPE OF ARTICLES: **Empirical research; theoretical articles; reviews**

MAJOR CONTENT AREAS: **Multiple studies; multiple methods; multiple**
settings; policy; practical; interdisciplinary
implications

TOPICS PREFERRED:

REVIEW PERIOD: **3 mo**   EARLY PUB OPTION:
PUBLICATION LAG TIME: **< 1 yr**

ACCEPT WITHOUT REVISION: REJECTION RATE:
ACCEPT WITH REVISION:

THEMATIC ISSUES USED:

CIRCULATION

NUMBER: FREQUENCY: **6 X yr.**

CURRENT RATES (INDIVIDUAL): **$115**
(INSTITUTIONAL):   (ASSOCIATE/STUDENT):

ANNUAL INDEX AVAILABILITY: COST:
SPECIAL SUPPLEMENTS: COST:
SUBSCRIPTION ADDRESS: **University of Chicago Press**
5720 S. Woodlawn Ave.
Chicago, IL 60637

STYLE/SUBMISSION REQUIREMENTS

STYLE: **APA**   STYLE SHEET:
REVIEW CHARGE: **None**   COST:
NUMBER OF COPIES: **4**   PAGE LIMIT: **15-25**
RESPONSE TO QUERY LETTERS:

GENERAL INFORMATION

JOURNAL TITLE: **CHILD AND FAMILY BEHAVIOR THERAPY**

MANUSCRIPT ADDRESS: **Cyril M. Franks, Ph.D., Editor**
Graduate School of Applied &
Professional Psychology
Rutgers University
Busch Campus
P.O. Box 819
Piscataway, NJ 08854

TYPE OF ARTICLES: **Research; reviews; theoretical; case studies;**
commentaries; book reviews
MAJOR CONTENT AREAS: **Behavior therapy (broadly interpreted) as it**
relates to young people, families, couples

TOPICS PREFERRED:

REVIEW PERIOD: **<2 mo**   EARLY PUB OPTION: **No**
PUBLICATION LAG TIME: **>6 mo**

ACCEPT WITHOUT REVISION: **5%**   REJECTION RATE: **65%**
ACCEPT WITH REVISION: **30%**

THEMATIC ISSUES USED: **No**

CIRCULATION

NUMBER: **2000**   FREQUENCY: **Quarterly**

CURRENT RATES (INDIVIDUAL): **$45**
(INSTITUTIONAL): **$95**   (ASSOCIATE/STUDENT):

ANNUAL INDEX AVAILABILITY: **Yes**   COST: **None**
SPECIAL SUPPLEMENTS: **No**   COST:
SUBSCRIPTION ADDRESS: **The Haworth Press, Inc.**
10 Alice St.
Binghamton, NY 13904-1580

STYLE/SUBMISSION REQUIREMENTS

STYLE: **APA**   STYLE SHEET: **Yes**
REVIEW CHARGE: **No**   COST:
NUMBER OF COPIES: **2 + diskette**   PAGE LIMIT: **20**
RESPONSE TO QUERY LETTERS: **Yes**

GENERAL INFORMATION

JOURNAL TITLE: **CHILD PSYCHIATRY & HUMAN DEVELOPMEN**

MANUSCRIPT ADDRESS: **Jack C. Westman, M.D., Editor**
600 Highland Ave.
Madison, WI 53791

TYPE OF ARTICLES: **Clinical, research, and review articles in child**
psychiatry and human development

MAJOR CONTENT AREAS: **Treatment; diagnosis; etiology**

TOPICS PREFERRED:

REVIEW PERIOD: **3-6 wk**   EARLY PUB OPTION: **No**
PUBLICATION LAG TIME: **9-12 mo**

ACCEPT WITHOUT REVISION: **No**   REJECTION RATE: **40%**
ACCEPT WITH REVISION:
THEMATIC ISSUES USED:

CIRCULATION

NUMBER: **900**   FREQUENCY: **Quarterly**

CURRENT RATES (INDIVIDUAL): **$39**
(INSTITUTIONAL): **$94**   (ASSOCIATE/STUDENT):

ANNUAL INDEX AVAILABILITY: **Yes**   COST:
SPECIAL SUPPLEMENTS: **No**   COST:
SUBSCRIPTION ADDRESS: **Human Sciences Press**
233 Spring St.
New York, NY 10013-1378

STYLE/SUBMISSION REQUIREMENTS

STYLE: **Index Medicus**   STYLE SHEET: **Yes**
REVIEW CHARGE: COST:
NUMBER OF COPIES: **2**   PAGE LIMIT: **16**
RESPONSE TO QUERY LETTERS:

GENERAL INFORMATION

JOURNAL TITLE: **CHILD STUDY JOURNAL**

MANUSCRIPT ADDRESS: **Child Study Journal**
Bacon 306
Buffalo State College
1300 Elmwood Ave.
Buffalo, NY 14222

TYPE OF ARTICLES: **Research; theoretical; book reviews**

MAJOR CONTENT AREAS: **Theory and research on child and adolescent**
development

TOPICS PREFERRED: **Those devoted to educational and psychological**
aspects of human development

REVIEW PERIOD: **3-5 mo**   EARLY PUB OPTION: **No**
PUBLICATION LAG TIME: **>6 mo**

ACCEPT WITHOUT REVISION: **20%**   REJECTION RATE:
ACCEPT WITH REVISION:

THEMATIC ISSUES USED:

CIRCULATION

NUMBER: FREQUENCY: **Quarterly**

CURRENT RATES (INDIVIDUAL): **$6**
(INSTITUTIONAL): **$32**   (ASSOCIATE/STUDENT): **$16**

ANNUAL INDEX AVAILABILITY: COST:
SPECIAL SUPPLEMENTS: COST:
SUBSCRIPTION ADDRESS:

STYLE/SUBMISSION REQUIREMENTS

STYLE: **APA**   STYLE SHEET: **No**
REVIEW CHARGE: **No**   COST:
NUMBER OF COPIES: **2**   PAGE LIMIT:
RESPONSE TO QUERY LETTERS: **Yes**

GENERAL INFORMATION

JOURNAL TITLE: **CHILD WELFARE**

MANUSCRIPT ADDRESS: **Child Welfare Legue of America, Inc.**
440 First Street, N.W., Suite 310
Washington, DC 20001

TYPE OF ARTICLES: **Policy; practice; program articles; theoretical; research; case studies; book reviews; book briefs**

MAJOR CONTENT AREAS: **Needs and goals of personnel associated with the field of child welfare**

TOPICS PREFERRED: **Health, education, and psychosocial needs of children**

REVIEW PERIOD: **3-5 mo** EARLY PUB OPTION: **Yes**
PUBLICATION LAG TIME: **>6 mo**

ACCEPT WITHOUT REVISION: **Few** REJECTION RATE: **80%**
ACCEPT WITH REVISION:

THEMATIC ISSUES USED: **Yes**

CIRCULATION

NUMBER: **8000** FREQUENCY: **Bimonthly**

CURRENT RATES (INDIVIDUAL):
(INSTITUTIONAL): (ASSOCIATE/STUDENT):

ANNUAL INDEX AVAILABILITY: COST:
SPECIAL SUPPLEMENTS: COST:
SUBSCRIPTION ADDRESS:

STYLE/SUBMISSION REQUIREMENTS

STYLE: **Chicago** STYLE SHEET: **Yes**
REVIEW CHARGE: COST:
NUMBER OF COPIES: **4** PAGE LIMIT: **12-16**
RESPONSE TO QUERY LETTERS:

GENERAL INFORMATION

JOURNAL TITLE: **CHILD AND YOUTH SERVICES**

MANUSCRIPT ADDRESS: **Jerome Beker, Editor**
Director
Center for Youth Development & Research
University of Minnesota
386 Mc Neal Hall
1985 Buford Avenue
St. Paul, MN 55108

TYPE OF ARTICLES: **Full length articles, current research & policy notes, book reviews**

MAJOR CONTENT AREAS: **Interdisciplinary forum for critical scholarship regarding service programs for children & youth**

TOPICS PREFERRED:

REVIEW PERIOD: EARLY PUB OPTION:
PUBLICATION LAG TIME:

ACCEPT WITHOUT REVISION: REJECTION RATE:
ACCEPT WITH REVISION:

THEMATIC ISSUES USED: **Yes**

CIRCULATION

NUMBER: **221**   FREQUENCY: **Biannual**

CURRENT RATES (INDIVIDUAL): **$40**
(INSTITUTIONAL): **$85**   (ASSOCIATE/STUDENT):

ANNUAL INDEX AVAILABILITY: **No**   COST:
SPECIAL SUPPLEMENTS: COST:
SUBSCRIPTION ADDRESS: **The Haworth Press, Inc.**
10 Alice Street
Binghamton, NY 13904-1580

STYLE/SUBMISSION REQUIREMENTS

STYLE: **APA**   STYLE SHEET:
REVIEW CHARGE: **No**   COST:
NUMBER OF COPIES: **5 + diskette**   PAGE LIMIT: **20**
RESPONSE TO QUERY LETTERS:

GENERAL INFORMATION

JOURNAL TITLE: **CHILDREN AND YOUTH SCIENCES REVIEW**

MANUSCRIPT ADDRESS: **Duncan Lindsey**
Children and Youth Services Review
College of Human Dev. & Performance
University of Oregon
Eugene, OR 97403

TYPE OF ARTICLES: **Articles; research; policy notes; book reviews**

MAJOR CONTENT AREAS: **Service programs for children and youth**

TOPICS PREFERRED: **Foster care; child abuse & neglect**

REVIEW PERIOD: **2-3 mo**　　EARLY PUB OPTION: **Yes**
PUBLICATION LAG TIME: **6-9 mo**

ACCEPT WITHOUT REVISION:　　　　　REJECTION RATE: **90%**
ACCEPT WITH REVISION:

THEMATIC ISSUES USED: **Sometimes**

CIRCULATION

NUMBER: **3,500**　　　　　FREQUENCY: **6 X yr**

CURRENT RATES (INDIVIDUAL):
(INSTITUTIONAL):　　　　　(ASSOCIATE/STUDENT):

ANNUAL INDEX AVAILABILITY: **Yes**　　　　COST:
SPECIAL SUPPLEMENTS: **Sometimes**　　　　COST:
SUBSCRIPTION ADDRESS: **Pergamon**
Maxwell House
Fairview Park
Elmsford, NY 10523

STYLE/SUBMISSION REQUIREMENTS

STYLE: **APA**　　　　　STYLE SHEET: **APA**
REVIEW CHARGE: **No**　　　　　COST: **None**
NUMBER OF COPIES: **5**　　　　PAGE LIMIT: **None**
RESPONSE TO QUERY LETTERS: **Yes**

GENERAL INFORMATION

JOURNAL TITLE: **CLINICAL GERONTOLOGIST**

MANUSCRIPT ADDRESS: **Terry L. Brink
1103 Church Street
Redlands, CA 92374**

TYPE OF ARTICLES: **Research; reviews; case studies; commentaries; book reviews; reviews of films, cassettes and software**

MAJOR CONTENT AREAS: **Aging and mental health**

TOPICS PREFERRED: **Dementia; depression; medications; behavior therapy; psychotherapy; Alzheimer's**

REVIEW PERIOD: **<2 mo**   EARLY PUB OPTION: **No**
PUBLICATION LAG TIME: **>6 mo**

ACCEPT WITHOUT REVISION: **20%**   REJECTION RATE: **75%**
ACCEPT WITH REVISION: **5%**

THEMATIC ISSUES USED: **Yes**

CIRCULATION

NUMBER: FREQUENCY: **Quarterly**

CURRENT RATES (INDIVIDUAL): **$45**
(INSTITUTIONAL): **$95**   (ASSOCIATE/STUDENT):

ANNUAL INDEX AVAILABILITY: COST:
SPECIAL SUPPLEMENTS: COST:
SUBSCRIPTION ADDRESS: **The Haworth Press, Inc.
10 Alice St.
Binghamton, NY 13904-1580**

STYLE/SUBMISSION REQUIREMENTS

STYLE: **APA**   STYLE SHEET:
REVIEW CHARGE: **No**   COST:
NUMBER OF COPIES: **3 + diskette**   PAGE LIMIT: **20**
RESPONSE TO QUERY LETTERS:

GENERAL INFORMATION

JOURNAL TITLE: **CLINICAL PSYCHOLOGY REVIEW**

MANUSCRIPT ADDRESS: **Alan S. Bellack**
Medical College of Penn at EEPI
3300 Henry Ave.
Philadelphia, PA 19129

TYPE OF ARTICLES: **Reviews of topics germane to clinical psychology**
(not individual research)
MAJOR CONTENT AREAS: **Psychopathology; psychotherapy; behavior**
therapy; behavioral medicine; community
assesssment; child development
TOPICS PREFERRED:

REVIEW PERIOD: **12 wk**   EARLY PUB OPTION: **No**
PUBLICATION LAG TIME: **9 mo**

ACCEPT WITHOUT REVISION: REJECTION RATE: **51%**
ACCEPT WITH REVISION:

THEMATIC ISSUES USED: **By invitation only**

CIRCULATION

NUMBER: FREQUENCY: **Bimonthly**

CURRENT RATES (INDIVIDUAL): **$60**
(INSTITUTIONAL): **$200**   (ASSOCIATE/STUDENT):

ANNUAL INDEX AVAILABILITY: COST:
SPECIAL SUPPLEMENTS: **No**   COST:
SUBSCRIPTION ADDRESS: **Pergamon Press**
Maxwell House, Fairview Park
Elmsford, NY 10523

STYLE/SUBMISSION REQUIREMENTS

STYLE: **APA**   STYLE SHEET:
REVIEW CHARGE: **No**   COST:
NUMBER OF COPIES: **3**   PAGE LIMIT: **50**
RESPONSE TO QUERY LETTERS: **Yes**

GENERAL INFORMATION

JOURNAL TITLE: **CLINICAL SOCIAL WORK JOURNAL**

MANUSCRIPT ADDRESS: **Jean Sanville, Ph.D., Editor**
1300 Tigertail Rd.
Los Angeles, CA 90049

TYPE OF ARTICLES: **Theoretical; case studies; research**
MAJOR CONTENT AREAS: **Articles of concern to clinicians; relating to**
practice and education; psychotherapy of
individual, group or family
TOPICS PREFERRED: **Psychodynamically oriented accounts to**
treatment modes

REVIEW PERIOD: **<2 mo**   EARLY PUB OPTION: **No**
PUBLICATION LAG TIME: **6 mo-1 yr**

ACCEPT WITHOUT REVISION: **10%**   REJECTION RATE: **50%**
ACCEPT WITH REVISION: **40%**

THEMATIC ISSUES USED: **Yes**

CIRCULATION

NUMBER: **7000**   FREQUENCY: **Quarterly**

CURRENT RATES (INDIVIDUAL): **$34**
(INSTITUTIONAL): **$110**   (ASSOCIATE/STUDENT):

ANNUAL INDEX AVAILABILITY: **Yes**   COST: **None**
SPECIAL SUPPLEMENTS: **No**   COST:
SUBSCRIPTION ADDRESS: **Human Sciences Press**
233 Spring St.
New York, NY 10013-1578

STYLE/SUBMISSION REQUIREMENTS

STYLE: **APA**   STYLE SHEET: **Yes**
REVIEW CHARGE: **NO**   COST:
NUMBER OF COPIES: **3**   PAGE LIMIT: **20-24**
RESPONSE TO QUERY LETTERS: **In limited cases**

GENERAL INFORMATION

JOURNAL TITLE: **CLINICAL SOCIOLOGY REVIEW**

MANUSCRIPT ADDRESS: **Dr. Clifford Black, Editor**
2125 Fairfax St.
Denton, TX 76205

TYPE OF ARTICLES: **Research; reviews; theoretical; case studies; commentaries; book reviews; teaching; practice**
MAJOR CONTENT AREAS: **Intervention at all levels (e.g., counseling; sociotherapy; family case work; social policies affecting families**
TOPICS PREFERRED:

REVIEW PERIOD: **<2 mo**   EARLY PUB OPTION: **No**
PUBLICATION LAG TIME: **3-5 mo**

ACCEPT WITHOUT REVISION: **Varies**   REJECTION RATE:
ACCEPT WITH REVISION:

THEMATIC ISSUES USED: **No**

CIRCULATION

NUMBER: **600+**   FREQUENCY: **Yearly**

CURRENT RATES (INDIVIDUAL): **$18**
(INSTITUTIONAL): **$18**   (ASSOCIATE/STUDENT):

ANNUAL INDEX AVAILABILITY: **No**   COST:
SPECIAL SUPPLEMENTS: **No**   COST:
SUBSCRIPTION ADDRESS: **Michigan State University Press**
1405 South Harrison Rd.
25 Manly Miles Bldg.,
East Lansing, MI 48823-5202

STYLE/SUBMISSION REQUIREMENTS

STYLE: **ASA**   STYLE SHEET: **No**
REVIEW CHARGE: **Yes, if not SPA mem**   COST: **$10**
NUMBER OF COPIES: **4**   PAGE LIMIT: **Varies**
RESPONSE TO QUERY LETTERS: **Yes**

GENERAL INFORMATION

JOURNAL TITLE: **COGNITIVE THERAPY AND RESEARCH**

MANUSCRIPT ADDRESS: **Dr. Philip C. Kendall, Editor**
Department of Psychology
Temple University
Philadelphia, PA 19122

TYPE OF ARTICLES: **Experimental studies; theoretical; reviews; technical; methodological; case studies; brief reports**

MAJOR CONTENT AREAS: **Clinical; cognitive; counseling; development; experimental; learning; personality; social psychology**

TOPICS PREFERRED:

REVIEW PERIOD: EARLY PUB OPTION:
PUBLICATION LAG TIME:

ACCEPT WITHOUT REVISION: REJECTION RATE:
ACCEPT WITH REVISION:

THEMATIC ISSUES USED:

CIRCULATION

NUMBER: FREQUENCY: **6 X yr**

CURRENT RATES (INDIVIDUAL): **$36**
(INSTITUTIONAL): **$180**   (ASSOCIATE/STUDENT):

ANNUAL INDEX AVAILABILITY: COST:
SPECIAL SUPPLEMENTS: COST:
SUBSCRIPTION ADDRESS: **Plenum Publishing**
233 Spring St.
New York, NY 10013

STYLE/SUBMISSION REQUIREMENTS

STYLE: **APA**   STYLE SHEET: **Yes**
REVIEW CHARGE: **No**   COST:
NUMBER OF COPIES: **4**   PAGE LIMIT:
RESPONSE TO QUERY LETTERS:

GENERAL INFORMATION

JOURNAL TITLE: **COMPREHENSIVE PSYCHIATRY**

MANUSCRIPT ADDRESS: **Ralph A. O'Connell, M.D.**
144 West 12th St.
New York, NY 10011

TYPE OF ARTICLES:

MAJOR CONTENT AREAS:

TOPICS PREFERRED:

REVIEW PERIOD: EARLY PUB OPTION:
PUBLICATION LAG TIME:

ACCEPT WITHOUT REVISION: REJECTION RATE:
ACCEPT WITH REVISION:

THEMATIC ISSUES USED:

CIRCULATION

NUMBER: FREQUENCY: **Bimonthly**

CURRENT RATES (INDIVIDUAL): **$99**
(INSTITUTIONAL): **$132**   (ASSOCIATE/STUDENT):

ANNUAL INDEX AVAILABILITY: COST:
SPECIAL SUPPLEMENTS: COST:
SUBSCRIPTION ADDRESS: **W.B. Saunders Co.**
One East First St.
Duluth, MN 55802

STYLE/SUBMISSION REQUIREMENTS

STYLE: STYLE SHEET: **Yes**
REVIEW CHARGE: COST:
NUMBER OF COPIES: **3**   PAGE LIMIT:
RESPONSE TO QUERY LETTERS:

GENERAL INFORMATION

JOURNAL TITLE: **CONTEMPORARY FAMILY THERAPY: AN INTERNATIONAL JOURNAL**

MANUSCRIPT ADDRESS: **William C. Nichols, Ed.D., Editor**
Box 3667
Tallahassee, FL 3215-3667

TYPE OF ARTICLES: **Research; theoretical; case studies; clinical reports**

MAJOR CONTENT AREAS: **Marital and family therapy**

TOPICS PREFERRED:

REVIEW PERIOD: **2-5 mo**   EARLY PUB OPTION: **No**
PUBLICATION LAG TIME: **>6 mo**

ACCEPT WITHOUT REVISION: **40%**   REJECTION RATE: **40-50%**
ACCEPT WITH REVISION: **60%**

THEMATIC ISSUES USED: **Yes**

CIRCULATION

NUMBER: **600**   FREQUENCY: **6 x yr**

CURRENT RATES (INDIVIDUAL): **$44**
(INSTITUTIONAL): **$145**   (ASSOCIATE/STUDENT): **NA**

ANNUAL INDEX AVAILABILITY: **No**   COST:
SPECIAL SUPPLEMENTS: **No**   COST:
SUBSCRIPTION ADDRESS: **Contemporary Family Therapy**
Human Sciences Press
233 Spring St.
New York, NY 10013-1578

STYLE/SUBMISSION REQUIREMENTS

STYLE: **APA**   STYLE SHEET: **Yes**
REVIEW CHARGE: **No**   COST:
NUMBER OF COPIES: **3**   PAGE LIMIT: **25**
RESPONSE TO QUERY LETTERS: **In limited cases**

GENERAL INFORMATION

JOURNAL TITLE: **CRIME AND DELINQUENCY**

MANUSCRIPT ADDRESS: **Kathryn A. Farr, Editor**
Dept. of Sociology
Portland State University
Portland, OR 97207

TYPE OF ARTICLES:

MAJOR CONTENT AREAS:

TOPICS PREFERRED: **Address specific policy or program implications**

REVIEW PERIOD: EARLY PUB OPTION:
PUBLICATION LAG TIME:

ACCEPT WITHOUT REVISION: REJECTION RATE:
ACCEPT WITH REVISION:

THEMATIC ISSUES USED:

CIRCULATION

NUMBER: FREQUENCY: **4 X yr**

CURRENT RATES (INDIVIDUAL): **$38**
(INSTITUTIONAL): **$108**   (ASSOCIATE/STUDENT):

ANNUAL INDEX AVAILABILITY: COST:
SPECIAL SUPPLEMENTS: COST:
SUBSCRIPTION ADDRESS: **Sage Publications, Inc.**
2455 Teller Rd.
Newbury Park, CA 91320

STYLE/SUBMISSION REQUIREMENTS

STYLE: **ASA**   STYLE SHEET:
REVIEW CHARGE: **Yes**   COST: **$10**
NUMBER OF COPIES: **4**   PAGE LIMIT: **30**
RESPONSE TO QUERY LETTERS:

GENERAL INFORMATION

JOURNAL TITLE: **DAY CARE AND EARLY EDUCATION**

MANUSCRIPT ADDRESS: **R. Nachbar, Editor**
233 Spring St.
New York, NY 10013

TYPE OF ARTICLES: **Research; reviews; theoretical; case studies;**
commentaries; book reviews
MAJOR CONTENT AREAS: **Early childhood education for teachers and**
administrators

TOPICS PREFERRED: **Curriculum; practical ideas**

REVIEW PERIOD: **3-5 mo**   EARLY PUB OPTION: **No**
PUBLICATION LAG TIME: **>6 mo**

ACCEPT WITHOUT REVISION: **30%**   REJECTION RATE: **40%**
ACCEPT WITH REVISION: **30%**

THEMATIC ISSUES USED: **No**

CIRCULATION

NUMBER: **5000**   FREQUENCY: **Quarterly**

CURRENT RATES (INDIVIDUAL): **$21**
(INSTITUTIONAL): **$65**   (ASSOCIATE/STUDENT):

ANNUAL INDEX AVAILABILITY: **No**   COST:
SPECIAL SUPPLEMENTS: **No**   COST:
SUBSCRIPTION ADDRESS: **Plenum Publishing**
233 Spring St.
New York, NY 10013

STYLE/SUBMISSION REQUIREMENTS

STYLE: **See guide**   STYLE SHEET: **Yes**
REVIEW CHARGE: **No**   COST:
NUMBER OF COPIES: **3**   PAGE LIMIT: **6-15**
RESPONSE TO QUERY LETTERS: **Yes**

GENERAL INFORMATION

JOURNAL TITLE: **DEATH STUDIES**

MANUSCRIPT ADDRESS: **Hannelore Wass, Editor**
1418 Norman Hall
University of Florida
Gainesville, FL 32611

TYPE OF ARTICLES: **Research; issues papers; program**
implementation; personal and professional
experiences

MAJOR CONTENT AREAS: **Death education; death-related counseling;**
terminal care

TOPICS PREFERRED: **Death attitudes; bereavement and loss; suicide;**
medical crisis; life-threatening illness

REVIEW PERIOD: **3 mo**   EARLY PUB OPTION: **No**
PUBLICATION LAG TIME: **9 mo**

ACCEPT WITHOUT REVISION: REJECTION RATE: **70%**
ACCEPT WITH REVISION:

THEMATIC ISSUES USED: **Yes**

CIRCULATION

NUMBER: **1000**   FREQUENCY: **Bimonthly**

CURRENT RATES (INDIVIDUAL): **$54**
(INSTITUTIONAL): **$120**   (ASSOCIATE/STUDENT):

ANNUAL INDEX AVAILABILITY: COST:
SPECIAL SUPPLEMENTS: COST:
SUBSCRIPTION ADDRESS: **Taylor: Frances Ltd.**
4 John St.
London WC1N 2ET
United Kingdom

STYLE/SUBMISSION REQUIREMENTS

STYLE: **Modified APA**   STYLE SHEET:
REVIEW CHARGE: **None**   COST:
NUMBER OF COPIES: **1 orig; 2 copies**   PAGE LIMIT: **2500 words**
RESPONSE TO QUERY LETTERS:

GENERAL INFORMATION

JOURNAL TITLE: **DEMOGRAPHY**

MANUSCRIPT ADDRESS: **Editor,** *Demography*
Department of Sociology, DE-40
University of Washington
Seattle, Washington, 98195

TYPE OF ARTICLES: **Scientific literature in population studies**

MAJOR CONTENT AREAS: **Social sciences; geography; biology; public health**

TOPICS PREFERRED:

REVIEW PERIOD: **2-3 mo**   EARLY PUB OPTION: **None**
PUBLICATION LAG TIME: **5-6 mo**

ACCEPT WITHOUT REVISION: **5%**   REJECTION RATE: **80%**
ACCEPT WITH REVISION: **15%**

THEMATIC ISSUES USED: **No**

CIRCULATION

NUMBER: **4400**   FREQUENCY: **Quarterly**

CURRENT RATES (INDIVIDUAL): **$85**
(INSTITUTIONAL):   (ASSOCIATE/STUDENT):

ANNUAL INDEX AVAILABILITY: **None**   COST:
SPECIAL SUPPLEMENTS: **None**   COST:
SUBSCRIPTION ADDRESS: **Demography Population Association of America**
1722 N St. NW
Washington, DC 20036

STYLE/SUBMISSION REQUIREMENTS

STYLE: STYLE SHEET: **Yes**
REVIEW CHARGE: **None**   COST:
NUMBER OF COPIES: **4**   PAGE LIMIT: **None, within reason**
RESPONSE TO QUERY LETTERS: **Yes, but depend heavily on 2-3 outside reviewers**

GENERAL INFORMATION

JOURNAL TITLE: **DEVELOPMENTAL PSYCHOLOGY**

MANUSCRIPT ADDRESS: **Ross D. Parke, Editor**
Department of Psychology
University of California
Riverside, CA 92521

TYPE OF ARTICLES: **Research; theoretical; case studies;**
commentaries;

MAJOR CONTENT AREAS: **Developmental psychology—social, cognitive,**
perceptual, emotional, motoric; transition to
parenthood; parent-child interaction

TOPICS PREFERRED: **Any topic on development is acceptable at all**
stages of development; psycho-pathological
aspects of families such as abuse and depression

REVIEW PERIOD: **<2 mo**   EARLY PUB OPTION: **No**
PUBLICATION LAG TIME: **>6 mo**

ACCEPT WITHOUT REVISION: **0%**   REJECTION RATE: **75%**
ACCEPT WITH REVISION: **25%**

THEMATIC ISSUES USED: **Yes**

CIRCULATION

NUMBER: **4800**   FREQUENCY: **6 X yr**

CURRENT RATES (INDIVIDUAL): **$100 non-member/$40 APA member**
(INSTITUTIONAL): **$200**   (ASSOCIATE/STUDENT):

ANNUAL INDEX AVAILABILITY: **Yes**   COST:
SPECIAL SUPPLEMENTS: **No**   COST:
SUBSCRIPTION ADDRESS: **Subscription Section**
1400 North Uhle St.
Arlington, VA 22201

STYLE/SUBMISSION REQUIREMENTS

STYLE: **APA**   STYLE SHEET: **No**
REVIEW CHARGE: **No**   COST:
NUMBER OF COPIES: **5**   PAGE LIMIT: **None**
RESPONSE TO QUERY LETTERS: **Yes**

GENERAL INFORMATION

JOURNAL TITLE: **ECONOMIC DEVELOPMENT AND SOCIAL CHANGE**

MANUSCRIPT ADDRESS: **1130 East 59th St.**
Chicago, IL 60637

TYPE OF ARTICLES:

MAJOR CONTENT AREAS:

TOPICS PREFERRED:

REVIEW PERIOD: EARLY PUB OPTION:
PUBLICATION LAG TIME:

ACCEPT WITHOUT REVISION: REJECTION RATE:
ACCEPT WITH REVISION:

THEMATIC ISSUES USED:

CIRCULATION

NUMBER: FREQUENCY: **4 X yr**

CURRENT RATES (INDIVIDUAL): **$30**
(INSTITUTIONAL): **$60**   (ASSOCIATE/STUDENT):

ANNUAL INDEX AVAILABILITY: COST:
SPECIAL SUPPLEMENTS: COST:
SUBSCRIPTION ADDRESS: **University of Chicago Press**
Journals Division
PO Box 37005
Chicago, IL 60637

STYLE/SUBMISSION REQUIREMENTS

STYLE: STYLE SHEET: **Request**
REVIEW CHARGE: COST:
NUMBER OF COPIES: PAGE LIMIT:
RESPONSE TO QUERY LETTERS:

GENERAL INFORMATION

JOURNAL TITLE: **ECONOMY AND SOCIETY**

MANUSCRIPT ADDRESS: **Sami Zubaida**
Dept. of Politics and Sociology
Birkbeck College
Malet St., London WCIE 71TX, U.K.

TYPE OF ARTICLES:

MAJOR CONTENT AREAS:

TOPICS PREFERRED:

REVIEW PERIOD:	EARLY PUB OPTION:
PUBLICATION LAG TIME:	
ACCEPT WITHOUT REVISION:	REJECTION RATE:
ACCEPT WITH REVISION:	
THEMATIC ISSUES USED:	

CIRCULATION

NUMBER:	FREQUENCY:
CURRENT RATES (INDIVIDUAL): **$50**	
(INSTITUTIONAL): **$72**	(ASSOCIATE/STUDENT):
ANNUAL INDEX AVAILABILITY:	COST:
SPECIAL SUPPLEMENTS:	COST:
SUBSCRIPTION ADDRESS:	**Economy and Society**

Routledge Journals
11 New Fetter Lane
London, EC4P 4EE, U.K.

STYLE/SUBMISSION REQUIREMENTS

STYLE:	STYLE SHEET: **Request**
REVIEW CHARGE:	COST:
NUMBER OF COPIES:	PAGE LIMIT:
RESPONSE TO QUERY LETTERS:	

GENERAL INFORMATION

JOURNAL TITLE: **EDUCATIONAL GERONTOLOGY**

MANUSCRIPT ADDRESS: **D. Bary Lumsden
Department of Higher and
Adult Education
P.O. Box 13857
Denton, TX 76203**

TYPE OF ARTICLES: **Research articles; timely reviews of subjects and books of interest to adult educators, gerontologists, Psychologists, and other scholars and practitioners will be considered**

MAJOR CONTENT AREAS: **Original papers in gerontology, adult education, social and behavioral sciences**

TOPICS PREFERRED:

REVIEW PERIOD:　　　　　　　　　EARLY PUB OPTION:
PUBLICATION LAG TIME:

ACCEPT WITHOUT REVISION:　　　　　　REJECTION RATE:
ACCEPT WITH REVISION:

THEMATIC ISSUES USED:

CIRCULATION

NUMBER:　　　　　　　　FREQUENCY: **Bimonthly**

CURRENT RATES (INDIVIDUAL): **$45**
(INSTITUTIONAL): **$95**　　(ASSOCIATE/STUDENT):

ANNUAL INDEX AVAILABILITY:　　　　　　COST:
SPECIAL SUPPLEMENTS:　　　　　　　COST:
SUBSCRIPTION ADDRESS:

STYLE/SUBMISSION REQUIREMENTS

STYLE: **APA**　　　　STYLE SHEET:
REVIEW CHARGE:　　　　　　COST:
NUMBER OF COPIES: **3**　　　PAGE LIMIT:
RESPONSE TO QUERY LETTERS:

GENERAL INFORMATION

JOURNAL TITLE: **ETHNOLOGY**

MANUSCRIPT ADDRESS: **Dr. George Barlow, Editor**
Department of Integrative Biology
University of California
Berkley, CA 94720

TYPE OF ARTICLES: **Animal behavior**

MAJOR CONTENT AREAS: **Broad audience; all types of papers on animal**
behavior, including humans, but no psychology

TOPICS PREFERRED: **No preference**

REVIEW PERIOD: **1-4 mo**   EARLY PUB OPTION: **None**
PUBLICATION LAG TIME: **6-8 mo**

ACCEPT WITHOUT REVISION: REJECTION RATE: **60-65%**
ACCEPT WITH REVISION:

THEMATIC ISSUES USED:

CIRCULATION

NUMBER: **500**   FREQUENCY: **12 x yr**

CURRENT RATES (INDIVIDUAL):
(INSTITUTIONAL):   (ASSOCIATE/STUDENT):

ANNUAL INDEX AVAILABILITY: COST:
SPECIAL SUPPLEMENTS: **"Advances in Ethnology"** COST:
SUBSCRIPTION ADDRESS: **Paul Parey**
Scientific Publishers/IR Unltd
35 West 38th St., Suite 3W
New York, NY 10018

STYLE/SUBMISSION REQUIREMENTS

STYLE: STYLE SHEET: **Yes**
REVIEW CHARGE: COST:
NUMBER OF COPIES: **3**   PAGE LIMIT: **25**
RESPONSE TO QUERY LETTERS:

GENERAL INFORMATION

JOURNAL TITLE: **EUROPEAN JOURNAL OF SOCIAL PSYCHOLOGY**

MANUSCRIPT ADDRESS: **Prof. Nicholas Emler, Chief Editor**
Department of Psychology
The University of Dundee
Dundee, DD1 4HN, U. K.

TYPE OF ARTICLES: **Theoretical; empirical research; major articles; short notes; book reviews**

MAJOR CONTENT AREAS: **Self-contained research studies; replication research; methodological suggestions; critiques of research**

TOPICS PREFERRED:

REVIEW PERIOD: EARLY PUB OPTION:
PUBLICATION LAG TIME:

ACCEPT WITHOUT REVISION: REJECTION RATE:
ACCEPT WITH REVISION:

THEMATIC ISSUES USED:

CIRCULATION

NUMBER: FREQUENCY: **Bimonthly**

CURRENT RATES (INDIVIDUAL):
(INSTITUTIONAL): **$205**   (ASSOCIATE/STUDENT): **$20**

ANNUAL INDEX AVAILABILITY: COST:
SPECIAL SUPPLEMENTS: COST:
SUBSCRIPTION ADDRESS: **Subscriptions Department**
John Wiley and Sons Limited
Baffins Lane
Chichester, Sussex P019 1UD
England, U. K.

STYLE/SUBMISSION REQUIREMENTS

STYLE: **Harvard System**   STYLE SHEET:
REVIEW CHARGE: COST:
NUMBER OF COPIES: **4**   PAGE LIMIT: **None**
RESPONSE TO QUERY LETTERS:

GENERAL INFORMATION

JOURNAL TITLE: **EXPERIMENTAL AGING RESEARCH**

MANUSCRIPT ADDRESS: **Merrill F. Elias, Ph.D.**
Editor-in-Chief
Experimental Aging Research
P.O. Box 40
Mount Desert, Maine 04660 USA

TYPE OF ARTICLES: **Research in the behavioral and biobehavioral**
sciences; theoretical papers; review articles
MAJOR CONTENT AREAS: **Combination of an interest in aging with an**
interest in experimental psychology, health
psychology, and biopsychology
TOPICS PREFERRED: **Research in the behavioral and biobehavioral**

REVIEW PERIOD: EARLY PUB OPTION:
PUBLICATION LAG TIME:

ACCEPT WITHOUT REVISION: REJECTION RATE:
ACCEPT WITH REVISION:
THEMATIC ISSUES USED: **Yes**

CIRCULATION

NUMBER: FREQUENCY: **Quarterly**

CURRENT RATES (INDIVIDUAL): **$110**
(INSTITUTIONAL):   (ASSOCIATE/STUDENT):

ANNUAL INDEX AVAILABILITY: COST:
SPECIAL SUPPLEMENTS: **Yes**   COST:
SUBSCRIPTION ADDRESS: **Beech Hill Publishing Company**

STYLE/SUBMISSION REQUIREMENTS

STYLE: **APA**   STYLE SHEET:
REVIEW CHARGE: COST:
NUMBER OF COPIES: **4**   PAGE LIMIT: **12-35**
RESPONSE TO QUERY LETTERS:

GENERAL INFORMATION

JOURNAL TITLE: **EXPERIMENTAL GERONTOLOGY**

MANUSCRIPT ADDRESS: **Dr. Leonard Hayflick, Editor-in-Chief**
Experimental Gerontology
University of California
San Francisco School of Medicine
Cell Biology and Aging Section (151E)
4150 Clement St.
San Francisco, CA 94121

TYPE OF ARTICLES: **Research; reviews; theoretical; meeting reports; news items; book reviews; reports**

MAJOR CONTENT AREAS: **Processes of biological aging in plants, animals and humans from molecular level to that of the whole organism**

TOPICS PREFERRED:

REVIEW PERIOD: **4-6 wk**   EARLY PUB OPTION:
PUBLICATION LAG TIME: **6 mo**

ACCEPT WITHOUT REVISION: REJECTION RATE:
ACCEPT WITH REVISION:

THEMATIC ISSUES USED:

CIRCULATION

NUMBER: FREQUENCY: **Bimonthly**

CURRENT RATES (INDIVIDUAL): **$72**
(INSTITUTIONAL): **$310**   (ASSOCIATE/STUDENT):

ANNUAL INDEX AVAILABILITY: COST:
SPECIAL SUPPLEMENTS: COST:
SUBSCRIPTION ADDRESS: **Pergamon Press, Inc.**
Fairview Park
Elmsford, NY 10523

STYLE/SUBMISSION REQUIREMENTS

STYLE: **CBE**   STYLE SHEET: **Yes**
REVIEW CHARGE: COST:
NUMBER OF COPIES: **3**   PAGE LIMIT:
RESPONSE TO QUERY LETTERS:

GENERAL INFORMATION

JOURNAL TITLE: **FAMILY AND COMMUNITY HEALTH**

MANUSCRIPT ADDRESS: **Jeanette Lancaster, R.N., Ph.D., Editor**
Family and Community Health
School of Nursing
University of Virginia
Charlottesville, VA 22903-3395

TYPE OF ARTICLES: **Research; reviews; case studies; book reviews;**
examples of programs

MAJOR CONTENT AREAS: **Each issue has a specific theme**

TOPICS PREFERRED: **Family and community health; health promotion**
of children; community programs for the elderly

REVIEW PERIOD: **3-5 mo**   EARLY PUB OPTION: **Yes**
PUBLICATION LAG TIME: **>6 mo**

ACCEPT WITHOUT REVISION: **20%**   REJECTION RATE: **30%**
ACCEPT WITH REVISION: **50%**

THEMATIC ISSUES USED: **Yes**

CIRCULATION

NUMBER: **2000**   FREQUENCY: **Quarterly**

CURRENT RATES (INDIVIDUAL): **$79.50**
(INSTITUTIONAL):   (ASSOCIATE/STUDENT):

ANNUAL INDEX AVAILABILITY: **No**   COST:
SPECIAL SUPPLEMENTS: **No**   COST:
SUBSCRIPTION ADDRESS: **Aspen Publishers, Inc.**
7201 McKinney Circle
Frederick, MD 21701

STYLE/SUBMISSION REQUIREMENTS

STYLE: **AMA**   STYLE SHEET: **Yes**
REVIEW CHARGE: **No**   COST:
NUMBER OF COPIES: **3**   PAGE LIMIT: **None**
RESPONSE TO QUERY LETTERS: **Yes**

GENERAL INFORMATION

JOURNAL TITLE: **FAMILY DYNAMICS OF ADDICTION QUARTERLY**

ANUSCRIPT ADDRESS: **Gary Lawson, Ph.D., Editor**
Ann Lawson, Ph.D., Editor
United States International University
School of Human Behavior, M2
10455 Pomerado Rd.
San Diego, CA 92131

TYPE OF ARTICLES: **Research; reviews; theoretical; case studies; commentaries; book reviews**

MAJOR CONTENT AREAS: **Interpreting and applying the results of research to everyday working situations**

TOPICS PREFERRED: **Effectiveness of the treatment, intervention, and prevention of drug, alcohol, and other addictions**

REVIEW PERIOD: **<2 mo**   EARLY PUB OPTION: **No**
PUBLICATION LAG TIME: **3-5 mo**

ACCEPT WITHOUT REVISION: **25%**   REJECTION RATE: **37%**
ACCEPT WITH REVISION: **37%**

THEMATIC ISSUES USED: **Yes**

CIRCULATION

NUMBER: FREQUENCY: **Quarterly**

CURRENT RATES (INDIVIDUAL):
(INSTITUTIONAL):   (ASSOCIATE/STUDENT):

ANNUAL INDEX AVAILABILITY: **No**   COST:
SPECIAL SUPPLEMENTS: **No**   COST:
SUBSCRIPTION ADDRESS: **Aspen Publishers**
200 Orchard Ridge Dr., Suite 200
Gaithersburg, MD 20878

STYLE/SUBMISSION REQUIREMENTS

STYLE: **APA**   STYLE SHEET: **Yes**
REVIEW CHARGE: **No**   COST:
NUMBER OF COPIES: **3**   PAGE LIMIT: **None**
RESPONSE TO QUERY LETTERS: **Yes**

GENERAL INFORMATION

JOURNAL TITLE: **FAMILY HISTORY**

MANUSCRIPT ADDRESS: **Cecil R. Humphery-Smith, F.S.A., Editor**
79-82 Northgate
Canterbury, Kent
CT1 1BA, U.K.

TYPE OF ARTICLES: **Research; theoretical; case studies;**
commentaries; book reviews; news; demography

MAJOR CONTENT AREAS: **Research**

TOPICS PREFERRED: **Family history and structure; genetically**
inherited disease research reports

REVIEW PERIOD: **<2 mo**   EARLY PUB OPTION: **Yes**
PUBLICATION LAG TIME: **3-5 mo**

ACCEPT WITHOUT REVISION: REJECTION RATE:
ACCEPT WITH REVISION: **50%**

THEMATIC ISSUES USED: **Yes**

CIRCULATION

NUMBER: **1300**   FREQUENCY: **Quarterly**

CURRENT RATES (INDIVIDUAL): **£20**
(INSTITUTIONAL):   (ASSOCIATE/STUDENT):

ANNUAL INDEX AVAILABILITY: **No**   COST:
SPECIAL SUPPLEMENTS: **Yes**   COST:
SUBSCRIPTION ADDRESS: **Same as above**

STYLE/SUBMISSION REQUIREMENTS

STYLE: STYLE SHEET: **No**
REVIEW CHARGE: **No**   COST:
NUMBER OF COPIES: **2**   PAGE LIMIT: **2-16**
RESPONSE TO QUERY LETTERS: **Yes**

GENERAL INFORMATION

JOURNAL TITLE: **FAMILY LIFE EDUCATOR**

MANUSCRIPT ADDRESS: **Kay Clark, Editor**
P.O. Box 1830
Santa Cruz, CA 95061-1830

TYPE OF ARTICLES: **Research; commentaries; book reviews; news**

MAJOR CONTENT AREAS: **Family life and sex education issues for**
secondary education teachers and other
educators who work with adolescents
TOPICS PREFERRED: **Topics which provide family life and sex**
education teachers with background information

REVIEW PERIOD: **3 mo**   EARLY PUB OPTION: **No**
PUBLICATION LAG TIME: **3-5 mo**

ACCEPT WITHOUT REVISION: REJECTION RATE:
ACCEPT WITH REVISION:

THEMATIC ISSUES USED: **No**

CIRCULATION

NUMBER: **5000**   FREQUENCY: **Quarterly**

CURRENT RATES (INDIVIDUAL): **$35**
(INSTITUTIONAL): **$55**   (ASSOCIATE/STUDENT):

ANNUAL INDEX AVAILABILITY: **No**   COST:
SPECIAL SUPPLEMENTS: **No**   COST:
SUBSCRIPTION ADDRESS: **P.O. Box 1830**
Santa Cruz, CA 95061-1830

STYLE/SUBMISSION REQUIREMENTS

STYLE: **Chicago**   STYLE SHEET: **Yes**
REVIEW CHARGE: **No**   COST:
NUMBER OF COPIES: **2**   PAGE LIMIT: **16**
RESPONSE TO QUERY LETTERS: **Yes**

GENERAL INFORMATION

JOURNAL TITLE: **FAMILY PLANNING PERSPECTIVES**

MANUSCRIPT ADDRESS: **111 Fifth Ave.**
New York, NY 10003

TYPE OF ARTICLES: **Research; commentaries**

MAJOR CONTENT AREAS: **All aspects of reproductive health**

TOPICS PREFERRED: **Teenage pregnancy; STDs; abortion; prenatal**
care; contraceptive practice; evaluation of
family planning and sex education programs
REVIEW PERIOD: **3-5 mo**   EARLY PUB OPTION: **No**
PUBLICATION LAG TIME: **3-5 mo**

ACCEPT WITHOUT REVISION: **None**   REJECTION RATE: **55%**
ACCEPT WITH REVISION: **45%**

THEMATIC ISSUES USED: **Yes, but rarely**

CIRCULATION

NUMBER: **15,000**   FREQUENCY: **6 X yr**

CURRENT RATES (INDIVIDUAL): **$28**
(INSTITUTIONAL): **$38**   (ASSOCIATE/STUDENT):

ANNUAL INDEX AVAILABILITY: **Yes**   COST: **None**
SPECIAL SUPPLEMENTS: **No**   COST:
SUBSCRIPTION ADDRESS: **111 Fifth Ave.**
New York, NY 10003

STYLE/SUBMISSION REQUIREMENTS

STYLE: **Chicago**   STYLE SHEET: **Yes**
REVIEW CHARGE: **No**   COST:
NUMBER OF COPIES: **1**   PAGE LIMIT: **35**
RESPONSE TO QUERY LETTERS: **Yes**

GENERAL INFORMATION

JOURNAL TITLE: **FAMILY PROCESS**

MANUSCRIPT ADDRESS: **Peter Steinglass, M.D., Editor**
Family Process
149 E. 78th St.
New York, NY 10021

TYPE OF ARTICLES: **Clinical research, training and theoretical**
contributions in the broad area of family
therapy

MAJOR CONTENT AREAS:

TOPICS PREFERRED:

REVIEW PERIOD: **2-6 mo**   EARLY PUB OPTION: **No**
PUBLICATION LAG TIME: **6-12 mo**

ACCEPT WITHOUT REVISION: **10%**   REJECTION RATE: **60%**
ACCEPT WITH REVISION: **30%**

THEMATIC ISSUES USED: **No**

CIRCULATION

NUMBER: **10,000**   FREQUENCY: **Quarterly**

CURRENT RATES (INDIVIDUAL): **$27**
(INSTITUTIONAL): **$44**   (ASSOCIATE/STUDENT):

ANNUAL INDEX AVAILABILITY: **Dec. issue ea yr**   COST: **NA**
SPECIAL SUPPLEMENTS: **Index 1962-1986**   COST: **per request**
SUBSCRIPTION ADDRESS: **Family Process**
P.O. Box 6889
Syracuse, NY 13217

STYLE/SUBMISSION REQUIREMENTS

STYLE: STYLE SHEET:
REVIEW CHARGE: COST:
NUMBER OF COPIES: **4**   PAGE LIMIT: **Avg: 25**
RESPONSE TO QUERY LETTERS: **Discouraged**

GENERAL INFORMATION

JOURNAL TITLE: **FAMILY RELATIONS**

MANUSCRIPT ADDRESS: **Timothy Brubaker**
Family and Child Studies Center
Miami University
Oxford OH 45056

TYPE OF ARTICLES: **Research; reviews; theoretical; case studies**

MAJOR CONTENT AREAS: **Any applied issues related to the family and child areas**

TOPICS PREFERRED: **Experiences in education, counseling and family services; evaluation research focusing on family life programs**
REVIEW PERIOD: **3-5 mo**   EARLY PUB OPTION: **No**
PUBLICATION LAG TIME: **3-5 mo**

ACCEPT WITHOUT REVISION: **1%**   REJECTION RATE: **75%**
ACCEPT WITH REVISION: **20%**

THEMATIC ISSUES USED: **Yes**

CIRCULATION

NUMBER: **5200+**   FREQUENCY: **Quarterly**

CURRENT RATES (INDIVIDUAL): **$45**
(INSTITUTIONAL):   (ASSOCIATE/STUDENT):

ANNUAL INDEX AVAILABILITY: **Yes**   COST:
SPECIAL SUPPLEMENTS: **No**   COST:
SUBSCRIPTION ADDRESS: **National Council of Family Relations**
3989 Central Ave., Suite 550
Minnepolis, MN 55421

STYLE/SUBMISSION REQUIREMENTS

STYLE: **APA**   STYLE SHEET: **Yes**
REVIEW CHARGE: **Yes**   COST: **$15**
NUMBER OF COPIES: **3**   PAGE LIMIT: **20-25**
RESPONSE TO QUERY LETTERS: **Yes**

GENERAL INFORMATION

JOURNAL TITLE: **FAMILY SAFETY AND HEALTH**

MANUSCRIPT ADDRESS: **Family Safety and Health**
444 N. Michigan Ave.
Chicago, IL 60611

TYPE OF ARTICLES: **Case studies; commentaries**

MAJOR CONTENT AREAS: **Home accident prevention (fires, poisoning,**
falls); physical and psychological health topics

TOPICS PREFERRED: **No preference**

REVIEW PERIOD: **< 2 mo**   EARLY PUB OPTION: **NO**
PUBLICATION LAG TIME: **6 mo or more**

ACCEPT WITHOUT REVISION: **70%**   REJECTION RATE: **10%**
ACCEPT WITH REVISION: **20%**

THEMATIC ISSUES USED: **Yes**

CIRCULATION

NUMBER: **2 million**   FREQUENCY: **Quarterly**

CURRENT RATES (INDIVIDUAL): **$10**
(INSTITUTIONAL):   (ASSOCIATE/STUDENT):

ANNUAL INDEX AVAILABILITY: **No**   COST:
SPECIAL SUPPLEMENTS: **No**   COST:
SUBSCRIPTION ADDRESS: **Same as above**

STYLE/SUBMISSION REQUIREMENTS

STYLE: **APA**   STYLE SHEET: **Yes**
REVIEW CHARGE: **No**   COST:
NUMBER OF COPIES: **2**   PAGE LIMIT: **8**
RESPONSE TO QUERY LETTERS: **Yes, but prefer phone calls**

GENERAL INFORMATION

JOURNAL TITLE: **FAMILY SYSTEMS MEDICINE**

MANUSCRIPT ADDRESS: **Donald A. Bloch, M.D., Editor**
40 West 12th St.
New York, NY 10021

TYPE OF ARTICLES: **Research; reviews; theoretical; commentaries;**
case studies; book reviews
MAJOR CONTENT AREAS: **Family and health care systems**

TOPICS PREFERRED:

REVIEW PERIOD: **<2 mo**   EARLY PUB OPTION: **No**
PUBLICATION LAG TIME: **3-5 mo**

ACCEPT WITHOUT REVISION: **10%**   REJECTION RATE: **70%**
ACCEPT WITH REVISION: **20%**

THEMATIC ISSUES USED: **No**

CIRCULATION

NUMBER: **1300**   FREQUENCY: **Quarterly**

CURRENT RATES (INDIVIDUAL): **$35**
(INSTITUTIONAL): **$70**   (ASSOCIATE/STUDENT):

ANNUAL INDEX AVAILABILITY: **No**   COST:
SPECIAL SUPPLEMENTS: **No**   COST:
SUBSCRIPTION ADDRESS: **841 Broadway, Suite 504**
New York, NY 10011

STYLE/SUBMISSION REQUIREMENTS

STYLE: **MLA**   STYLE SHEET: **Yes**
REVIEW CHARGE: **No**   COST:
NUMBER OF COPIES: **4**   PAGE LIMIT: **None**
RESPONSE TO QUERY LETTERS: **Yes**

GENERAL INFORMATION

JOURNAL TITLE: **FEMINIST ISSUES**

MANUSCRIPT ADDRESS: **Editor,** *Feminist Issues*
2948 Hillegass
Berkeley, CA 94705

TYPE OF ARTICLES: **Feminist social and political analysis; emphasis on international exchange of ideas**

MAJOR CONTENT AREAS:

TOPICS PREFERRED:

REVIEW PERIOD: EARLY PUB OPTION:
PUBLICATION LAG TIME:

ACCEPT WITHOUT REVISION: REJECTION RATE:
ACCEPT WITH REVISION:

THEMATIC ISSUES USED:

CIRCULATION

NUMBER: FREQUENCY: **2 X yr**

CURRENT RATES (INDIVIDUAL): **$15**
(INSTITUTIONAL): **$34**   (ASSOCIATE/STUDENT):

ANNUAL INDEX AVAILABILITY: COST:
SPECIAL SUPPLEMENTS: COST:
SUBSCRIPTION ADDRESS: **Transaction Periodicals Consortium**
Dept. 8010, Rutgers Univ.
New Brunswick, NJ 80903

STYLE/SUBMISSION REQUIREMENTS

STYLE: STYLE SHEET:
REVIEW CHARGE: COST:
NUMBER OF COPIES: PAGE LIMIT:
RESPONSE TO QUERY LETTERS:

GENERAL INFORMATION

JOURNAL TITLE: **FEMINIST STUDIES**

MANUSCRIPT ADDRESS: **C/O Women's Studies Program
University of Maryland
College Park, CA 20742**

TYPE OF ARTICLES: **Research; review; theoretical; book reviews**

MAJOR CONTENT AREAS:

TOPICS PREFERRED: **Topics relating to women for our
interdisciplinary audience**

REVIEW PERIOD: **3-5 mo**   EARLY PUB OPTION: **No**
PUBLICATION LAG TIME: **>6 mo**

ACCEPT WITHOUT REVISION: **0%**   REJECTION RATE: **93%**
ACCEPT WITH REVISION: **7%**

THEMATIC ISSUES USED: **Yes**

CIRCULATION

NUMBER: **7500**   FREQUENCY: **3 X yr**

CURRENT RATES (INDIVIDUAL): **$21**
(INSTITUTIONAL): **$48**   (ASSOCIATE/STUDENT):

ANNUAL INDEX AVAILABILITY: **No**   COST:
SPECIAL SUPPLEMENTS: **No**   COST:
SUBSCRIPTION ADDRESS: **Same as above**

STYLE/SUBMISSION REQUIREMENTS

STYLE: **Chicago**   STYLE SHEET: **Yes**
REVIEW CHARGE: **No**   COST:
NUMBER OF COPIES: **3**   PAGE LIMIT: **35**
RESPONSE TO QUERY LETTERS: **Yes**

GENERAL INFORMATION

JOURNAL TITLE: **FAMILY THERAPY**

MANUSCRIPT ADDRESS: **Martin Blinder,M.D., Editor
50 Idalia Rd.
San Anselmo, CA 94960**

TYPE OF ARTICLES: **Research; review; theoretical; case studies; commentaries**

MAJOR CONTENT AREAS: **Therapy and counseling; marriage and family; divorce; law; alcohol; drug use; aging; children; sexuality; social psychology; domestic violence;**
TOPICS PREFERRED: **ethnicity; codependency; sex roles; deviancy; religion and values; human development**

REVIEW PERIOD: **<2 mo**   EARLY PUB OPTION: **No**
PUBLICATION LAG TIME: **3-5 mo**

ACCEPT WITHOUT REVISION: **20%**   REJECTION RATE: **60%**
ACCEPT WITH REVISION: **20%**

THEMATIC ISSUES USED: **Yes**

CIRCULATION

NUMBER: **1500**   FREQUENCY: **3 X yr**

CURRENT RATES (INDIVIDUAL): **$44**
(INSTITUTIONAL): **$50**   (ASSOCIATE/STUDENT):

ANNUAL INDEX AVAILABILITY: **No**   COST:
SPECIAL SUPPLEMENTS: **No**   COST:
SUBSCRIPTION ADDRESS: **Libra Publishers
3089-C Clairemont Dr.
Suite 383
San Diego, CA 92117**

STYLE/SUBMISSION REQUIREMENTS

STYLE: **APA**   STYLE SHEET: **No**
REVIEW CHARGE: **No**   COST:
NUMBER OF COPIES: **2**   PAGE LIMIT: **None**
RESPONSE TO QUERY LETTERS: **Yes**

GENERAL INFORMATION

JOURNAL TITLE: **FOCUS: EDUCATING POROFESSIONALS IN FAMILY RECOVERY**

MANUSCRIPT ADDRESS: **3201 SW 15th St.
Deerfield Beach, FL 33442**

TYPE OF ARTICLES: **Research; theoretical; case studies; tips for therapists**

MAJOR CONTENT AREAS: **Family therapy styles; addiction therapy; crossover between spirituality and psychotherapy**

TOPICS PREFERRED:

REVIEW PERIOD: **<2 mo**   EARLY PUB OPTION: **No**
PUBLICATION LAG TIME: **>6mo**

ACCEPT WITHOUT REVISION: **0%**   REJECTION RATE: **25%**
ACCEPT WITH REVISION: **75%**

THEMATIC ISSUES USED: **Yes**

CIRCULATION

NUMBER: **12,000**   FREQUENCY: **Bimonthly**

CURRENT RATES (INDIVIDUAL): **$22**
(INSTITUTIONAL):   (ASSOCIATE/STUDENT):

ANNUAL INDEX AVAILABILITY: **No**   COST:
SPECIAL SUPPLEMENTS: **No**   COST:
SUBSCRIPTION ADDRESS: **Same as above**

STYLE/SUBMISSION REQUIREMENTS

STYLE: **APA**   STYLE SHEET: **No**
REVIEW CHARGE: **No**   COST:
NUMBER OF COPIES: **1**   PAGE LIMIT: **10**
RESPONSE TO QUERY LETTERS: **Yes**

GENERAL INFORMATION

JOURNAL TITLE: **GENDER AND SOCIETY**

MANUSCRIPT ADDRESS: **Margaret L. Anderson, Editor**
Gender and Society
Department of Sociology
University of Delaware
Newark, DE 19716

TYPE OF ARTICLES: **Research; theoretical**

MAJOR CONTENT AREAS: **Gender**

TOPICS PREFERRED:

REVIEW PERIOD: **<2 mo**   EARLY PUB OPTION: **No**
PUBLICATION LAG TIME: **>6 mo**

ACCEPT WITHOUT REVISION: REJECTION RATE:
ACCEPT WITH REVISION:

THEMATIC ISSUES USED: **Yes**

CIRCULATION

NUMBER: FREQUENCY: **Quarterly**

CURRENT RATES (INDIVIDUAL): **$32**
(INSTITUTIONAL): **$84**   (ASSOCIATE/STUDENT): **NA**

ANNUAL INDEX AVAILABILITY: **No**   COST:
SPECIAL SUPPLEMENTS: **No**   COST:
SUBSCRIPTION ADDRESS: **Sage Publications**
2111 W. Hillcrest Dr.
Newbury Park, CA 91320

STYLE/SUBMISSION REQUIREMENTS

STYLE: **Chicago**   STYLE SHEET: **Yes**
REVIEW CHARGE: **Yes**   COST: **$10**
NUMBER OF COPIES: **5**   PAGE LIMIT: **25**
RESPONSE TO QUERY LETTERS: **No**

GENERAL INFORMATION

JOURNAL TITLE: **GROUP AND ORGANIZATIONAL STUDIES**

MANUSCRIPT ADDRESS: **Michael J. Kavanaugh, Editor**
School of Business
State University of New York at Albany
Albany, NY 12222

TYPE OF ARTICLES: **Data-based research articles, research review reports, research and evaluation studies, action research reports, critiques of research**

MAJOR CONTENT AREAS: **Leadership, management development, group processes, communication in organizations, consultation, organizational development**

TOPICS PREFERRED: **Studies with cross cultural implications**

REVIEW PERIOD: EARLY PUB OPTION:
PUBLICATION LAG TIME:

ACCEPT WITHOUT REVISION: REJECTION RATE:
ACCEPT WITH REVISION:

THEMATIC ISSUES USED:

CIRCULATION

NUMBER: FREQUENCY: **4 X year**

CURRENT RATES (INDIVIDUAL): **$42**
(INSTITUTIONAL): **$100**   (ASSOCIATE/STUDENT):

ANNUAL INDEX AVAILABILITY: COST:
SPECIAL SUPPLEMENTS: COST:
SUBSCRIPTION ADDRESS: **Sage Publications Inc.**
2111 West Hillcrest Dr.
Newbury Park, CA 91320

STYLE/SUBMISSION REQUIREMENTS

STYLE: **APA**   STYLE SHEET:
REVIEW CHARGE: COST:
NUMBER OF COPIES: **5**   PAGE LIMIT: **12-20**
RESPONSE TO QUERY LETTERS:

GENERAL INFORMATION

JOURNAL TITLE: **HARVARD EDUCATIONAL REVIEW**

MANUSCRIPT ADDRESS: **Gutman Library Suite 349**
6 Appian Way
Cambridge, MA 02138

TYPE OF ARTICLES: **Research; reviews; theoretical; commentaries;**
book reviews; teacher's column
MAJOR CONTENT AREAS: **Opinion and research in the field of education**

TOPICS PREFERRED: **Anything related to education**

REVIEW PERIOD: **3-5 mo**   EARLY PUB OPTION: **No**
PUBLICATION LAG TIME: **>6 mo**

ACCEPT WITHOUT REVISION: **8%**   REJECTION RATE: **72%**
ACCEPT WITH REVISION: **20%**

THEMATIC ISSUES USED: **Yes**

CIRCULATION

NUMBER: **12,000**   FREQUENCY: **Quarterly**

CURRENT RATES (INDIVIDUAL): **$35**
(INSTITUTIONAL): **$64**   (ASSOCIATE/STUDENT): **$24**

ANNUAL INDEX AVAILABILITY: **Yes**   COST: **NA**
SPECIAL SUPPLEMENTS: **No**   COST:
SUBSCRIPTION ADDRESS: **Gutman Library Suite 349**
6 Appian Way
Cambridge, MA 02138

STYLE/SUBMISSION REQUIREMENTS

STYLE: **APA/Chicago**   STYLE SHEET: **Yes**
REVIEW CHARGE: **No**   COST:
NUMBER OF COPIES: **3**   PAGE LIMIT: **35**
RESPONSE TO QUERY LETTERS: **Yes**

GENERAL INFORMATION

JOURNAL TITLE: **HEALTH EDUCATION QUARTERLY**

MANUSCRIPT ADDRESS: **Noreen M. Clark, Ph.D., Editor**
Dept. of Health Behavior & Health
University of Michigan
School of Public Health
1420 Washington Heights
Ann Arbor, MI 48109

TYPE OF ARTICLES: **Empirical research; case studies; program**
evaluation; review articles; book reviews; letters
to the editor

MAJOR CONTENT AREAS: **Articles directed toward researchers and/or**
practitioners in health behavior and health
education

TOPICS PREFERRED:

REVIEW PERIOD: EARLY PUB OPTION:
PUBLICATION LAG TIME:

ACCEPT WITHOUT REVISION: REJECTION RATE:
ACCEPT WITH REVISION:

THEMATIC ISSUES USED: **Contact the editor for information**
on substantive issues in progress

CIRCULATION

NUMBER: FREQUENCY: **Quarterly**

CURRENT RATES (INDIVIDUAL): **$50**
(INSTITUTIONAL): **$125**   (ASSOCIATE/STUDENT):

ANNUAL INDEX AVAILABILITY: COST:
SPECIAL SUPPLEMENTS: COST:
SUBSCRIPTION ADDRESS: **John Wiley & Sons, Inc.**
605 Third Ave.
New York, NY 10158

STYLE/SUBMISSION REQUIREMENTS

STYLE: **Index Medicus**   STYLE SHEET:
REVIEW CHARGE: COST:
NUMBER OF COPIES: **1 orig, 3 copies**   PAGE LIMIT:
RESPONSE TO QUERY LETTERS:

GENERAL INFORMATION

JOURNAL TITLE: **HISPANIC JOURNAL OF BEHAVIORAL SCIENCES**
MANUSCRIPT ADDRESS: **Amado M. Padilla, Editor**
Center for Educational Research at Stanford
Stanford Universtiy
Stanford, CA 94305

TYPE OF ARTICLES: **Research; reviews; theoretical; case studies;**
commentaries; book reviews
MAJOR CONTENT AREAS: **Articles that address Hispanic Americans in any**
of the behavioral or educational disciplines

TOPICS PREFERRED: **No preference**

REVIEW PERIOD: **<2 mo**   EARLY PUB OPTION: **No**
PUBLICATION LAG TIME: **>6 mo**

ACCEPT WITHOUT REVISION: **5-10%**   REJECTION RATE: **50%**
ACCEPT WITH REVISION: **40-45%**

THEMATIC ISSUES USED: **Yes**

CIRCULATION

NUMBER: **750-800**   FREQUENCY: **Quarterly**

CURRENT RATES (INDIVIDUAL): **$30**
(INSTITUTIONAL): **$60**   (ASSOCIATE/STUDENT): **NA**

ANNUAL INDEX AVAILABILITY: **No**   COST:
SPECIAL SUPPLEMENTS: **No**   COST:
SUBSCRIPTION ADDRESS:

STYLE/SUBMISSION REQUIREMENTS

STYLE: **APA**   STYLE SHEET: **No**
REVIEW CHARGE: **No**   COST:
NUMBER OF COPIES: **3**   PAGE LIMIT: **25-30**
RESPONSE TO QUERY LETTERS: **In limited cases**

GENERAL INFORMATION

JOURNAL TITLE: **HOLISTIC NURSING PRACTICE**

MANUSCRIPT ADDRESS: **Editor, Nursing Publications, HNP**
Aspen Publishers Inc.
200 Orchard Ridge Drive
Gaithersburg, MD 20878

TYPE OF ARTICLES: **Reports on research and practice that provide information to nurse clinicians and educators about holistic nursing approaches to nursing practice in clinical settings**

MAJOR CONTENT AREAS:

TOPICS PREFERRED:

REVIEW PERIOD: EARLY PUB OPTION:
PUBLICATION LAG TIME:

ACCEPT WITHOUT REVISION: REJECTION RATE:
ACCEPT WITH REVISION:

THEMATIC ISSUES USED:

CIRCULATION

NUMBER: FREQUENCY: **Quarterly**

CURRENT RATES (INDIVIDUAL): **$59**
(INSTITUTIONAL):   (ASSOCIATE/STUDENT):

ANNUAL INDEX AVAILABILITY: COST:
SPECIAL SUPPLEMENTS: COST:
SUBSCRIPTION ADDRESS: **Aspen Publishers Inc.**
7201 McKinney Circle
Frederick, MD 21701

STYLE/SUBMISSION REQUIREMENTS

STYLE: STYLE SHEET: **On req**
REVIEW CHARGE: COST:
NUMBER OF COPIES: PAGE LIMIT:
RESPONSE TO QUERY LETTERS:

GENERAL INFORMATION

JOURNAL TITLE: **HOME ECONOMICS RESEARCH JOURNAL**

MANUSCRIPT ADDRESS: **Dr. Stephen R. Jorgensen, Editor**
Home Economics Research Journal
Texas Tech University
P.O. Box 4170
Lubbock, TX 79409-4107

TYPE OF ARTICLES: **Original research; scholarly reviews**

MAJOR CONTENT AREAS: **All areas of home economics and related**
disciplines concerned with the general well-being
of families and individuals
TOPICS PREFERRED:

REVIEW PERIOD: EARLY PUB OPTION:
PUBLICATION LAG TIME:

ACCEPT WITHOUT REVISION: REJECTION RATE:
ACCEPT WITH REVISION:

THEMATIC ISSUES USED:

CIRCULATION

NUMBER: FREQUENCY: **4 X yr**

CURRENT RATES (INDIVIDUAL): **$25**
(INSTITUTIONAL):   (ASSOCIATE/STUDENT):

ANNUAL INDEX AVAILABILITY: COST:
SPECIAL SUPPLEMENTS: COST:
SUBSCRIPTION ADDRESS: **Managing Editor**
Home Economics Research Journal
American Home Economics Assoc.
1555 King Street
Alexandria, VA 22314

STYLE/SUBMISSION REQUIREMENTS

STYLE: **APA**   STYLE SHEET:
REVIEW CHARGE: **Yes**   COST: **$25**
NUMBER OF COPIES: **3**   PAGE LIMIT:
RESPONSE TO QUERY LETTERS:

GENERAL INFORMATION

JOURNAL TITLE: **HOME HEALTH CARE SERVICES QUARTERLY**

MANUSCRIPT ADDRESS: **Brahna Trager**
P.O. Box 96
San Geronimo, CA 94963

TYPE OF ARTICLES:

MAJOR CONTENT AREAS:

TOPICS PREFERRED:

REVIEW PERIOD: EARLY PUB OPTION:
PUBLICATION LAG TIME:

ACCEPT WITHOUT REVISION: REJECTION RATE:
ACCEPT WITH REVISION:

THEMATIC ISSUES USED:

CIRCULATION

NUMBER: **500**   FREQUENCY: **Quarterly**

CURRENT RATES (INDIVIDUAL): **$40**
(INSTITUTIONAL): **$95**   (ASSOCIATE/STUDENT):

ANNUAL INDEX AVAILABILITY: **No**   COST:
SPECIAL SUPPLEMENTS: COST:
SUBSCRIPTION ADDRESS: **The Haworth Press Inc.**
10 Alice Street
Binghamton, NY 13904-1580

STYLE/SUBMISSION REQUIREMENTS

STYLE: **APA**   STYLE SHEET:
REVIEW CHARGE: **No**   COST:
NUMBER OF COPIES: **3 + diskette**   PAGE LIMIT: **20**
RESPONSE TO QUERY LETTERS:

GENERAL INFORMATION

JOURNAL TITLE: **HUMAN COMMUNICATION RESEARCH**

MANUSCRIPT ADDRESS: **James J. Bradac**
Comm. Studies Program
U of CA, Santa Barbara
Santa Barbara, CA 93106

TYPE OF ARTICLES:

MAJOR CONTENT AREAS:

TOPICS PREFERRED: **Original research, methodologies relevant to**
study of human comm., critical syntheses of
research and theoretical and philosophical
perspectives on human comm. activity

REVIEW PERIOD: EARLY PUB OPTION:
PUBLICATION LAG TIME:

ACCEPT WITHOUT REVISION: REJECTION RATE:
ACCEPT WITH REVISION:

THEMATIC ISSUES USED:

CIRCULATION

NUMBER: FREQUENCY: **Quarterly**

CURRENT RATES (INDIVIDUAL): **$40**
(INSTITUTIONAL): **$106**   (ASSOCIATE/STUDENT):

ANNUAL INDEX AVAILABILITY: COST:
SPECIAL SUPPLEMENTS: COST:
SUBSCRIPTION ADDRESS: **International Communication Assoc.**
8140 Burnet Rd.
Austin, TX 78758

STYLE/SUBMISSION REQUIREMENTS

STYLE: **APA**   STYLE SHEET:
REVIEW CHARGE: COST:
NUMBER OF COPIES: **3**   PAGE LIMIT:
RESPONSE TO QUERY LETTERS:

GENERAL INFORMATION

JOURNAL TITLE: **HUMAN ECOLOGY**

MANUSCRIPT ADDRESS: **Hunter College Rm 723 N
695 Park Ave.
New York, NY 10021**

TYPE OF ARTICLES: **Research; case studies**

MAJOR CONTENT AREAS: **Human ecology; anthropology; geography;
psychology; biology; sociology; urban planning**

TOPICS PREFERRED: **Papers concerned with complex and varied
systems of interaction between people and
environment**

REVIEW PERIOD: **3-5 mo**   EARLY PUB OPTION: **No**
PUBLICATION LAG TIME: **>6 mo**

ACCEPT WITHOUT REVISION: REJECTION RATE:
ACCEPT WITH REVISION:

THEMATIC ISSUES USED: **Rarely**

CIRCULATION

NUMBER: FREQUENCY: **Quarterly**

CURRENT RATES (INDIVIDUAL): **$42**
(INSTITUTIONAL): **$185**   (ASSOCIATE/STUDENT):

ANNUAL INDEX AVAILABILITY: COST:
SPECIAL SUPPLEMENTS: COST:
SUBSCRIPTION ADDRESS: **Plenum Publications
233 Spring St.
New York, NY 10013-1578**

STYLE/SUBMISSION REQUIREMENTS

STYLE: STYLE SHEET: **No**
REVIEW CHARGE: **No**   COST:
NUMBER OF COPIES: **3**   PAGE LIMIT: **None**
RESPONSE TO QUERY LETTERS:

GENERAL INFORMATION

JOURNAL TITLE: **HUMAN RELATIONS**

MANUSCRIPT ADDRESS: **Tavistock Institute of Human Relations**
Tavistock Centre
120 Belsize Lane
London NW35BA, U.K.

TYPE OF ARTICLES: **Research; reviews; theoretical; case studies;**
commentaries

MAJOR CONTENT AREAS: **Interpersonal; intergroup relations**

TOPICS PREFERRED: **Action research on work and/or family**

REVIEW PERIOD: **3-5 mo**   EARLY PUB OPTION: **No**
PUBLICATION LAG TIME: **3-5 mo**

ACCEPT WITHOUT REVISION: **0%**   REJECTION RATE: **40%**
ACCEPT WITH REVISION: **60%**

THEMATIC ISSUES USED: **Yes**

CIRCULATION

NUMBER: **2000**   FREQUENCY: **Monthly**

CURRENT RATES (INDIVIDUAL): **$125**
(INSTITUTIONAL): **$295**   (ASSOCIATE/STUDENT):

ANNUAL INDEX AVAILABILITY: **Yes**   COST: **None**
SPECIAL SUPPLEMENTS: **Yes**   COST: **Varies**
SUBSCRIPTION ADDRESS: **Plenum Press Journals**
Plenum Publishing Co.
233 Spring St.
New York, NY 10013

STYLE/SUBMISSION REQUIREMENTS

STYLE: **APA**   STYLE SHEET: **Yes**
REVIEW CHARGE: **No**   COST:
NUMBER OF COPIES: **3**   PAGE LIMIT: **5000 words**
RESPONSE TO QUERY LETTERS: **In limited cases**

GENERAL INFORMATION

JOURNAL TITLE: **HUMAN STUDIES**

MANUSCRIPT ADDRESS: **Kluwer Academic Publishers**
PO Box 17
3300 AA Dordrecht
Netherlands

TYPE OF ARTICLES: **General; theoretical**

MAJOR CONTENT AREAS: **Human sciences and philosophy**

TOPICS PREFERRED: **Theoretical studies; empirical studies with strong**
theoretical emphasis

REVIEW PERIOD: **6 mo**   EARLY PUB OPTION: **No**
PUBLICATION LAG TIME: **18 mo**

ACCEPT WITHOUT REVISION: **10%**   REJECTION RATE: **60%**
ACCEPT WITH REVISION: **30%**

THEMATIC ISSUES USED: **Yes**

CIRCULATION

NUMBER: **450**   FREQUENCY: **Quarterly**

CURRENT RATES (INDIVIDUAL): **$48**
(INSTITUTIONAL): **$90**   (ASSOCIATE/STUDENT):

ANNUAL INDEX AVAILABILITY: **Yes**   COST:
SPECIAL SUPPLEMENTS: **No**   COST:
SUBSCRIPTION ADDRESS: **Kluwer Academic Publishers Group**
PO Box 322
3300 AH Dordrecht
Netherlands

STYLE/SUBMISSION REQUIREMENTS

STYLE: **See style sheet**   STYLE SHEET: **On Request**
REVIEW CHARGE: **None**   COST:
NUMBER OF COPIES: **3**   PAGE LIMIT: **25-30**
RESPONSE TO QUERY LETTERS: **Yes**

GENERAL INFORMATION

JOURNAL TITLE: **ILLINOIS TEACHER OF HOME ECONOMICS**

MANUSCRIPT ADDRESS: **Mildred Barnes Griggs, Editor**
University of Illinois
347 Education Bldg.
1310 S. Sixth St.
Champaign, IL 61820

TYPE OF ARTICLES: **Case studies; commentaries; book reviews**

MAJOR CONTENT AREAS: **Curriculum development; program and student eval; teaching techniques**

TOPICS PREFERRED: **Nutrition; child development; consumer education; family relations; clothing; occupational home economics**

REVIEW PERIOD: **<2 mo**   EARLY PUB OPTION: **No**
PUBLICATION LAG TIME: **3-5 mo**

ACCEPT WITHOUT REVISION: **20%**   REJECTION RATE: **20%**
ACCEPT WITH REVISION: **60%**

THEMATIC ISSUES USED: **Yes**

CIRCULATION

NUMBER: **3750**   FREQUENCY: **Bimonthly**

CURRENT RATES (INDIVIDUAL): **$15**
(INSTITUTIONAL): **$15**   (ASSOCIATE/STUDENT): **$10**

ANNUAL INDEX AVAILABILITY: **Yes**   COST: **Free**
SPECIAL SUPPLEMENTS: **No**   COST:
SUBSCRIPTION ADDRESS: **University of Illinois**
Illinois Teacher
Room 105
51 East Armory Ave.
Champaign, IL 61820

STYLE/SUBMISSION REQUIREMENTS

STYLE: **APA**   STYLE SHEET: **Yes**
REVIEW CHARGE: **No**   COST:
NUMBER OF COPIES: **2**   PAGE LIMIT: **None**
RESPONSE TO QUERY LETTERS: **Yes**

GENERAL INFORMATION

JOURNAL TITLE: **INTERNATIONAL JOURNAL OF THE ADDICTIONS**

MANUSCRIPT ADDRESS: **Nancy Reid-Rapport, Editorial Assistant C/O 15 Pine Tree Circle Cotati, CA 94931**

TYPE OF ARTICLES: **Research**

MAJOR CONTENT AREAS: **Training and treatment in field of addiction and substance abuse**

TOPICS PREFERRED:

REVIEW PERIOD: EARLY PUB OPTION:
PUBLICATION LAG TIME:

ACCEPT WITHOUT REVISION: REJECTION RATE:
ACCEPT WITH REVISION:

THEMATIC ISSUES USED:

CIRCULATION

NUMBER: FREQUENCY: **Monthly**

CURRENT RATES (INDIVIDUAL): **$675**
(INSTITUTIONAL): **$1350**   (ASSOCIATE/STUDENT):

ANNUAL INDEX AVAILABILITY: COST:
SPECIAL SUPPLEMENTS: COST:
SUBSCRIPTION ADDRESS: **Marcel Dekker, Inc. 270 Madison Ave. New York, NY 10016**

STYLE/SUBMISSION REQUIREMENTS

STYLE: STYLE SHEET:
REVIEW CHARGE: COST:
NUMBER OF COPIES: **2**   PAGE LIMIT:
RESPONSE TO QUERY LETTERS:

GENERAL INFORMATION

JOURNAL TITLE: **INTERNATIONAL JOURNAL OF AGING AND HUMAN DEVELOPMENT**
MANUSCRIPT ADDRESS: **Dr. Robert J. Kastenbaum**
Department of Communication
Arizona State University
Tempe, AZ 85287-1205

TYPE OF ARTICLES:

MAJOR CONTENT AREAS: **Psychological and social studies of aging and the aged**

TOPICS PREFERRED:

REVIEW PERIOD: EARLY PUB OPTION:
PUBLICATION LAG TIME:

ACCEPT WITHOUT REVISION: REJECTION RATE:
ACCEPT WITH REVISION:

HEMATIC ISSUES USED:

CIRCULATION

NUMBER: FREQUENCY: **8 X yr**

CURRENT RATES (INDIVIDUAL): **$54**
(INSTITUTIONAL): **$137** (ASSOCIATE/STUDENT):

ANNUAL INDEX AVAILABILITY: **Yes** COST: **$150**
SPECIAL SUPPLEMENTS: COST:
SUBSCRIPTION ADDRESS: **Baywood Publishing Company, Inc.**
26 Austin Ave.
P.O. Box 337
Amityville, NY 11701

STYLE/SUBMISSION REQUIREMENTS

STYLE: STYLE SHEET:
REVIEW CHARGE: COST:
NUMBER OF COPIES: **3** PAGE LIMIT:
RESPONSE TO QUERY LETTERS:

GENERAL INFORMATION

JOURNAL TITLE: **INTERNATIONAL JOURNAL OF
COMPARATIVE SOCIOLOGY**

MANUSCRIPT ADDRESS: **K. Ishwaran, General Editor
Dept. of Sociology
York University
Downsview, Ontario M3J 1P3
Canada**

TYPE OF ARTICLES: **Social sciences, comparative**

MAJOR CONTENT AREAS: **Serves all areas of social sciences, including
family sociology**

TOPICS PREFERRED:

REVIEW PERIOD: **3 mo** EARLY PUB OPTION:
PUBLICATION LAG TIME: **12-16 mo**

ACCEPT WITHOUT REVISION: REJECTION RATE:
ACCEPT WITH REVISION:

THEMATIC ISSUES USED:

CIRCULATION

NUMBER: FREQUENCY: **Quarterly**

CURRENT RATES (INDIVIDUAL):
(INSTITUTIONAL): (ASSOCIATE/STUDENT):

ANNUAL INDEX AVAILABILITY: COST:
SPECIAL SUPPLEMENTS: COST:
SUBSCRIPTION ADDRESS: **E. J. Brill Publishers
PO Box 9000
2300 PA Leiden
Netherlands**

STYLE/SUBMISSION REQUIREMENTS

STYLE: **AJS** STYLE SHEET: **Yes**
REVIEW CHARGE: **No** COST:
NUMBER OF COPIES: **3** PAGE LIMIT: **20-22**
RESPONSE TO QUERY LETTERS: **Usually**

GENERAL INFORMATION

JOURNAL TITLE: **INTERNATIONAL JOURNAL OF EATING DISORDERS**

MANUSCRIPT ADDRESS: **Michael Strober, PhD**
Editor-in-Chief
Department of Psychiatry and
Biobehavioral Sciences-UCLA
760 Westwood Plaza
Los Angeles, CA 90024

TYPE OF ARTICLES: **Basic research; theoretical articles**

MAJOR CONTENT AREAS: **Variety of aspects of anorexia, bulemia, obesity and other atypical patterns of eating behavior**

TOPICS PREFERRED:

REVIEW PERIOD: EARLY PUB OPTION:
PUBLICATION LAG TIME:

ACCEPT WITHOUT REVISION: REJECTION RATE:
ACCEPT WITH REVISION:

THEMATIC ISSUES USED:

CIRCULATION

NUMBER: FREQUENCY: **Bimonthly**

CURRENT RATES (INDIVIDUAL): **$95**
(INSTITUTIONAL): **$230** (ASSOCIATE/STUDENT):

ANNUAL INDEX AVAILABILITY: COST:
SPECIAL SUPPLEMENTS: COST:
SUBSCRIPTION ADDRESS: **John Wiley and Sons, Inc.**
605 Third Ave.
New York, NY 10158

STYLE/SUBMISSION REQUIREMENTS

STYLE: **APA** STYLE SHEET:
REVIEW CHARGE: COST:
NUMBER OF COPIES: PAGE LIMIT:
RESPONSE TO QUERY LETTERS:

GENERAL INFORMATION

JOURNAL TITLE: **INTERNATIONAL JOURNAL OF LAW AND THE FAMILY**

MANUSCRIPT ADDRESS: **John Eekelaar**
Pembroke College
Oxford OX1 1DW, U.K.

TYPE OF ARTICLES: **Research; theoretical; commentaries; book reviews**

MAJOR CONTENT AREAS: **Family issues (worldwide), especially where they have relevance to law and legal policy**

TOPICS PREFERRED: **All topics considered**

REVIEW PERIOD: **<2 mo**   EARLY PUB OPTION: **No**
PUBLICATION LAG TIME: **>6 mo**

ACCEPT WITHOUT REVISION: **20%**   REJECTION RATE: **25%**
ACCEPT WITH REVISION: **75%**

THEMATIC ISSUES USED: **No**

CIRCULATION

NUMBER: **350**   FREQUENCY: **3 X yr**

CURRENT RATES (INDIVIDUAL): **£40 (U.K.); £44 (E.C.); $60 (U.S.)**
(INSTITUTIONAL):   (ASSOCIATE/STUDENT):

ANNUAL INDEX AVAILABILITY: **No**   COST:
SPECIAL SUPPLEMENTS: **No**   COST:
SUBSCRIPTION ADDRESS:

STYLE/SUBMISSION REQUIREMENTS

STYLE: **Flexible**   STYLE SHEET: **Yes**
REVIEW CHARGE: **No**   COST:
NUMBER OF COPIES: **3**   PAGE LIMIT: **None**
RESPONSE TO QUERY LETTERS: **Yes**

GENERAL INFORMATION

JOURNAL TITLE: **INTERNATIONAL JOURNAL OF SOCIOLOGY OF THE FAMILY**
MANUSCRIPT ADDRESS: **Man Singh Das, Ph.D., Editor**
Department of Sociology
Northern Illinois University
Dekalb, IL 60115

TYPE OF ARTICLES: **Research; review; theoretical; commentaries; book reviews; case studies**
MAJOR CONTENT AREAS: **Cross-national, cross-cultural and interdisciplinary research in marriage and the family**

TOPICS PREFERRED:

REVIEW PERIOD: **<2 mo**   EARLY PUB OPTION: **No**
PUBLICATION LAG TIME: **>6 mo**

ACCEPT WITHOUT REVISION: **20%**   REJECTION RATE: **30%**
ACCEPT WITH REVISION: **50%**

THEMATIC ISSUES USED: **Yes**

CIRCULATION

NUMBER: **1500**   FREQUENCY: **2 X yr**

CURRENT RATES (INDIVIDUAL): **$50**
(INSTITUTIONAL): **$50**   (ASSOCIATE/STUDENT): **$50**

ANNUAL INDEX AVAILABILITY: **No**   COST:
SPECIAL SUPPLEMENTS: **Yes**   COST: **$25**
SUBSCRIPTION ADDRESS: **Prints India**
11 Darya Ganj
New Delhi- 110002
India

STYLE/SUBMISSION REQUIREMENTS

STYLE: **ASR**   STYLE SHEET: **Yes**
REVIEW CHARGE: **Yes**   COST: **$25**
NUMBER OF COPIES: **3**   PAGE LIMIT: **30**
RESPONSE TO QUERY LETTERS: **Yes**

GENERAL INFORMATION

JOURNAL TITLE: **INTERNATIONAL JOURNAL OF TECHNOLOGY AND AGING**

MANUSCRIPT ADDRESS: **Gari Lesnoff-Caravaglia, Ph.D.**
Director, National Clearinghouse
on Technology and Aging
College of Health and Human Services
Ohio University
Athens, OH 45701

TYPE OF ARTICLES:

MAJOR CONTENT AREAS: **Aspects of technology and aging**

TOPICS PREFERRED:

REVIEW PERIOD: EARLY PUB OPTION:
PUBLICATION LAG TIME:

ACCEPT WITHOUT REVISION: REJECTION RATE:
ACCEPT WITH REVISION:

THEMATIC ISSUES USED:

CIRCULATION

NUMBER: FREQUENCY: **2 X yr**

CURRENT RATES (INDIVIDUAL): **$29**
(INSTITUTIONAL): **$65**   (ASSOCIATE/STUDENT):

ANNUAL INDEX AVAILABILITY: COST:
SPECIAL SUPPLEMENTS: COST:
SUBSCRIPTION ADDRESS: **International Journal of**
Technology and Aging
Human Sciences Press
233 Spring St.
New York, NY 10013-1578

STYLE/SUBMISSION REQUIREMENTS

STYLE: **APA**   STYLE SHEET:
REVIEW CHARGE: COST:
NUMBER OF COPIES: **3**   PAGE LIMIT:
RESPONSE TO QUERY LETTERS:

GENERAL INFORMATION

JOURNAL TITLE: **INTERNATIONAL JOURNAL ON WORLD PEACE**

MANUSCRIPT ADDRESS: **Dr. Panos D. Bardis**
University of Toledo
Toledo, OH 43606

TYPE OF ARTICLES: **Research; reviews; theoretical; case studies; commentaries; book reviews poems and short essays**

MAJOR CONTENT AREAS: **All social sciences and humanities plus peace and war**

TOPICS PREFERRED:

REVIEW PERIOD: **<2 mo**   EARLY PUB OPTION: **No**
PUBLICATION LAG TIME: **3-5 mo**

ACCEPT WITHOUT REVISION: **10%**   REJECTION RATE: **80%**
ACCEPT WITH REVISION: **10%**

THEMATIC ISSUES USED: **No**

CIRCULATION

NUMBER: **10,000**   FREQUENCY: **Quarterly**

CURRENT RATES (INDIVIDUAL): **$15**
(INSTITUTIONAL): **$30**   (ASSOCIATE/STUDENT): **$10**

ANNUAL INDEX AVAILABILITY: **Yes**   COST: None
SPECIAL SUPPLEMENTS: COST:
SUBSCRIPTION ADDRESS: **Box 1311**
New York, NY 10116

STYLE/SUBMISSION REQUIREMENTS

STYLE: STYLE SHEET: **Yes**
REVIEW CHARGE: **No**   COST:
NUMBER OF COPIES: **3**   PAGE LIMIT: **10-30**
RESPONSE TO QUERY LETTERS: **Yes**

GENERAL INFORMATION

JOURNAL TITLE: **INTERNATIONAL SOCIAL SCIENCE JOURNAL**

MANUSCRIPT ADDRESS: **Editor**
Unesco, 7 place de Fontenoy
75700 Paris, France

TYPE OF ARTICLES: **Scholarly**

MAJOR CONTENT AREAS: **All social science fields**

TOPICS PREFERRED:

REVIEW PERIOD: **8 wk**   EARLY PUB OPTION: **No**
PUBLICATION LAG TIME: **14 mo**

ACCEPT WITHOUT REVISION: REJECTION RATE:
ACCEPT WITH REVISION: **X**

THEMATIC ISSUES USED: **All issues thematic**

CIRCULATION

NUMBER: **3,600**   FREQUENCY: **4 X yr**

CURRENT RATES (INDIVIDUAL): **$38**
(INSTITUTIONAL): **$69**   (ASSOCIATE/STUDENT):

ANNUAL INDEX AVAILABILITY: **Yes**   COST:
SPECIAL SUPPLEMENTS: COST:
SUBSCRIPTION ADDRESS: **Basil Blackwell Ltd.**
108 Cowley Rd.
Oxford OX4 1JF, U.K.

STYLE/SUBMISSION REQUIREMENTS

STYLE: STYLE SHEET: **Yes**
REVIEW CHARGE: COST:
NUMBER OF COPIES: **3**   PAGE LIMIT: **306**
RESPONSE TO QUERY LETTERS: **Yes**

GENERAL INFORMATION

JOURNAL TITLE: **INTERNATIONAL SOCIAL SCIENCE REVIEW**

MANUSCRIPT ADDRESS: **Dr. Panos D. Bardis**
University of Toledo
Toldeo, OH 43606

TYPE OF ARTICLES: **Research; reviews; theoretical; case studies; commentaries; book reviews**

MAJOR CONTENT AREAS: **All social sciences and humanities**

TOPICS PREFERRED: **Cross-cultural; sociohistorical**

REVIEW PERIOD: **< 2 mo**   EARLY PUB OPTION: **No**
PUBLICATION LAG TIME: **3-5 mo**

ACCEPT WITHOUT REVISION: **10%**   REJECTION RATE: **80%**
ACCEPT WITH REVISION: **10%**

THEMATIC ISSUES USED: **No**

CIRCULATION

NUMBER: **14,000**   FREQUENCY: **Quarterly**

CURRENT RATES (INDIVIDUAL): **$10**
(INSTITUTIONAL): **$10**   (ASSOCIATE/STUDENT):

ANNUAL INDEX AVAILABILITY: **Yes**   COST: **Free**
SPECIAL SUPPLEMENTS: COST:
SUBSCRIPTION ADDRESS: **1717 Ames**
Winfield, Kansas 67156

STYLE/SUBMISSION REQUIREMENTS

STYLE: STYLE SHEET: **Yes**
REVIEW CHARGE: **No**   COST:
NUMBER OF COPIES: **3**   PAGE LIMIT: **10-30**
RESPONSE TO QUERY LETTERS: **Yes**

GENERAL INFORMATION

JOURNAL TITLE: **INTERNATIONAL SOCIOLOGY**

MANUSCRIPT ADDRESS: **Martin Albrow, Editor**
University College
P.O. Box 78
Cardiff, CF1 1XL, U. K.

TYPE OF ARTICLES:

MAJOR CONTENT AREAS:

TOPICS PREFERRED:

REVIEW PERIOD: EARLY PUB OPTION:
PUBLICATION LAG TIME:

ACCEPT WITHOUT REVISION: REJECTION RATE:
ACCEPT WITH REVISION:

THEMATIC ISSUES USED:

CIRCULATION

NUMBER: FREQUENCY:

CURRENT RATES (INDIVIDUAL): **£22**
(INSTITUTIONAL): **£40**   (ASSOCIATE/STUDENT):

ANNUAL INDEX AVAILABILITY: COST:
SPECIAL SUPPLEMENTS: COST:
SUBSCRIPTION ADDRESS: **Sage Publications, Ltd.**
28 Banner St.
London EC1Y 8QE, U. K.

STYLE/SUBMISSION REQUIREMENTS

STYLE: STYLE SHEET: **Yes**
REVIEW CHARGE: COST:
NUMBER OF COPIES: **2**   PAGE LIMIT: **6000 words**
RESPONSE TO QUERY LETTERS:

GENERAL INFORMATION

JOURNAL TITLE: **JABS**

MANUSCRIPT ADDRESS: **Catherine Messina**
NTL Institute
1240 N. Pitt St., Suite 100
Alexandria, VA 22314-1403

TYPE OF ARTICLES:

MAJOR CONTENT AREAS:

TOPICS PREFERRED:

REVIEW PERIOD: **3-12 wk**   EARLY PUB OPTION:
PUBLICATION LAG TIME:

ACCEPT WITHOUT REVISION: REJECTION RATE:
ACCEPT WITH REVISION:

THEMATIC ISSUES USED:

CIRCULATION

NUMBER: FREQUENCY:

CURRENT RATES (INDIVIDUAL):
(INSTITUTIONAL): (ASSOCIATE/STUDENT):

ANNUAL INDEX AVAILABILITY: COST:
SPECIAL SUPPLEMENTS: COST:
SUBSCRIPTION ADDRESS: **JAI Press, Inc.**
55 Old Post Rd. #2
P.O. Box 1678
Greenwich, CT 06836

STYLE/SUBMISSION REQUIREMENTS

STYLE: **APA**   STYLE SHEET:
REVIEW CHARGE: COST:
NUMBER OF COPIES: **5**   PAGE LIMIT:
RESPONSE TO QUERY LETTERS:

GENERAL INFORMATION

JOURNAL TITLE: **JOURNAL OF ABNORMAL CHILD PSYCHOLOGY**

MANUSCRIPT ADDRESS: **Herbert C. Quay**
P.O. Box 24-8074
Coral Gables, FL 33124

TYPE OF ARTICLES:

MAJOR CONTENT AREAS: **Behavioral pathology in childhood & adolescence**

TOPICS PREFERRED:

REVIEW PERIOD: EARLY PUB OPTION:
PUBLICATION LAG TIME:

ACCEPT WITHOUT REVISION: REJECTION RATE:
ACCEPT WITH REVISION:

THEMATIC ISSUES USED:

CIRCULATION

NUMBER: FREQUENCY: **Bimonthly**

CURRENT RATES (INDIVIDUAL): **$49.50**
(INSTITUTIONAL): **$225**   (ASSOCIATE/STUDENT):

ANNUAL INDEX AVAILABILITY: COST:
SPECIAL SUPPLEMENTS: COST:
SUBSCRIPTION ADDRESS: **Plenum Publishing Corp.**
233 Spring St.
New York, NY 10013

STYLE/SUBMISSION REQUIREMENTS

STYLE: **APA**   STYLE SHEET:
REVIEW CHARGE: COST:
NUMBER OF COPIES: **3**   PAGE LIMIT:
RESPONSE TO QUERY LETTERS:

GENERAL INFORMATION

JOURNAL TITLE: **JOURNAL OF ABNORMAL CLINICAL PSYCHOLOGY**

MANUSCRIPT ADDRESS: **Herbert C. Quoz**
Box 248074
University of Miami
Corol Gaslen, FL 33124

TYPE OF ARTICLES: **Research; reviews; theoretical**

MAJOR CONTENT AREAS: **Child and adolescent psychology**

TOPICS PREFERRED:

REVIEW PERIOD: **3-5 mo**   EARLY PUB OPTION: **No**
PUBLICATION LAG TIME: **>6 mo**

ACCEPT WITHOUT REVISION: **1%**   REJECTION RATE: **70%**
ACCEPT WITH REVISION: **29%**

THEMATIC ISSUES USED: **No**

CIRCULATION

NUMBER: **1100**   FREQUENCY: **6 X yr**

CURRENT RATES (INDIVIDUAL): **$67**
(INSTITUTIONAL): **$245**   (ASSOCIATE/STUDENT):

ANNUAL INDEX AVAILABILITY: **No**   COST:
SPECIAL SUPPLEMENTS: **No**   COST:
SUBSCRIPTION ADDRESS: **Journal of Abnormal Child Psychology**
Plenum Publishers
233 Spring St.
New York, NY 10013

STYLE/SUBMISSION REQUIREMENTS

STYLE: **APA**   STYLE SHEET: **Yes**
REVIEW CHARGE: **No**   COST:
NUMBER OF COPIES: **3**   PAGE LIMIT: **None**
RESPONSE TO QUERY LETTERS:

GENERAL INFORMATION

JOURNAL TITLE: **JOURNAL OF ABNORMAL PSYCHOLOGY**

MANUSCRIPT ADDRESS: **Susan Mineka, Editor**
Northwestern University
Dept. of Psychology
102 Swift Hall
Evanston, IL 60208

TYPE OF ARTICLES: **Basic research and theory**

MAJOR CONTENT AREAS:

TOPICS PREFERRED:

REVIEW PERIOD: EARLY PUB OPTION:
PUBLICATION LAG TIME:

ACCEPT WITHOUT REVISION: REJECTION RATE:
ACCEPT WITH REVISION:

THEMATIC ISSUES USED:

CIRCULATION

NUMBER: FREQUENCY: **Quarterly**

CURRENT RATES (INDIVIDUAL): **$60**
(INSTITUTIONAL): **$120**   (ASSOCIATE/STUDENT):

ANNUAL INDEX AVAILABILITY: COST:
SPECIAL SUPPLEMENTS: COST:
SUBSCRIPTION ADDRESS: **APA, Inc.**
1400 North Uhle St.
Arlington, VA 22201

STYLE/SUBMISSION REQUIREMENTS

STYLE: STYLE SHEET:
REVIEW CHARGE: COST:
NUMBER OF COPIES: **5**   PAGE LIMIT:
RESPONSE TO QUERY LETTERS:

GENERAL INFORMATION

JOURNAL TITLE: **JOURNAL OF ADOLESCENCE**

MANUSCRIPT ADDRESS: **Dr. Alan Waterman**
Trenton State College
Hillwood Lakes, CN 08650

TYPE OF ARTICLES: **Theory; research; clinical practice; reviews**

MAJOR CONTENT AREAS: **Adolescent development; treatment and**
management of adolescent disorders

TOPICS PREFERRED:

REVIEW PERIOD: EARLY PUB OPTION:
PUBLICATION LAG TIME:

ACCEPT WITHOUT REVISION: REJECTION RATE:
ACCEPT WITH REVISION:

THEMATIC ISSUES USED:

CIRCULATION

NUMBER: FREQUENCY:

CURRENT RATES (INDIVIDUAL):
(INSTITUTIONAL):   (ASSOCIATE/STUDENT):

ANNUAL INDEX AVAILABILITY: COST:
SPECIAL SUPPLEMENTS: COST:
SUBSCRIPTION ADDRESS:

STYLE/SUBMISSION REQUIREMENTS

STYLE: **APA**   STYLE SHEET:
REVIEW CHARGE: COST:
NUMBER OF COPIES: **4**   PAGE LIMIT: **5000 words**
RESPONSE TO QUERY LETTERS:

GENERAL INFORMATION

JOURNAL TITLE: **JOURNAL OF ADOLESCENT RESEARCH**

MANUSCRIPT ADDRESS: **E. Ellen Thornburg, Editor**
H.E.L.P. Books, Inc.
1201 E. Calle Elena
Tucson, AZ 85718

TYPE OF ARTICLES: **Major theoretical papers, state-of-the-art papers, and current research**

MAJOR CONTENT AREAS: **Increase understanding of individuals 11-22**

TOPICS PREFERRED:

REVIEW PERIOD: EARLY PUB OPTION:
PUBLICATION LAG TIME:

ACCEPT WITHOUT REVISION: REJECTION RATE:
ACCEPT WITH REVISION:

THEMATIC ISSUES USED:

CIRCULATION

NUMBER: FREQUENCY: **4 X yr**

CURRENT RATES (INDIVIDUAL): **$38**
(INSTITUTIONAL): **$84**   (ASSOCIATE/STUDENT):

ANNUAL INDEX AVAILABILITY: COST:
SPECIAL SUPPLEMENTS: COST:
SUBSCRIPTION ADDRESS: **Sage Publications, Inc.**
2455 Teller Rd.
Newbury Park, Ca 91320

STYLE/SUBMISSION REQUIREMENTS

STYLE: **APA**   STYLE SHEET:
REVIEW CHARGE: COST:
NUMBER OF COPIES: **5**   PAGE LIMIT:
RESPONSE TO QUERY LETTERS:

GENERAL INFORMATION

JOURNAL TITLE: **JOURNAL OF AGING AND HEALTH**

MANUSCRIPT ADDRESS: **Kyriakos S. Markides, PhD, editor**
Dept. of Preventative Medicine
and Community Health
U of Texas Medical Branch
Galveston, TX 77550

TYPE OF ARTICLES: **Research; reviews; theoretical**

MAJOR CONTENT AREAS: **Behavioral and social factors related to aging and health**

TOPICS PREFERRED: **Deal with social and behavioral factors related to health and aging (original research)**

REVIEW PERIOD: **< 2 mo**   EARLY PUB OPTION: **No**
PUBLICATION LAG TIME: **6 mo or more**

ACCEPT WITHOUT REVISION: **5%**   REJECTION RATE: **80%**
ACCEPT WITH REVISION: **15%**

THEMATIC ISSUES USED: **Yes**

CIRCULATION

NUMBER: FREQUENCY: **4 X yr**

CURRENT RATES (INDIVIDUAL): **$35.10**
(INSTITUTIONAL): **$79.20**   (ASSOCIATE/STUDENT):

ANNUAL INDEX AVAILABILITY: COST:
SPECIAL SUPPLEMENTS: COST:
SUBSCRIPTION ADDRESS: **Sage Publications, Inc.**
2455 Teller Rd.
Newbury Park, CA 91320

STYLE/SUBMISSION REQUIREMENTS

STYLE: **APA**   STYLE SHEET:
REVIEW CHARGE: COST:
NUMBER OF COPIES: **4**   PAGE LIMIT: **30**
RESPONSE TO QUERY LETTERS:

GENERAL INFORMATION

JOURNAL TITLE: **JOURNAL OF AGING & SOCIAL POLICY**

MANUSCRIPT ADDRESS: **Scott A. Bass and Robert Morris, Editors**
Journal of Aging and Social Policy
Gerontology Institute
University of Massachussetts at Boston
Downtown Center
Boston, MA 02125

TYPE OF ARTICLES:

MAJOR CONTENT AREAS: **Highlights issues and problems of elders due to**
contemporary policy by providing critical
analysis of policy

TOPICS PREFERRED: **History of contemporary issues; evolution of**
policy; examinations of literature related to
policy

REVIEW PERIOD: EARLY PUB OPTION:
PUBLICATION LAG TIME:

ACCEPT WITHOUT REVISION: REJECTION RATE:
ACCEPT WITH REVISION:

THEMATIC ISSUES USED:

CIRCULATION

NUMBER: FREQUENCY: **Quarterly**

CURRENT RATES (INDIVIDUAL): **$28**
(INSTITUTIONAL): **$32**   (ASSOCIATE/STUDENT):

ANNUAL INDEX AVAILABILITY: **Yes**   COST:
SPECIAL SUPPLEMENTS: COST:
SUBSCRIPTION ADDRESS: **The Haworth Press, Inc.**
10 Alice St.
Binghamton, NY 13904-1580

STYLE/SUBMISSION REQUIREMENTS

STYLE: **APA**   STYLE SHEET:
REVIEW CHARGE: **No**   COST:
NUMBER OF COPIES: **4 + diskette**   PAGE LIMIT: **20**
RESPONSE TO QUERY LETTERS:

GENERAL INFORMATION

JOURNAL TITLE: **JOURNAL OF AGING STUDIES**

MANUSCRIPT ADDRESS: **Jaber F. Gubrium, Editor**
Dept. of Sociology
U of Florida
Gainesville, FL 32611

TYPE OF ARTICLES:

MAJOR CONTENT AREAS:

TOPICS PREFERRED: **Critical, empirical, theoretical contributions**
welcome

REVIEW PERIOD: EARLY PUB OPTION:
PUBLICATION LAG TIME:

ACCEPT WITHOUT REVISION: REJECTION RATE:
ACCEPT WITH REVISION:

THEMATIC ISSUES USED:

CIRCULATION

NUMBER: FREQUENCY:

CURRENT RATES (INDIVIDUAL): **On request**
(INSTITUTIONAL): (ASSOCIATE/STUDENT):

ANNUAL INDEX AVAILABILITY: COST:
SPECIAL SUPPLEMENTS: COST:
SUBSCRIPTION ADDRESS: **JAI Press, Inc.**
55 Old Post Rd. No. 2
PO Box 1678
Greenwich, CT 06836-1678

STYLE/SUBMISSION REQUIREMENTS

STYLE: **ASA** STYLE SHEET:
REVIEW CHARGE: COST:
NUMBER OF COPIES: **4** PAGE LIMIT:
RESPONSE TO QUERY LETTERS:

GENERAL INFORMATION

JOURNAL TITLE: **JOURNAL OF ALCOHOL AND DRUG EDUCATION**

MANUSCRIPT ADDRESS: **Department of Sociology
Box 870219
University of Alabama
Tuscaloosa, AL 35487-0219**

TYPE OF ARTICLES: **Research; reviews; theoretical; case studies; commentaries; book reviews**

MAJOR CONTENT AREAS: **Research on usage and programs for prevention in alcohol/drugs**

TOPICS PREFERRED: **Usage studies; education/prevention including intervention programs (DWI; employee assistance; family); treatment programs for youth**

REVIEW PERIOD: **<2 mo**   EARLY PUB OPTION: **No**
PUBLICATION LAG TIME: **>6mo**

ACCEPT WITHOUT REVISION: **25%**   REJECTION RATE: **50%**
ACCEPT WITH REVISION: **25%**

THEMATIC ISSUES USED: **No**

CIRCULATION

NUMBER: **1000**   FREQUENCY: **3 X yr**

CURRENT RATES (INDIVIDUAL): **$35/$25 ADPA mem**
(INSTITUTIONAL):   (ASSOCIATE/STUDENT):

ANNUAL INDEX AVAILABILITY: **No**   COST:
SPECIAL SUPPLEMENTS: **No**   COST:
SUBSCRIPTION ADDRESS: **Journal Executive
1120 East Oakland
P.O. Box 1-212
Lansing, MI 48901**

STYLE/SUBMISSION REQUIREMENTS

STYLE: **APA**   STYLE SHEET: **Yes**
REVIEW CHARGE: **No**   COST:
NUMBER OF COPIES: **3**   PAGE LIMIT: **10-15**
RESPONSE TO QUERY LETTERS: **Yes**

GENERAL INFORMATION

JOURNAL TITLE: **JOURNAL OF AMERICAN ETHNIC HISTORY**

MANUSCRIPT ADDRESS: **Professor Ronald Baylor**
Social Science
Georgia Tech
Atlanta, GA 30332

TYPE OF ARTICLES: **Research; case studies; historiographical**

MAJOR CONTENT AREAS: **Ethnicity; race; immigration in North America**

TOPICS PREFERRED: **Historically based essays which are analytical or interpretive; any topic which focuses on ethnicity or race**
REVIEW PERIOD: **3-5 mo**   EARLY PUB OPTION: **No**
PUBLICATION LAG TIME: **>6 mo**

ACCEPT WITHOUT REVISION: **10%**   REJECTION RATE: **50%**
ACCEPT WITH REVISION: **40%**

THEMATIC ISSUES USED: **Yes**

CIRCULATION

NUMBER: **1000**   FREQUENCY: **Quarterly**

CURRENT RATES (INDIVIDUAL): **$30**
(INSTITUTIONAL): **$60**   (ASSOCIATE/STUDENT): **$15**

ANNUAL INDEX AVAILABILITY: **No**   COST:
SPECIAL SUPPLEMENTS: **No**   COST:
SUBSCRIPTION ADDRESS: **Transaction Periodicals**
Rutgers University
New Brunswick, NJ 08903

STYLE/SUBMISSION REQUIREMENTS

STYLE: **Chicago**   STYLE SHEET: **No**
REVIEW CHARGE: **No**   COST:
NUMBER OF COPIES: **3**   PAGE LIMIT: **30-35**
RESPONSE TO QUERY LETTERS: **Yes**

GENERAL INFORMATION

JOURNAL TITLE: **JOURNAL OF APPLIED GERONTOLOGY**

MANUSCRIPT ADDRESS: **Miles Simpson, Editor**
PO Box 51026
Durham, NC 27717-1026

TYPE OF ARTICLES: **Focus explicitly on application of knowledge to improvement of quality of life of older persons**

MAJOR CONTENT AREAS: **Major goal—publish findings, recomendations, and promising ideas that have general applicability to and significance for older persons everywhere**

TOPICS PREFERRED:

REVIEW PERIOD: EARLY PUB OPTION:
PUBLICATION LAG TIME:

ACCEPT WITHOUT REVISION: REJECTION RATE:
ACCEPT WITH REVISION:

THEMATIC ISSUES USED:

CIRCULATION

NUMBER: FREQUENCY: **Quarterly**

CURRENT RATES (INDIVIDUAL): **$39**
(INSTITUTIONAL): **$98**   (ASSOCIATE/STUDENT):

ANNUAL INDEX AVAILABILITY: COST:
SPECIAL SUPPLEMENTS: COST:
SUBSCRIPTION ADDRESS: **Sage Publications, Inc.**
2455 Teller Rd.
Newbury Park, CA 91320

STYLE/SUBMISSION REQUIREMENTS

STYLE: **APA**   STYLE SHEET:
REVIEW CHARGE: COST:
NUMBER OF COPIES: **4**   PAGE LIMIT: **20**
RESPONSE TO QUERY LETTERS:

GENERAL INFORMATION

JOURNAL TITLE: **JOURNAL OF APPLIED PSYCHOLOGY**

MANUSCRIPT ADDRESS: **Neal Schmitt, Editor**
Dept. of Psychology
Michigan State University
East Lansing, MI 48824-1117

TYPE OF ARTICLES:

MAJOR CONTENT AREAS: **Original, investigations that contribute new knowledge and understanding to any field of applied psychology except clinical psychology**

TOPICS PREFERRED:

REVIEW PERIOD: EARLY PUB OPTION:
PUBLICATION LAG TIME:

ACCEPT WITHOUT REVISION: REJECTION RATE:
ACCEPT WITH REVISION:

THEMATIC ISSUES USED:

CIRCULATION

NUMBER: FREQUENCY: **Bimonthly**

CURRENT RATES (INDIVIDUAL): **$100**
(INSTITUTIONAL): **$200**   (ASSOCIATE/STUDENT): **$50**

ANNUAL INDEX AVAILABILITY: COST:
SPECIAL SUPPLEMENTS: COST:
SUBSCRIPTION ADDRESS: **APA, Inc.**
1400 North Uhle St.
Arlington, VA 22201

STYLE/SUBMISSION REQUIREMENTS

STYLE: STYLE SHEET:
REVIEW CHARGE: COST:
NUMBER OF COPIES: **4**   PAGE LIMIT:
RESPONSE TO QUERY LETTERS:

GENERAL INFORMATION

JOURNAL TITLE: **JOURNAL OF ASIAN AND AFRICAN STUDIES**

MANUSCRIPT ADDRESS: **Yoendra Malik**
Dept. of Political Science
University of Akron
Akron, OH

TYPE OF ARTICLES: **Presents scholarly accounts of studies of humankind and society in developing nations of Asia and Africa**

MAJOR CONTENT AREAS: **Invites contributions from anthropology, sociology, history, and other social sciences**

TOPICS PREFERRED:

REVIEW PERIOD: EARLY PUB OPTION:
PUBLICATION LAG TIME:

ACCEPT WITHOUT REVISION: REJECTION RATE:
ACCEPT WITH REVISION:

THEMATIC ISSUES USED:

CIRCULATION

NUMBER: FREQUENCY: **Quarterly**

CURRENT RATES (INDIVIDUAL):
(INSTITUTIONAL):   (ASSOCIATE/STUDENT):

ANNUAL INDEX AVAILABILITY: COST:
SPECIAL SUPPLEMENTS: COST:
SUBSCRIPTION ADDRESS: **E. J. Brill Publishers**
PO Box 9000
2300 PA Leiden
Netherlands

STYLE/SUBMISSION REQUIREMENTS

STYLE: STYLE SHEET:
REVIEW CHARGE: COST:
NUMBER OF COPIES: PAGE LIMIT:
RESPONSE TO QUERY LETTERS:

GENERAL INFORMATION

JOURNAL TITLE: **JOURNAL OF BUSINESS AND PSYCHOLOGY**

MANUSCRIPT ADDRESS: **London House/SRD**
1550 Northwest Highway
Park Ridge, IL 60068

TYPE OF ARTICLES: **Research; theoretical; book reviews**

MAJOR CONTENT AREAS: **Psychology issues in the workplace**

TOPICS PREFERRED: **Employee health psychology; experiential studies; health care cost containment; impact of workplace on family**

REVIEW PERIOD: **3-5 mo**   EARLY PUB OPTION: **Yes**
PUBLICATION LAG TIME: **3-5 mo**

ACCEPT WITHOUT REVISION: **5%**   REJECTION RATE: **70%**
ACCEPT WITH REVISION: **25%**

THEMATIC ISSUES USED: **Yes**

CIRCULATION

NUMBER: FREQUENCY:

CURRENT RATES (INDIVIDUAL):
(INSTITUTIONAL):   (ASSOCIATE/STUDENT):

ANNUAL INDEX AVAILABILITY: COST:
SPECIAL SUPPLEMENTS: COST:
SUBSCRIPTION ADDRESS:

STYLE/SUBMISSION REQUIREMENTS

STYLE: STYLE SHEET:
REVIEW CHARGE: COST:
NUMBER OF COPIES: PAGE LIMIT:
RESPONSE TO QUERY LETTERS:

GENERAL INFORMATION

JOURNAL TITLE: **JOURNAL OF CLINICAL PSYCHOLOGY**

MANUSCRIPT ADDRESS: **Dr. Vladimir Pishkin, Editor**
3113 NW 62nd St.
Oklahoma City, OK 73112

TYPE OF ARTICLES: **Research; reviews**

MAJOR CONTENT AREAS: **Psychopathology**

TOPICS PREFERRED: **Experimental research**

REVIEW PERIOD: **> 6 mo**   EARLY PUB OPTION: **No**
PUBLICATION LAG TIME: **> 6 mo**

ACCEPT WITHOUT REVISION: **5%**   REJECTION RATE: **80%**
ACCEPT WITH REVISION: **15%**

THEMATIC ISSUES USED: **Yes**

CIRCULATION

NUMBER: **4500**   FREQUENCY: **Bimonthly**

CURRENT RATES (INDIVIDUAL): **$40**
(INSTITUTIONAL): **$100**   (ASSOCIATE/STUDENT):

ANNUAL INDEX AVAILABILITY: **Yes**   COST:
SPECIAL SUPPLEMENTS: **Yes**   COST:
SUBSCRIPTION ADDRESS: **CPPC**
4 Conant Square
Brandon, VT 05733

STYLE/SUBMISSION REQUIREMENTS

STYLE: **APA**   STYLE SHEET: **No**
REVIEW CHARGE: **No**   COST:
NUMBER OF COPIES: **4**   PAGE LIMIT: **N/A**
RESPONSE TO QUERY LETTERS: **Yes**

GENERAL INFORMATION

JOURNAL TITLE: **JOURNAL OF COMPARITIVE FAMILY STUDIES**

MANUSCRIPT ADDRESS: **Attn: Carol Cairns**
Department of Sociology
University of Calgary
2500 University Dr., NW
Calgary, Alberta T2N 1N4
Canda

TYPE OF ARTICLES: **Research; reviews; commentaries; book reviews; case studies; theoretical**

MAJOR CONTENT AREAS: **Cross-cultural research; national; as well as international comparative family studies**

TOPICS PREFERRED: **Cross-cultural perspective on the study of the family**

REVIEW PERIOD: **3-5 mo** EARLY PUB OPTION: **No**
PUBLICATION LAG TIME: **>6 mo**

ACCEPT WITHOUT REVISION: REJECTION RATE: **70%**
ACCEPT WITH REVISION: **30%**

THEMATIC ISSUES USED: **Yes**

CIRCULATION

NUMBER: **800** FREQUENCY: **3 X yr**

CURRENT RATES (INDIVIDUAL): **$40**
(INSTITUTIONAL): **$55** (ASSOCIATE/STUDENT):

ANNUAL INDEX AVAILABILITY: **Yes** COST: **No**
SPECIAL SUPPLEMENTS: **No** COST:
SUBSCRIPTION ADDRESS: **Same as above**

STYLE/SUBMISSION REQUIREMENTS

STYLE: **ASA** STYLE SHEET: **Yes**
REVIEW CHARGE: **No** COST:
NUMBER OF COPIES: **3** PAGE LIMIT: **5000 words**
RESPONSE TO QUERY LETTERS: **Yes**

GENERAL INFORMATION

JOURNAL TITLE: **JOURNAL OF CONSULTING AND CLINICAL PSYCHOLOGY**

MANUSCRIPT ADDRESS: **Larry E. Beutler**
Graduate School Of Education
U of CA at Santa Barbara
Santa Barbara, CA 93106

TYPE OF ARTICLES:

MAJOR CONTENT AREAS:

TOPICS PREFERRED: **Diagnosis or treatment of abnormal behavior**

REVIEW PERIOD: EARLY PUB OPTION:
PUBLICATION LAG TIME:

ACCEPT WITHOUT REVISION: REJECTION RATE:
ACCEPT WITH REVISION:

THEMATIC ISSUES USED:

CIRCULATION

NUMBER: FREQUENCY: **Bimonthly**
CURRENT RATES (INDIVIDUAL): **$120**
(INSTITUTIONAL): **$240**   (ASSOCIATE/STUDENT): **$60**

ANNUAL INDEX AVAILABILITY: COST:
SPECIAL SUPPLEMENTS: COST:
SUBSCRIPTION ADDRESS: **APA, Inc.**
Subscription Section
1400 North Uhle St.
Arlington, VA 22201

STYLE/SUBMISSION REQUIREMENTS

STYLE: STYLE SHEET:
REVIEW CHARGE: COST:
NUMBER OF COPIES: **4**   PAGE LIMIT:
RESPONSE TO QUERY LETTERS:

GENERAL INFORMATION

JOURNAL TITLE: **JOURNAL OF CONSUMER STUDIES & HOME ECONOMICS**

MANUSCRIPT ADDRESS: **Ann Maree Rees**
School of Home Economics
University of Wales
College of Cardiff
P.O. Box 7
Cardiff CF1 1XL, U.K.

TYPE OF ARTICLES: **Research reports, v. occasional review papers**

MAJOR CONTENT AREAS: **Food studies; textile studies; housing; sociological studies; consumer studies; energy and fuels; materials science; education;**

TOPICS PREFERRED: **Multiple**

REVIEW PERIOD: **Up to 6 mo** EARLY PUB OPTION: **Depending**
PUBLICATION LAG TIME: **Apx. 1 yr** **on topic**

ACCEPT WITHOUT REVISION: **If suitable** REJECTION RATE: **Appx. 50%**
ACCEPT WITH REVISION: **If necessary**

THEMATIC ISSUES USED: **No**

CIRCULATION

NUMBER: FREQUENCY: **Quarterly**

CURRENT RATES (INDIVIDUAL): **£78**
(INSTITUTIONAL): **£78** (ASSOCIATE/STUDENT):

ANNUAL INDEX AVAILABILITY: COST:
SPECIAL SUPPLEMENTS: COST:
SUBSCRIPTION ADDRESS: **Journal Subscriptions Dept.,**
Marston Book Services,
P.O. Box 87
Oxford, U.K.

STYLE/SUBMISSION REQUIREMENTS

STYLE: **JF** STYLE SHEET: **Yes**
REVIEW CHARGE: **No** COST:
NUMBER OF COPIES: **1** PAGE LIMIT:
RESPONSE TO QUERY LETTERS:

GENERAL INFORMATION

JOURNAL TITLE: **JOURNAL OF COUNSELING PSYCHOLOGY**

MANUSCRIPT ADDRESS: **Lenore W. Harmon**
U of Illinois at Urbana-Champaign
College of Ed.
1310 S. Sixth Ave. Room 210
Champaign, IL 61820

TYPE OF ARTICLES:

MAJOR CONTENT AREAS:

TOPICS PREFERRED: **Reports of empirical studies, theoretical articles,**
and studies on evalution of applications of
counseling programs

REVIEW PERIOD: EARLY PUB OPTION:
PUBLICATION LAG TIME:

ACCEPT WITHOUT REVISION: REJECTION RATE:
ACCEPT WITH REVISION:

THEMATIC ISSUES USED:

CIRCULATION

NUMBER: FREQUENCY: **Quarterly**

CURRENT RATES (INDIVIDUAL): **$50**
(INSTITUTIONAL): **$100**   (ASSOCIATE/STUDENT): **$25**

ANNUAL INDEX AVAILABILITY: COST:
SPECIAL SUPPLEMENTS: COST:
SUBSCRIPTION ADDRESS: **APA Inc. Sub. section**
1400 North Uhle St.
Arlington, VA 22201

STYLE/SUBMISSION REQUIREMENTS

STYLE: STYLE SHEET:
REVIEW CHARGE: COST:
NUMBER OF COPIES: **5**   PAGE LIMIT:
RESPONSE TO QUERY LETTERS:

GENERAL INFORMATION

JOURNAL TITLE: **JOURNAL OF COUPLES THERAPY**

MANUSCRIPT ADDRESS: **Barbara Jo Brothers, Editor**
3500 St. Charles St.
New Orleans, LA 70115

TYPE OF ARTICLES: **Research; reviews; theoretical; case studies;**
commentaries; book reviews; interviews
MAJOR CONTENT AREAS: **Psychotherapy with couples; issues relative to**
establishing intimate relationships

TOPICS PREFERRED: **Focus on health and "what works" as opposed**
to focus on pathology

REVIEW PERIOD: **3-5 mo**   EARLY PUB OPTION: **No**
PUBLICATION LAG TIME: **>6 mo**

ACCEPT WITHOUT REVISION: **20%**   REJECTION RATE: **30%**
ACCEPT WITH REVISION: **50%**

THEMATIC ISSUES USED: **Yes**

CIRCULATION

NUMBER: FREQUENCY: **Quarterly**

CURRENT RATES (INDIVIDUAL): **$24**
(INSTITUTIONAL): **$32**   (ASSOCIATE/STUDENT): **N/A**

ANNUAL INDEX AVAILABILITY: **No**   COST:
SPECIAL SUPPLEMENTS: **Yes**   COST:
SUBSCRIPTION ADDRESS: **The Haworth Press, Inc.**
10 Alice St.
Binghamton, NY 13904-1580

STYLE/SUBMISSION REQUIREMENTS

STYLE: **APA**   STYLE SHEET: **Yes**
REVIEW CHARGE: **No**   COST:
NUMBER OF COPIES: **3 + diskette**   PAGE LIMIT: **15**
RESPONSE TO QUERY LETTERS: **Yes**

GENERAL INFORMATION

JOURNAL TITLE: **JOURNAL OF CROSS CULTURAL GERONTOLOGY**

MANUSCRIPT ADDRESS: **Editors**
Dept. of Anthropology
Case Western Reserve University
Cleveland, OH 44106

TYPE OF ARTICLES: **Research findings; theoretical issues; applied approaches to non-Western populations**

MAJOR CONTENT AREAS: **International & interdisciplinary journal providing a forum for scholarly discussion of the aging process & the problems of the aged throughout the world**

TOPICS PREFERRED: **Sub-cultural groupings of Western minority ethnic groups are also welcomed**

REVIEW PERIOD: EARLY PUB OPTION:
PUBLICATION LAG TIME:

ACCEPT WITHOUT REVISION: REJECTION RATE:
ACCEPT WITH REVISION:

THEMATIC ISSUES USED:

CIRCULATION

NUMBER: FREQUENCY: **4 X yr**

CURRENT RATES (INDIVIDUAL): **$41**
(INSTITUTIONAL): **$127.50**   (ASSOCIATE/STUDENT):

ANNUAL INDEX AVAILABILITY: COST:
SPECIAL SUPPLEMENTS: COST:
SUBSCRIPTION ADDRESS: **Klower Academic Publishers Group**
P.O. Box 322
3300 AH Dordrecht
Netherlands

STYLE/SUBMISSION REQUIREMENTS

STYLE: STYLE SHEET: **On request**
REVIEW CHARGE: **None**   COST:
NUMBER OF COPIES: **4**   PAGE LIMIT:
RESPONSE TO QUERY LETTERS:

GENERAL INFORMATION

JOURNAL TITLE: **JOURNAL OF CROSS-CULTURAL PSYCHOLOGY**

MANUSCRIPT ADDRESS: **John E. Williams, Editor**
Dept. of Psychology
Box 7778
Wake Forest University
Winston-Salem, NC 27109

TYPE OF ARTICLES:

MAJOR CONTENT AREAS:

TOPICS PREFERRED: **Empirical research; exclusively cross-cultural**

REVIEW PERIOD: **2 mo**   EARLY PUB OPTION:
PUBLICATION LAG TIME: **1 yr**

ACCEPT WITHOUT REVISION: REJECTION RATE:
ACCEPT WITH REVISION:

THEMATIC ISSUES USED: **Yes**

CIRCULATION

NUMBER: FREQUENCY: **4 X yr**

CURRENT RATES (INDIVIDUAL): **$38**
(INSTITUTIONAL): **$104**   (ASSOCIATE/STUDENT):

ANNUAL INDEX AVAILABILITY: COST:
SPECIAL SUPPLEMENTS: COST:
SUBSCRIPTION ADDRESS: **Sage Publications, Inc.**
2455 Teller Rd.
Newbury Park, CA 01320

STYLE/SUBMISSION REQUIREMENTS

STYLE: **APA**   STYLE SHEET:
REVIEW CHARGE: COST:
NUMBER OF COPIES: **3**   PAGE LIMIT: **15-20**
RESPONSE TO QUERY LETTERS:

GENERAL INFORMATION

JOURNAL TITLE: **JOURNAL OF DIVORCE AND REMARRIAGE**

MANUSCRIPT ADDRESS: **Craig A. Everett, PhD**
Sonora Desert Professional Bldg., Suite 150
6060 N. Fountain Plaza Dr.
Suite 150
Tucson, AZ 85704

TYPE OF ARTICLES: **Research; theoretical; case studies; clinical articles**

MAJOR CONTENT AREAS: **All variables related to divorce and remarriage**

TOPICS PREFERRED: **All**

REVIEW PERIOD:	**3-5 mo**	EARLY PUB OPTION:	**No**
PUBLICATION LAG TIME:	**>6 mo**		
ACCEPT WITHOUT REVISION:		REJECTION RATE:	**60%**
ACCEPT WITH REVISION:	**40%**		
THEMATIC ISSUES USED:	**Yes**		

CIRCULATION

NUMBER:	**900**	FREQUENCY:	**Quarterly**
CURRENT RATES (INDIVIDUAL):	**$45**		
(INSTITUTIONAL):	**$125**	(ASSOCIATE/STUDENT):	
ANNUAL INDEX AVAILABILITY:	**No**	COST:	
SPECIAL SUPPLEMENTS:	**No**	COST:	

SUBSCRIPTION ADDRESS: **The Haworth Press, Inc.**
10 Alice St.
Binghamton, NY 13904-1580

STYLE/SUBMISSION REQUIREMENTS

STYLE:	**APA**	STYLE SHEET:	**Yes**
REVIEW CHARGE:	**No**	COST:	
NUMBER OF COPIES:	**3 + diskette**	PAGE LIMIT:	**20**
RESPONSE TO QUERY LETTERS:	**Yes**		

GENERAL INFORMATION

JOURNAL TITLE: **JOURNAL OF DRUG ISSUES**

MANUSCRIPT ADDRESS: **P.O. Box 4021**
Tallahassee, FL 32315

TYPE OF ARTICLES: **Research; theoretical; commentaries; book reviews**

MAJOR CONTENT AREAS: **Drug isses**

TOPICS PREFERRED: **Policy related**

REVIEW PERIOD: **<2 mo**   EARLY PUB OPTION: **No**
PUBLICATION LAG TIME: **>6 mo**

ACCEPT WITHOUT REVISION: **5%**   REJECTION RATE: **90%**
ACCEPT WITH REVISION: **5%**

THEMATIC ISSUES USED: **Yes**

CIRCULATION

NUMBER: **950**   FREQUENCY: **Quarterly**

CURRENT RATES (INDIVIDUAL): **$55**
(INSTITUTIONAL): **$70**   (ASSOCIATE/STUDENT):

ANNUAL INDEX AVAILABILITY: **Yes**   COST: **None**
SPECIAL SUPPLEMENTS: **Yes**   COST: **None**
SUBSCRIPTION ADDRESS: **P.O. Box 4021**
Tallahassee, FL 32315-4021

STYLE/SUBMISSION REQUIREMENTS

STYLE: **Chicago**   STYLE SHEET: **Yes**
REVIEW CHARGE: **No**   COST:
NUMBER OF COPIES: **3**   PAGE LIMIT: **Varies**
RESPONSE TO QUERY LETTERS: **In limited cases**

GENERAL INFORMATION

JOURNAL TITLE: **JOURNAL OF EARLY ADOLESCENCE**

MANUSCRIPT ADDRESS: **E. Ellen Thornburg**
1201 E. Calle Elena
Tucson, AZ 85718

TYPE OF ARTICLES: **Research; reviews; theoretical; commentaries; book reviews**

MAJOR CONTENT AREAS: **All areas pertaining to early adolescence ages10-14 years)**

TOPICS PREFERRED: **See above**

REVIEW PERIOD: **2-5mo**   EARLY PUB OPTION: **No**
PUBLICATION LAG TIME: **>6 mo**

ACCEPT WITHOUT REVISION: **0%**   REJECTION RATE:
ACCEPT WITH REVISION:

THEMATIC ISSUES USED: **Yes**

CIRCULATION

NUMBER: FREQUENCY: **Quarterly**

CURRENT RATES (INDIVIDUAL):
(INSTITUTIONAL):   (ASSOCIATE/STUDENT):
ANNUAL INDEX AVAILABILITY: **Yes**   COST: **None**
SPECIAL SUPPLEMENTS: **No**   COST:
SUBSCRIPTION ADDRESS: **Sage Publications, Inc.**
2455 Teller Rd.
Newbury Park, CA 91320

STYLE/SUBMISSION REQUIREMENTS

STYLE: **APA**   STYLE SHEET: **No**
REVIEW CHARGE: **No**   COST:
NUMBER OF COPIES: **4**   PAGE LIMIT: **30**
RESPONSE TO QUERY LETTERS: **No, telephone calls preferred**

GENERAL INFORMATION

JOURNAL TITLE: **JOURNAL OF EDUCATION RESEARCH**

MANUSCRIPT ADDRESS: **Editor**
Heldref Publications
4000 Albemarle St., N.W.
Washington, D.C. 20016

TYPE OF ARTICLES: **Describe or synthesize research of direct**
relevance to educational practice in elementary
& secondary schools (especially where variables
are manipulated)

MAJOR CONTENT AREAS: **Educational practice in elementary and**
secondary schools; rigorous assessments of
claims for products; testing materials

TOPICS PREFERRED:

REVIEW PERIOD: **6 mo**   EARLY PUB OPTION:
PUBLICATION LAG TIME:

ACCEPT WITHOUT REVISION: REJECTION RATE:
ACCEPT WITH REVISION:

THEMATIC ISSUES USED:

CIRCULATION

NUMBER: FREQUENCY: **Bimonthly**

CURRENT RATES (INDIVIDUAL):
(INSTITUTIONAL): **$55**   (ASSOCIATE/STUDENT):

ANNUAL INDEX AVAILABILITY: COST:
SPECIAL SUPPLEMENTS: COST:
SUBSCRIPTION ADDRESS: **Same as above**

STYLE/SUBMISSION REQUIREMENTS

STYLE: **APA**   STYLE SHEET:
REVIEW CHARGE: COST:
NUMBER OF COPIES: **2**   PAGE LIMIT:
RESPONSE TO QUERY LETTERS:

GENERAL INFORMATION

JOURNAL TITLE: **JOURNAL OF ELDER ABUSE AND NEGLECT**

MANUSCRIPT ADDRESS: **Rosalie S. Wolf, PhD**
Institute on Aging
The Medical Center of Central
Massachusettes
119 Belmont St.
Worchester, MA 01605

TYPE OF ARTICLES: **Research; review; theoretical; case studies; commentaries; book reviews; conference proceedings**

MAJOR CONTENT AREAS: **Issues related to elder abuse and neglect, including guardianship, competency issues; delivery of care to abused and neglected elders**

TOPICS PREFERRED: **Topics with relevance to elder abuse and neglect; health; law enforcement; criminal justice; social services**

REVIEW PERIOD: **3-5 mo**   EARLY PUB OPTION: **No**
PUBLICATION LAG TIME: **>6 mo**

ACCEPT WITHOUT REVISION: **37%**   REJECTION RATE: **37%**
ACCEPT WITH REVISION: **24%**

THEMATIC ISSUES USED: **Yes**

CIRCULATION

NUMBER: **615**   FREQUENCY: **Quarterly**

CURRENT RATES (INDIVIDUAL): **$24**
(INSTITUTIONAL): **$32**   (ASSOCIATE/STUDENT):

ANNUAL INDEX AVAILABILITY: **No**   COST:
SPECIAL SUPPLEMENTS: **No**   COST:
SUBSCRIPTION ADDRESS: **The Haworth Press, Inc.**
10 Alice St.
Binghamton, NY 13904-1580

STYLE/SUBMISSION REQUIREMENTS

STYLE: **APA**   STYLE SHEET: **Yes**
REVIEW CHARGE: **No**   COST:
NUMBER OF COPIES: **3+diskette**   PAGE LIMIT: **20**
RESPONSE TO QUERY LETTERS: **Yes**

GENERAL INFORMATION

JOURNAL TITLE: **JOURNAL OF EXPERIMENTAL EDUCATION**

MANUSCRIPT ADDRESS:

TYPE OF ARTICLES:

MAJOR CONTENT AREAS: a) **Learning & instruction;**
b) **motivation & social processes;**
c) **measurement, statistics & research design**

TOPICS PREFERRED:

REVIEW PERIOD: EARLY PUB OPTION:
PUBLICATION LAG TIME:

ACCEPT WITHOUT REVISION: REJECTION RATE:
ACCEPT WITH REVISION:

THEMATIC ISSUES USED: **Yes**

CIRCULATION

NUMBER: FREQUENCY:

CURRENT RATES (INDIVIDUAL):
(INSTITUTIONAL):   (ASSOCIATE/STUDENT):

ANNUAL INDEX AVAILABILITY: COST:
SPECIAL SUPPLEMENTS: COST:
SUBSCRIPTION ADDRESS:

STYLE/SUBMISSION REQUIREMENTS

STYLE: **APA**   STYLE SHEET:
REVIEW CHARGE: COST:
NUMBER OF COPIES: **3**   PAGE LIMIT:
RESPONSE TO QUERY LETTERS:

GENERAL INFORMATION

JOURNAL TITLE: **JOURNAL OF FAMILY ISSUES**

MANUSCRIPT ADDRESS: **Center for the Study of Family Development**
University of Dayton
Dayton, OH 45469-1445

TYPE OF ARTICLES: **Research; theoretical**

MAJOR CONTENT AREAS: **Any topic related to family issues**

TOPICS PREFERRED: **Social problems related to marriage and family life; theoretical and professional issues relevant to family research and practice**

REVIEW PERIOD: **<2 mo**   EARLY PUB OPTION: **No**
PUBLICATION LAG TIME: **>6 mo**

ACCEPT WITHOUT REVISION: **0%**   REJECTION RATE: **82%**
ACCEPT WITH REVISION: **18%**

THEMATIC ISSUES USED: **Yes**

CIRCULATION

NUMBER: **2000**   FREQUENCY: **Quarterly**

CURRENT RATES (INDIVIDUAL): **$35**
(INSTITUTIONAL): **$95**   (ASSOCIATE/STUDENT):

ANNUAL INDEX AVAILABILITY: **Yes**   COST: **Lst issue**
SPECIAL SUPPLEMENTS: **No**   COST:
SUBSCRIPTION ADDRESS: **Sage Publications, Inc.**
2455 Teller Rd.
Newbury Park, CA 91320

STYLE/SUBMISSION REQUIREMENTS

STYLE: **APA**   STYLE SHEET: **Yes**
REVIEW CHARGE: **No**   COST:
NUMBER OF COPIES: **4**   PAGE LIMIT: **30**
RESPONSE TO QUERY LETTERS: **Yes**

GENERAL INFORMATION

JOURNAL TITLE: **JOURNAL OF FAMILY LAW**

MANUSCRIPT ADDRESS: **Donna F. Townsend, Editor-in-Chief**
University of Louisville
School of Law
2301 South Third St.
Louisville, KY 40292

TYPE OF ARTICLES: **Current and emerging issues; historical and theory**

MAJOR CONTENT AREAS: **All aspects of family law and domestic law problems**

TOPICS PREFERRED:

REVIEW PERIOD: EARLY PUB OPTION:
PUBLICATION LAG TIME:

ACCEPT WITHOUT REVISION: REJECTION RATE:
ACCEPT WITH REVISION:

THEMATIC ISSUES USED:

CIRCULATION

NUMBER: FREQUENCY: **Quarterly**

CURRENT RATES (INDIVIDUAL):
(INSTITUTIONAL): **$20**   (ASSOCIATE/STUDENT):

ANNUAL INDEX AVAILABILITY: COST:
SPECIAL SUPPLEMENTS: COST:
SUBSCRIPTION ADDRESS: **University of Louisville**
2301 South Third St.
Louisville, KY 40292

STYLE/SUBMISSION REQUIREMENTS

STYLE: **Harvard Law Rv**   STYLE SHEET: **Yes**
REVIEW CHARGE: COST:
NUMBER OF COPIES: PAGE LIMIT:
RESPONSE TO QUERY LETTERS:

GENERAL INFORMATION

JOURNAL TITLE: **JOURNAL OF FAMILY PRACTICE**

MANUSCRIPT ADDRESS: **Paul M. Fischer, M.D.**
Dept. of Family Medicine
Medical College of Georgia
Augusta, GA 30912

TYPE OF ARTICLES: **Research; clinical reviews; editorials**

MAJOR CONTENT AREAS: **Papers relevent to clinical family practice**

TOPICS PREFERRED:

REVIEW PERIOD: **2-3 mo**   EARLY PUB OPTION: **No**
PUBLICATION LAG TIME: **5 mo**

ACCEPT WITHOUT REVISION: **5%**   REJECTION RATE: **65%**
ACCEPT WITH REVISION: **30%**

THEMATIC ISSUES USED: **Rarely**

CIRCULATION

NUMBER: **38,000**   FREQUENCY: **Monthly**

CURRENT RATES (INDIVIDUAL): **Controlled circulation / $66**
(INSTITUTIONAL): **$87**   (ASSOCIATE/STUDENT): **$50**

ANNUAL INDEX AVAILABILITY: **No**   COST:
SPECIAL SUPPLEMENTS: **Rarely**   COST:
SUBSCRIPTION ADDRESS: **Journal of Family Practice**
25 Van Ront St.
Norwalk, CT 06856

STYLE/SUBMISSION REQUIREMENTS

STYLE: **AMA**   STYLE SHEET:
REVIEW CHARGE: COST:
NUMBER OF COPIES: **1**   PAGE LIMIT:
RESPONSE TO QUERY LETTERS: **Yes**

GENERAL INFORMATION

JOURNAL TITLE: **JOURNAL OF FAMILY PSYCHOLOGY**

MANUSCRIPT ADDRESS: **Howard A. Liddle, Editor**
Journal of Family Psychology
Temple University
249 Weiss Hall
Philadelphia, PA 19122

TYPE OF ARTICLES: **Theory; research; clinical practice**

MAJOR CONTENT AREAS: **Family and marital issues; therapeutic methods;**
evaluation training and supervision; policy and
legal issues
TOPICS PREFERRED:

REVIEW PERIOD: EARLY PUB OPTION:
PUBLICATION LAG TIME:

ACCEPT WITHOUT REVISION: REJECTION RATE:
ACCEPT WITH REVISION:

THEMATIC ISSUES USED:

CIRCULATION

NUMBER: FREQUENCY: **4 X yr**

CURRENT RATES (INDIVIDUAL):
(INSTITUTIONAL): **$90**   (ASSOCIATE/STUDENT):

ANNUAL INDEX AVAILABILITY: COST:
SPECIAL SUPPLEMENTS: COST:
SUBSCRIPTION ADDRESS: **Sage Publications, Inc.**
2455 Teller Rd.
Newbury Park, CA 91320

STYLE/SUBMISSION REQUIREMENTS

STYLE: **APA**   STYLE SHEET:
REVIEW CHARGE: COST:
NUMBER OF COPIES: **1 orig;3 copies**   PAGE LIMIT: **20–25**
RESPONSE TO QUERY LETTERS: **Yes**

GENERAL INFORMATION

JOURNAL TITLE: **JOURNAL OF FAMILY PSYCHOTHERAPY**

MANUSCRIPT ADDRESS: **Terry S. Trepper, Ph.D., Editor**
Director
Family Studies Center
Purdue University Calumet
Hammond, IN 46323-2094

TYPE OF ARTICLES: **Case studies; book reviews**

MAJOR CONTENT AREAS: **All schools of family therapy; innovations in clinical practice; clinical strategies**

TOPICS PREFERRED: **Open-only case studies or case oriented manuscripts**

REVIEW PERIOD: **3-5 mo**   EARLY PUB OPTION: **No**
PUBLICATION LAG TIME: **6 mo or more**

ACCEPT WITHOUT REVISION: **10%**   REJECTION RATE: **30%**
ACCEPT WITH REVISION: **60%**

THEMATIC ISSUES USED: **Yes**

CIRCULATION

NUMBER: **1000**   FREQUENCY: **Quarterly**

CURRENT RATES (INDIVIDUAL): **$32**
(INSTITUTIONAL): **$42**   (ASSOCIATE/STUDENT): **$75**

ANNUAL INDEX AVAILABILITY: **No**   COST:
SPECIAL SUPPLEMENTS: **No**   COST:
SUBSCRIPTION ADDRESS: **The Haworth Press, Inc.**
10 Alice Street
Binghamton, NY 13904-1580

STYLE/SUBMISSION REQUIREMENTS

STYLE: **APA**   STYLE SHEET: **Yes**
REVIEW CHARGE: **No**   COST:
NUMBER OF COPIES: **4 + diskette**   PAGE LIMIT: **20-25**
RESPONSE TO QUERY LETTERS: **Yes**

GENERAL INFORMATION

JOURNAL TITLE: **JOURNAL OF FAMILY THERAPY**

MANUSCRIPT ADDRESS: **The Editor**
Journal of Family Therapy
c/o Academic Press Limited
24-28 Oval Rd.
London, NW1 7DX, England, U.K.

TYPE OF ARTICLES: **Reviews; research; theory**

MAJOR CONTENT AREAS: **Family research and therapy**

TOPICS PREFERRED:

REVIEW PERIOD: EARLY PUB OPTION:
PUBLICATION LAG TIME:

ACCEPT WITHOUT REVISION: REJECTION RATE:
ACCEPT WITH REVISION:

THEMATIC ISSUES USED:

CIRCULATION

NUMBER: FREQUENCY:

CURRENT RATES (INDIVIDUAL):
(INSTITUTIONAL):   (ASSOCIATE/STUDENT):

ANNUAL INDEX AVAILABILITY: COST:
SPECIAL SUPPLEMENTS: COST:
SUBSCRIPTION ADDRESS:

STYLE/SUBMISSION REQUIREMENTS

STYLE: **APA**   STYLE SHEET:
REVIEW CHARGE: COST:
NUMBER OF COPIES: **3**   PAGE LIMIT:
RESPONSE TO QUERY LETTERS:

GENERAL INFORMATION

JOURNAL TITLE: **JOURNAL OF FAMILY VIOLENCE**

MANUSCRIPT ADDRESS: **Dr. Vincent B. Van Hasselt**
Western Psychiatric Institute & Clinic
3811 O'Hara St.
Pittsburgh, PA 15213

TYPE OF ARTICLES: **Clinical and research reports**

MAJOR CONTENT AREAS:

TOPICS PREFERRED: **Investigations utilizing group comparisons and**
also single-case experimental strategies

REVIEW PERIOD: EARLY PUB OPTION:
PUBLICATION LAG TIME:

ACCEPT WITHOUT REVISION: REJECTION RATE:
ACCEPT WITH REVISION:

THEMATIC ISSUES USED:

CIRCULATION

NUMBER: FREQUENCY: **Quarterly**

CURRENT RATES (INDIVIDUAL): **$32**
(INSTITUTIONAL): **$110**   (ASSOCIATE/STUDENT):

ANNUAL INDEX AVAILABILITY: COST:
SPECIAL SUPPLEMENTS: COST:
SUBSCRIPTION ADDRESS: **Plenum Publishing Corp.**
233 Spring St.
New York, NY 10013

STYLE/SUBMISSION REQUIREMENTS

STYLE: **APA**   STYLE SHEET:
REVIEW CHARGE: **None**   COST:
NUMBER OF COPIES: **1 orig; 2 copies**   PAGE LIMIT:
RESPONSE TO QUERY LETTERS:

GENERAL INFORMATION

JOURNAL TITLE: **JOURNAL OF FEMINIST FAMILY THERAPY**

MANUSCRIPT ADDRESS: **Lois Braverman, ACSW, Editor**
3833 Woods Drive
Des Moines, IA 50312

TYPE OF ARTICLES: **Research; reviews; theoretical; case studies; book reviews**

MAJOR CONTENT AREAS: **Feminist family therapy treatment areas and implications**

TOPICS PREFERRED: **All family issues with an emphasis on gender**

REVIEW PERIOD: **3-5 mo**   EARLY PUB OPTION: **No**
PUBLICATION LAG TIME: **>6 mo**
ACCEPT WITHOUT REVISION: **0%**   REJECTION RATE: **50%**
ACCEPT WITH REVISION: **50%**

THEMATIC ISSUES USED: **Yes**

CIRCULATION

NUMBER: **400**   FREQUENCY: **Quarterly**

CURRENT RATES (INDIVIDUAL): **$24**
(INSTITUTIONAL): **$40**   (ASSOCIATE/STUDENT):

ANNUAL INDEX AVAILABILITY: **No**   COST:
SPECIAL SUPPLEMENTS: **No**   COST:
SUBSCRIPTION ADDRESS: **The Haworth Press, Inc.**
10 Alice St.
Binghamton, NY 13904-1580

STYLE/SUBMISSION REQUIREMENTS

STYLE: **APA**   STYLE SHEET: **Yes**
REVIEW CHARGE: **No**   COST:
NUMBER OF COPIES: **3 + diskette**   PAGE LIMIT: **15-25**
RESPONSE TO QUERY LETTERS: **Yes**

GENERAL INFORMATION

JOURNAL TITLE: **JOURNAL OF GAY AND LESBIAN PSYCHOTHERAPY**

MANUSCRIPT ADDRESS: **David L. Scasta, MD**
1439 Pineville Rd.
New Hope, PA 18938

TYPE OF ARTICLES: **Practical information about gay and lesbian patients**

MAJOR CONTENT AREAS: **Information about gay and lesbian psychotherapy in psychiatry, psychology, and social work**

TOPICS PREFERRED: **Drug and alcohol counseling; family and couples therapy; adolescent therapy; bereavement**

REVIEW PERIOD: EARLY PUB OPTION:
PUBLICATION LAG TIME:

ACCEPT WITHOUT REVISION: REJECTION RATE:
ACCEPT WITH REVISION:

THEMATIC ISSUES USED:

CIRCULATION

NUMBER: **318**   FREQUENCY: **Quarterly**

CURRENT RATES (INDIVIDUAL): **$24**
(INSTITUTIONAL): **$30**   (ASSOCIATE/STUDENT):

ANNUAL INDEX AVAILABILITY: COST:
SPECIAL SUPPLEMENTS: COST:
SUBSCRIPTION ADDRESS: **The Haworth Press, Inc.**
10 Alice St.
Binghamton, NY 13904-1580

STYLE/SUBMISSION REQUIREMENTS

STYLE: **APA**   STYLE SHEET: **Yes**
REVIEW CHARGE: **No**   COST:
NUMBER OF COPIES: **4 + diskette**   PAGE LIMIT: **25**
RESPONSE TO QUERY LETTERS:

GENERAL INFORMATION

JOURNAL TITLE: **JOURNAL OF GENETIC PSYCHOLOGY**

MANUSCRIPT ADDRESS: **Managing Editor**
4000 Albemarle St., N.W.
Washington, DC 20016

TYPE OF ARTICLES: **Research; theory; occasional applied and**
descriptive articles

MAJOR CONTENT AREAS: **Research & theory in developmental & clinical**
psychology

TOPICS PREFERRED: **Empirical research & criticism of theory**

REVIEW PERIOD: **2-3 mo**   EARLY PUB OPTION:
PUBLICATION LAG TIME:

ACCEPT WITHOUT REVISION: REJECTION RATE:
ACCEPT WITH REVISION:

THEMATIC ISSUES USED:

CIRCULATION

NUMBER: FREQUENCY: **Quarterly**

CURRENT RATES (INDIVIDUAL):
(INSTITUTIONAL): **$65**   (ASSOCIATE/STUDENT):

ANNUAL INDEX AVAILABILITY: COST:
SPECIAL SUPPLEMENTS: COST:
SUBSCRIPTION ADDRESS: **Helfref Publications**
4000 Albemarle St. N.W.
Washington, DC 20016

STYLE/SUBMISSION REQUIREMENTS

STYLE: **APA**   STYLE SHEET:
REVIEW CHARGE: COST:
NUMBER OF COPIES: **1 orig; 1 copy**   PAGE LIMIT:
RESPONSE TO QUERY LETTERS:

GENERAL INFORMATION

JOURNAL TITLE: **JOURNAL OF GERIATRIC DRUG THERAPY**

MANUSCRIPT ADDRESS: **Dr. James W. Cooper, Editor**
Department of Pharmacy Practice
College of Pharmacy
University of Georgia
Athens, GA 30602

TYPE OF ARTICLES: **Research; reviews; theoretical; case studies; commentaries; book reviews; current primary lit**

MAJOR CONTENT AREAS: **Drug usage in geriatric patients**

TOPICS PREFERRED: **All aspects**

REVIEW PERIOD: **<2 mo**   EARLY PUB OPTION: **No**
PUBLICATION LAG TIME: **3-5 mo**

ACCEPT WITHOUT REVISION: **25%**   REJECTION RATE: **25%**
ACCEPT WITH REVISION: **50%**

THEMATIC ISSUES USED: **Yes**

CIRCULATION

NUMBER: **500**   FREQUENCY: **Quarterly**

CURRENT RATES (INDIVIDUAL): **$40**
(INSTITUTIONAL): **$60**   (ASSOCIATE/STUDENT):

ANNUAL INDEX AVAILABILITY: **No**   COST:
SPECIAL SUPPLEMENTS: **No**   COST:
SUBSCRIPTION ADDRESS: **The Haworth Press, Inc.**
10 Alice St.
Binghamton, NY 13904-1580

STYLE/SUBMISSION REQUIREMENTS

STYLE: **Index Medicus**   STYLE SHEET: **Yes**
REVIEW CHARGE: **No**   COST:
NUMBER OF COPIES: **3 + diskette**   PAGE LIMIT: **40-50**
RESPONSE TO QUERY LETTERS: **Yes**

GENERAL INFORMATION

JOURNAL TITLE: **JOURNAL OF GERONTOLOGICAL SOCIAL WORK**

MANUSCRIPT ADDRESS: **Dr. Rose Dobrof**
Professor, School of Social Work
Brookdale Center on Aging
Hunter College
425 E. 25th St., Room 909W
New York, NY 10010

TYPE OF ARTICLES: **Research; book reviews; case studies; theoretical articles**

MAJOR CONTENT AREAS: **Needs of special populations; practice and organizational issues in service delivery; policy issues**

TOPICS PREFERRED: **Studies of social work theory and practice in the field of aging**

REVIEW PERIOD: **3-5 mo**   EARLY PUB OPTION: **No**
PUBLICATION LAG TIME: **≥ 6 mo**

ACCEPT WITHOUT REVISION: **10%**   REJECTION RATE: **30-40%**
ACCEPT WITH REVISION: **50-60%**

THEMATIC ISSUES USED: **Yes**

CIRCULATION

NUMBER: **750**   FREQUENCY: **Quarterly**
CURRENT RATES (INDIVIDUAL): **$35**
(INSTITUTIONAL): **$85**   (ASSOCIATE/STUDENT):

ANNUAL INDEX AVAILABILITY: **No**   COST:
SPECIAL SUPPLEMENTS: **No**   COST:
SUBSCRIPTION ADDRESS: **The Haworth Press, Inc.**
10 Alice St.
Binghamton, NY 13904-1580

STYLE/SUBMISSION REQUIREMENTS

STYLE: **APA**   STYLE SHEET: **No**
REVIEW CHARGE: **No**   COST:
NUMBER OF COPIES: **3 + diskette**   PAGE LIMIT: **20**
RESPONSE TO QUERY LETTERS: **Yes**

GENERAL INFORMATION

JOURNAL TITLE:	**JOURNAL OF GROUP PSYCHODRAMA, PSYCHOTHERAPY, AND SOCIOMETRY**
MANUSCRIPT ADDRESS:	**Managing Editors, JGPPS**
	4000 Albermarle St., N.W.
	Washington, DC 200016

TYPE OF ARTICLES:	**Research; reviews; theoretical; case studies; commentaries; book reviews**
MAJOR CONTENT AREAS:	**Action methods in group work**
TOPICS PREFERRED:	**Related to psychodrama and group psychotherapy**

REVIEW PERIOD:	**>6 mo**	EARLY PUB OPTION:	**No**
PUBLICATION LAG TIME:	**6 mo or more**		

ACCEPT WITHOUT REVISION:	**5%**	REJECTION RATE:	**40%**
ACCEPT WITH REVISION:	**55%**		

THEMATIC ISSUES USED:	**Yes**

CIRCULATION

NUMBER:		FREQUENCY:	**Quarterly**

CURRENT RATES (INDIVIDUAL):	**$50**		
(INSTITUTIONAL):		(ASSOCIATE/STUDENT):	

ANNUAL INDEX AVAILABILITY:		COST:
SPECIAL SUPPLEMENTS:		COST:
SUBSCRIPTION ADDRESS:	**Same as above**	

STYLE/SUBMISSION REQUIREMENTS

STYLE:	**APA**	STYLE SHEET:	
REVIEW CHARGE:		COST:	
NUMBER OF COPIES:	**2**	PAGE LIMIT:	
RESPONSE TO QUERY LETTERS:			

GENERAL INFORMATION

JOURNAL TITLE: **JOURNAL OF HOMOSEXUALITY**

MANUSCRIPT ADDRESS: **John P. DeCecco, Ph.D., Editor**
CERES
Psychology Building, Room 502
San Francisco State University
San Francisco, CA 94132

TYPE OF ARTICLES: **Research; reviews; theoretical; book reviews**

MAJOR CONTENT AREAS: **Interdisciplinary-social sciences; humanities; arts**

TOPICS PREFERRED: **Anything relevant and usually non-clinical**

REVIEW PERIOD: EARLY PUB OPTION:
PUBLICATION LAG TIME: **>6 mo**

ACCEPT WITHOUT REVISION: REJECTION RATE:
ACCEPT WITH REVISION:

THEMATIC ISSUES USED: **Yes**

CIRCULATION

NUMBER: **612**   FREQUENCY: **8 X yr**

CURRENT RATES (INDIVIDUAL): **$40**
(INSTITUTIONAL): **$95**   (ASSOCIATE/STUDENT):

ANNUAL INDEX AVAILABILITY: **Yes**   COST:
SPECIAL SUPPLEMENTS: **Yes**   COST:
SUBSCRIPTION ADDRESS: **The Haworth Press, Inc.**
10 Alice Street
Binghamton, NY 13904-1580

STYLE/SUBMISSION REQUIREMENTS

STYLE: **Depends on subj**   STYLE SHEET: **Yes**
REVIEW CHARGE: **No**   COST:
NUMBER OF COPIES: **3 + diskette**   PAGE LIMIT: **25**
RESPONSE TO QUERY LETTERS: **Yes**

GENERAL INFORMATION

JOURNAL TITLE: **JOURNAL OF HOUSING FOR THE ELDERLY**

MANUSCRIPT ADDRESS: **Leon A. Pastalan, Ph.D.**
2226 Art & Architecture Bldg.
University of Michigan
Ann Arbor, MI 48109-2069

TYPE OF ARTICLES:

MAJOR CONTENT AREAS:

TOPICS PREFERRED: **Housing issues and innovative reports of interest to professionals in architecture, urban planning, and public policy who are responsible for improving the living environments of the elderly**

REVIEW PERIOD: EARLY PUB OPTION:
PUBLICATION LAG TIME:

ACCEPT WITHOUT REVISION: REJECTION RATE:
ACCEPT WITH REVISION:

THEMATIC ISSUES USED:

CIRCULATION

NUMBER: FREQUENCY: **Biannual**

CURRENT RATES (INDIVIDUAL): **$40**
(INSTITUTIONAL): **$95**   (ASSOCIATE/STUDENT):

ANNUAL INDEX AVAILABILITY: COST:
SPECIAL SUPPLEMENTS: COST:
SUBSCRIPTION ADDRESS: **The Haworth Press, Inc.**
10 Alice Street
Binghamton, NY 13904-1580

STYLE/SUBMISSION REQUIREMENTS

STYLE: STYLE SHEET:
REVIEW CHARGE: **No**   COST:
NUMBER OF COPIES: **3 + diskette**   PAGE LIMIT: **20**
RESPONSE TO QUERY LETTERS:

GENERAL INFORMATION

JOURNAL TITLE: **JOURNAL OF HUMAN RESOURCES**

MANUSCRIPT ADDRESS: **Social Science Bldg.**
1180 Observatory Drive
University of Wisconsin
Madison, WI 53706

TYPE OF ARTICLES: **State of the art economic articles in labor economics**

MAJOR CONTENT AREAS: **Econometrics**

TOPICS PREFERRED: **Labor; retirement; health**

REVIEW PERIOD: **>6 mo**   EARLY PUB OPTION: **No**
PUBLICATION LAG TIME: **6 mo or more**

ACCEPT WITHOUT REVISION: **0%**   REJECTION RATE: **90%**
ACCEPT WITH REVISION: **10%**

THEMATIC ISSUES USED: **Yes**

CIRCULATION

NUMBER: **2500**   FREQUENCY: **Quarterly**

CURRENT RATES (INDIVIDUAL): **$27**
(INSTITUTIONAL): **$54**   (ASSOCIATE/STUDENT):

ANNUAL INDEX AVAILABILITY: **Yes**   COST:
SPECIAL SUPPLEMENTS: **Yes**   COST:
SUBSCRIPTION ADDRESS: **UW Press**
114 N. Murray St.
Madison, WI 53715

STYLE/SUBMISSION REQUIREMENTS

STYLE: **Chicago**   STYLE SHEET: **No**
REVIEW CHARGE: **No**   COST:
NUMBER OF COPIES: **5**   PAGE LIMIT: **25**
RESPONSE TO QUERY LETTERS: **No**

GENERAL INFORMATION

JOURNAL TITLE: **JOURNAL OF HUMANISTIC PSYCHOLOGY**

MANUSCRIPT ADDRESS: **Thomas Greening, Ph.D.**
Suite 205
1314 Westwood Blvd.
Los Angeles, CA 90024

TYPE OF ARTICLES: **Research; reviews; theoretical; case studies;**
commentaries; book reviews

MAJOR CONTENT AREAS:

TOPICS PREFERRED:

REVIEW PERIOD: **<2 mo**   EARLY PUB OPTION: **No**
PUBLICATION LAG TIME: **>6 mo**

ACCEPT WITHOUT REVISION: **3%**   REJECTION RATE: **90%**
ACCEPT WITH REVISION: **7%**

THEMATIC ISSUES USED: **Yes**

CIRCULATION

NUMBER: **5000**   FREQUENCY: **Quarterly**

CURRENT RATES (INDIVIDUAL): **$36**
(INSTITUTIONAL): **$98**   (ASSOCIATE/STUDENT): **$27**

ANNUAL INDEX AVAILABILITY: **Yes**   COST:
SPECIAL SUPPLEMENTS: **No**   COST:
SUBSCRIPTION ADDRESS: **Sage Publications, Inc.**
2455 Teller Rd.
Newbury Park, CA 91320

STYLE/SUBMISSION REQUIREMENTS

STYLE: **APA**   STYLE SHEET: **No**
REVIEW CHARGE: **No**   COST:
NUMBER OF COPIES: **2**   PAGE LIMIT: **30**
RESPONSE TO QUERY LETTERS: **In limited cases**

GENERAL INFORMATION

JOURNAL TITLE: **JOURNAL OF INTERPERSONAL VIOLENCE**

MANUSCRIPT ADDRESS: **Jon R. Conte, Editor**
School of Social Science Administration
University of Chicago
969 East 60th Street
Chicago, IL 60637

TYPE OF ARTICLES: **Study and treatment of victims and perpetrators**
of interpersonal violence

MAJOR CONTENT AREAS: **Causes, effects, treatment, and prevention of all**
types of violence

TOPICS PREFERRED:

REVIEW PERIOD: EARLY PUB OPTION:
PUBLICATION LAG TIME:

ACCEPT WITHOUT REVISION: REJECTION RATE:
ACCEPT WITH REVISION:

THEMATIC ISSUES USED:

CIRCULATION

NUMBER: FREQUENCY: **4 X year**

CURRENT RATES (INDIVIDUAL): **$33**
(INSTITUTIONAL): **$75**   (ASSOCIATE/STUDENT):

ANNUAL INDEX AVAILABILITY: COST:
SPECIAL SUPPLEMENTS: COST:
SUBSCRIPTION ADDRESS: **Sage Publications, Inc.**
2455 Teller Rd.
Newbury Park, CA 91320

STYLE/SUBMISSION REQUIREMENTS

STYLE: **APA**   STYLE SHEET:
REVIEW CHARGE: COST:
NUMBER OF COPIES: **3**   PAGE LIMIT:
RESPONSE TO QUERY LETTERS:

GENERAL INFORMATION

JOURNAL TITLE: **JOURNAL OF LEISURE RESEARCH**

MANUSCRIPT ADDRESS: **Peter Witt, Editor**
Box 5446
University of North Texas
Denton, TX 76203-5446

TYPE OF ARTICLES: **Research; reviews; theoretical; commentaries**

MAJOR CONTENT AREAS: **All aspects of research where leisure/recreation**
is the dependent or independent variable

TOPICS PREFERRED: **No preference**

REVIEW PERIOD: **3-5 mo**   EARLY PUB OPTION: **No**
PUBLICATION LAG TIME: **6 mo or more**

ACCEPT WITHOUT REVISION: **5%**   REJECTION RATE: **60%**
ACCEPT WITH REVISION: **35%**

THEMATIC ISSUES USED: **Yes**

CIRCULATION

NUMBER: **1700**   FREQUENCY: **Quarterly**

CURRENT RATES (INDIVIDUAL): **$30**
(INSTITUTIONAL): **$50**   (ASSOCIATE/STUDENT):

ANNUAL INDEX AVAILABILITY: **No**   COST:
SPECIAL SUPPLEMENTS: **No**   COST:
SUBSCRIPTION ADDRESS: **National Recreation and Park Assn.**
3101 Park Center Drive
Alexandria, VA 22302

STYLE/SUBMISSION REQUIREMENTS

STYLE: **APA**   STYLE SHEET: **No**
REVIEW CHARGE: **No**   COST:
NUMBER OF COPIES: **4**   PAGE LIMIT: **20-25**
RESPONSE TO QUERY LETTERS: **Yes**

GENERAL INFORMATION

JOURNAL TITLE: **JOURNAL OF MARITAL AND FAMILY THERAPY**

MANUSCRIPT ADDRESS: **Douglas H. Sprenkle, PhD, Editor**
Journal of Marital and Family Therapy
Purdue University
Marriage and Family Therapy Program
523 Russell Street
West Lafayette, IN 47907

TYPE OF ARTICLES: **The *Journal of Marital and Family Therapy* seeks to advance the professional understanding of the practice marital & family therapy & improve the psychotherapeutic**

MAJOR CONTENT AREAS: **treatment of marital & family disharmony. Toward that end, the *Journal* publishes articles on research, theory, training, &**

TOPICS PREFERRED: **clinical practice in marital & family therapy.**

REVIEW PERIOD: **4 mo**   EARLY PUB OPTION:
PUBLICATION LAG TIME: **6-9 mo**

ACCEPT WITHOUT REVISION: REJECTION RATE: **85%**
ACCEPT WITH REVISION: **N/A**

THEMATIC ISSUES USED: **None**

CIRCULATION
NUMBER: **20,000**   FREQUENCY: **4 X yr.**

CURRENT RATES (INDIVIDUAL): **$45**
(INSTITUTIONAL): **$75**   (ASSOCIATE/STUDENT):

ANNUAL INDEX AVAILABILITY: **None**   COST: **Nohe**
SPECIAL SUPPLEMENTS: **None**   COST: **None**
SUBSCRIPTION ADDRESS: **Am. Association of Marriage & Family**
1100 17th St., NW
10th Floor
Washington, DC 20036

STYLE/SUBMISSION REQUIREMENTS
STYLE: **APA**   STYLE SHEET: **Yes(Ed)**
REVIEW CHARGE: **None**   COST: **None**
NUMBER OF COPIES: **4**   PAGE LIMIT: **20+**
RESPONSE TO QUERY LETTERS: **Yes**   **references**

GENERAL INFORMATION

JOURNAL TITLE: **JOURNAL OF MARRIAGE & THE FAMILY**

MANUSCRIPT ADDRESS: **Editor**
Dept. of Sociology
Univ. of Nebraska-Lincoln
Lincoln, NE 68588-0367

TYPE OF ARTICLES: **Original theory; research interpretation; critical**
discussion

MAJOR CONTENT AREAS: **Subjects related to marriage and the family**

TOPICS PREFERRED:

REVIEW PERIOD: EARLY PUB OPTION:
PUBLICATION LAG TIME:

ACCEPT WITHOUT REVISION: REJECTION RATE:
ACCEPT WITH REVISION:

THEMATIC ISSUES USED:

CIRCULATION

NUMBER: FREQUENCY: **Quarterly**

CURRENT RATES (INDIVIDUAL): **$50**
(INSTITUTIONAL): **$85**   (ASSOCIATE/STUDENT):

ANNUAL INDEX AVAILABILITY: COST:
SPECIAL SUPPLEMENTS: COST:
SUBSCRIPTION ADDRESS: **National Council on Family Relations**
3989 Central Avenue, NE
Suite 550
Minneapolis, MN 55421

STYLE/SUBMISSION REQUIREMENTS

STYLE: **APA**   STYLE SHEET: **In Journal**
REVIEW CHARGE: **$15**   COST:
NUMBER OF COPIES: **4**   PAGE LIMIT:
RESPONSE TO QUERY LETTERS:

GENERAL INFORMATION

JOURNAL TITLE: **JOURNAL OF MENTAL HEALTH COUNSELING**

MANUSCRIPT ADDRESS: **Ball State University**
Department of Counseling Psych TC 622
Muncie, IN 47306

TYPE OF ARTICLES: **Research; theoretical; case studies commentaries; practice articles**

MAJOR CONTENT AREAS: **Practice; theory; research; and professional exchange**

TOPICS PREFERRED: **Anything related to mental health counseling**

REVIEW PERIOD: **3-5 mo**   EARLY PUB OPTION: **No**
PUBLICATION LAG TIME: **> 6 mo**

ACCEPT WITHOUT REVISION: **<1%**   REJECTION RATE: **75%**
ACCEPT WITH REVISION: **24%**

THEMATIC ISSUES USED: **Yes**

CIRCULATION

NUMBER: **13,500+**   FREQUENCY: **Quarterly**

CURRENT RATES (INDIVIDUAL): **$27**
(INSTITUTIONAL): **$64.80**   (ASSOCIATE/STUDENT):

ANNUAL INDEX AVAILABILITY: **Yes**   COST: **Lst issue**
SPECIAL SUPPLEMENTS: **No**   COST:
SUBSCRIPTION ADDRESS: **Sage Publications, Inc.**
2455 Teller Rd.
Newbury Park, CA 91320

STYLE/SUBMISSION REQUIREMENTS

STYLE: **APA**   STYLE SHEET: **No**
REVIEW CHARGE: **No**   COST:
NUMBER OF COPIES: **4**   PAGE LIMIT: **20-25**
RESPONSE TO QUERY LETTERS: **Yes**

GENERAL INFORMATION

JOURNAL TITLE: **JOURNAL OF NEGRO EDUCATION**

MANUSCRIPT ADDRESS: **Howard University West Campus**
Rm 120 Holy Cross Hall
2900 Wan Ness St. N.W.
Washington, D.C. 20008

TYPE OF ARTICLES: **Those discussing and analysing issues incident to the education of black people.**

MAJOR CONTENT AREAS: **Educational policy**
Educational practice
Pedagogical issues

TOPICS PREFERRED:

REVIEW PERIOD: **8-12 wk**   EARLY PUB OPTION:
PUBLICATION LAG TIME: **12-16 mo**

ACCEPT WITHOUT REVISION: REJECTION RATE: **65%**
ACCEPT WITH REVISION:

THEMATIC ISSUES USED:

CIRCULATION

NUMBER: **2200**   FREQUENCY: **Quarterly**

CURRENT RATES (INDIVIDUAL): **$16**
(INSTITUTIONAL): **$20**   (ASSOCIATE/STUDENT):

ANNUAL INDEX AVAILABILITY: **Yes**   COST: **$13**
SPECIAL SUPPLEMENTS: COST:
SUBSCRIPTION ADDRESS: **Circulation Dept. (J of NE)**
P.O. Box 311
Howard University
Washington, D.C. 20059

STYLE/SUBMISSION REQUIREMENTS

STYLE: **APA/Chicago**   STYLE SHEET:
REVIEW CHARGE: COST:
NUMBER OF COPIES: **3**   PAGE LIMIT: **25**
RESPONSE TO QUERY LETTERS:

GENERAL INFORMATION

JOURNAL TITLE: **JOURNAL OF NONVERBAL BEHAVIOR**

MANUSCRIPT ADDRESS: **Miles L. Patterson, Editor**
Department of Psychology
University of Missouri-St. Louis
St. Louis, MO 63121-4499

TYPE OF ARTICLES: **Research; theoretical**

MAJOR CONTENT AREAS: **Methodological research on nonverbal**
behaviorism; social interaction; communication;
emotional expressiveness
TOPICS PREFERRED: **Understanding of interaction and**
communication focusing on gaze, facial
expressiveness, kinesics, paralanguage, posture,
gestures, etc.
REVIEW PERIOD: EARLY PUB OPTION:
PUBLICATION LAG TIME:

ACCEPT WITHOUT REVISION: REJECTION RATE:
ACCEPT WITH REVISION:

THEMATIC ISSUES USED:

CIRCULATION

NUMBER: FREQUENCY:

CURRENT RATES (INDIVIDUAL): **$41**
(INSTITUTIONAL): **$115**   (ASSOCIATE/STUDENT):

ANNUAL INDEX AVAILABILITY: COST:
SPECIAL SUPPLEMENTS: COST:
SUBSCRIPTION ADDRESS: **Human Sciences Press**
233 Spring St.
New York, NY 10013-1578

STYLE/SUBMISSION REQUIREMENTS

STYLE: **APA**   STYLE SHEET:
REVIEW CHARGE: COST:
NUMBER OF COPIES: **4**   PAGE LIMIT:
RESPONSE TO QUERY LETTERS:

GENERAL INFORMATION

JOURNAL TITLE: **JOURNAL OF NUTRITION FOR THE ELDERLY**

MANUSCRIPT ADDRESS: **Annette B. Notow**
Journal of Nutrition for the Edlerly
Box 169
Little Neck, NY 11363

TYPE OF ARTICLES: **Research; reviews; book reviews; commentaries; case studies; theory**

MAJOR CONTENT AREAS: **Nutrition and health issues**

TOPICS PREFERRED: **Same**

REVIEW PERIOD: **3-5 mo**   EARLY PUB OPTION: **No**
PUBLICATION LAG TIME: **>6 mo**

ACCEPT WITHOUT REVISION: **20%**   REJECTION RATE: **20%**
ACCEPT WITH REVISION: **60%**

THEMATIC ISSUES USED: **No**

CIRCULATION

NUMBER: **1500**   FREQUENCY: **Quarterly**

CURRENT RATES (INDIVIDUAL): **$40**
(INSTITUTIONAL): **$90**   (ASSOCIATE/STUDENT):

ANNUAL INDEX AVAILABILITY: **No**   COST:
SPECIAL SUPPLEMENTS: **No**   COST:
SUBSCRIPTION ADDRESS: **The Haworth Press, Inc.**
10 Alice. St.
Binghamton, NY 13904-1580

STYLE/SUBMISSION REQUIREMENTS

STYLE: **APA**   STYLE SHEET: **Yes**
REVIEW CHARGE: **No**   COST:
NUMBER OF COPIES: **3 + diskette**   PAGE LIMIT: **20**
RESPONSE TO QUERY LETTERS: **Yes**

GENERAL INFORMATION

JOURNAL TITLE: **JOURNAL OF OFFENDER REHABILITATION**

MANUSCRIPT ADDRESS: **Nathanial J. Pallone, Ph.D.**
133A Lucy Stone Hall
Livingston College Campus
New Brunswick, NJ 08903

TYPE OF ARTICLES:

MAJOR CONTENT AREAS:

TOPICS PREFERRED:

REVIEW PERIOD: EARLY PUB OPTION:
PUBLICATION LAG TIME:

ACCEPT WITHOUT REVISION: REJECTION RATE:
ACCEPT WITH REVISION:

THEMATIC ISSUES USED:

CIRCULATION

NUMBER: **305**   FREQUENCY: **Quarterly**

CURRENT RATES (INDIVIDUAL): **$40**
(INSTITUTIONAL): **$75**   (ASSOCIATE/STUDENT):

ANNUAL INDEX AVAILABILITY: **No**   COST:
SPECIAL SUPPLEMENTS: COST:
SUBSCRIPTION ADDRESS: **The Haworth Press, Inc.**
10 Alice Street
Binghamton, NY 13904-1580

STYLE/SUBMISSION REQUIREMENTS

STYLE: STYLE SHEET:
REVIEW CHARGE: **No**   COST:
NUMBER OF COPIES: **3 + diskette**   PAGE LIMIT:
RESPONSE TO QUERY LETTERS:

GENERAL INFORMATION

JOURNAL TITLE: **JOURNAL OF ORGANIZATIONAL BEHAVIOR**

MANUSCRIPT ADDRESS: **Professor Cary L. Cooper**
Manchester School of Management
University of Manchester
Institute of Science and Technology
P.O. Box 88 Sackville St.
Manchester M60 1QD England, U. K.

TYPE OF ARTICLES: **Research; theory; research methodolog; book reviews**

MAJOR CONTENT AREAS: **Research in industrial/organizational psychology and organizational behavior fields throughout the world**

TOPICS PREFERRED: **Topics related to occupational/organizational behavior including motivation, work performance, equal opportunities at work, job design, career processes, occupational stress, personnel selection, training, organizational change, job analysis, behavioral aspects of industrial relations, organizational sructure and climate, leadership, and power**

REVIEW PERIOD: EARLY PUB OPTION:
PUBLICATION LAG TIME:
ACCEPT WITHOUT REVISION: REJECTION RATE:
ACCEPT WITH REVISION:
THEMATIC ISSUES USED:

CIRCULATION

NUMBER: FREQUENCY: **7 X yr**

CURRENT RATES (INDIVIDUAL):
(INSTITUTIONAL): **$250**   (ASSOCIATE/STUDENT):
ANNUAL INDEX AVAILABILITY: COST:
SPECIAL SUPPLEMENTS: COST:
SUBSCRIPTION ADDRESS: **John Wiley and Sons, Ltd.**
Subscription Department
Baffins Lane, Chichester
West Sussex P019 1UD, England, U. K.

STYLE/SUBMISSION REQUIREMENTS

STYLE: **Harvard System**   STYLE SHEET:
REVIEW CHARGE: COST:
NUMBER OF COPIES: **3**   PAGE LIMIT: **None**
RESPONSE TO QUERY LETTERS:

GENERAL INFORMATION

JOURNAL TITLE: **JOURNAL OF PEDIATRIC PSYCHOLOGY**

MANUSCRIPT ADDRESS: **Michael C. Roberts, Ph.D.**
Box 870348, Psychology
University of Alabama
Tuscaloosa, AL 35487-0348

TYPE OF ARTICLES: **Research; reviews; theoretical articles; a few case studies**

MAJOR CONTENT AREAS: **Interface of psychology and pediatrics; concommitants of physical disorders and conditions; psychological interventions**
TOPICS PREFERRED: **Must be pediatric psychology physical and mental health; illness issues affecting children adolescents and families**
REVIEW PERIOD: **< 2 mo**   EARLY PUB OPTION: **No**
PUBLICATION LAG TIME: **> 6 mo**

ACCEPT WITHOUT REVISION: **0%**   REJECTION RATE: **75%**
ACCEPT WITH REVISION: **25%**

THEMATIC ISSUES USED: **Yes**

CIRCULATION

NUMBER: **2000**   FREQUENCY: **6 X yr**

CURRENT RATES (INDIVIDUAL): **$39/$28 if member of Soc. of Ped. Psy.**
(INSTITUTIONAL): **$225**   (ASSOCIATE/STUDENT):

ANNUAL INDEX AVAILABILITY: **No**   COST:
SPECIAL SUPPLEMENTS: **No**   COST:
SUBSCRIPTION ADDRESS: **Plenum Publishing Corp.**
233 Spring St.
New York, NY 10013

STYLE/SUBMISSION REQUIREMENTS

STYLE: **APA**   STYLE SHEET: **No**
REVIEW CHARGE: **No**   COST:
NUMBER OF COPIES: **3**   PAGE LIMIT: **20**
RESPONSE TO QUERY LETTERS: **In limited cases**

GENERAL INFORMATION

JOURNAL TITLE: **JOURNAL OF PERINATAL AND NEONATAL NURSING**

MANUSCRIPT ADDRESS: **Rita Gibbs, Advising Editor**
291 Depot Rd.
Boxborough, MA 01719

TYPE OF ARTICLES: **Research; reviews; theoretical; case studies; commentaries; book reviews**

MAJOR CONTENT AREAS: **Neonatal and perinatal nursing**

TOPICS PREFERRED: **No limit**

REVIEW PERIOD: **<2 mo**   EARLY PUB OPTION: **No**

PUBLICATION LAG TIME: **6 mo or more**

ACCEPT WITHOUT REVISION: REJECTION RATE:

ACCEPT WITH REVISION:

THEMATIC ISSUES USED: **Yes**

CIRCULATION

NUMBER: **2400**   FREQUENCY: **Quarterly**

CURRENT RATES (INDIVIDUAL): **$53**

(INSTITUTIONAL):   (ASSOCIATE/STUDENT):

ANNUAL INDEX AVAILABILITY: **No**   COST:

SPECIAL SUPPLEMENTS: **No**   COST:

SUBSCRIPTION ADDRESS: **Aspen Publishers, Inc.**
7201 McKinney Circle
Frederick, MD 21701

STYLE/SUBMISSION REQUIREMENTS

STYLE: **AMA**   STYLE SHEET: **No**

REVIEW CHARGE: **No**   COST:

NUMBER OF COPIES: **3**   PAGE LIMIT: **20-25**

RESPONSE TO QUERY LETTERS: **Yes**

GENERAL INFORMATION

JOURNAL TITLE: **JOURNAL OF PERSONALITY**

MANUSCRIPT ADDRESS: **Editor-Elect**
Howard Tennen
Department of Psychiatry
University of Connecticut
 Health Center
Farmington, CT 06032

TYPE OF ARTICLES: **Research; short reports; theoretical**

MAJOR CONTENT AREAS: **Experimental studies of personality and behavior dynamics, personality development, and individual differences in cognitive, affective and interpersonal domains**

TOPICS PREFERRED:

REVIEW PERIOD: **3-5 mo**   EARLY PUB OPTION: **No**
PUBLICATION LAG TIME: **>6 mo**

ACCEPT WITHOUT REVISION: **0%**   REJECTION RATE: **80%**
ACCEPT WITH REVISION: **20%**

THEMATIC ISSUES USED: **Yes**

CIRCULATION

NUMBER: **2000**   FREQUENCY: **Quarterly**

CURRENT RATES (INDIVIDUAL): **$30**
(INSTITUTIONAL): **$60**   (ASSOCIATE/STUDENT): **$15**

ANNUAL INDEX AVAILABILITY: **Yes**   COST:
SPECIAL SUPPLEMENTS: **No**   COST:
SUBSCRIPTION ADDRESS: **Duke University Press**
Box 6697 College Station
Durham, NC 27708

STYLE/SUBMISSION REQUIREMENTS

STYLE: **APA**   STYLE SHEET: **No**
REVIEW CHARGE: **No**   COST:
NUMBER OF COPIES: **4**   PAGE LIMIT: **None**
RESPONSE TO QUERY LETTERS: **Yes**

GENERAL INFORMATION

JOURNAL TITLE: **JOURNAL OF PERSONALITY ASSESSMENT**

MANUSCRIPT ADDRESS: **Irving A. Weiner, PhD.**
U of South Florida Psychiatry Center
3515 E. Fletcher Ave.
Tampa, FL 33613

TYPE OF ARTICLES: **Commentaries, case reports, and research**
dealing with the evaluation and application of
method of personality assessment

MAJOR CONTENT AREAS:

TOPICS PREFERRED:

REVIEW PERIOD: EARLY PUB OPTION:
PUBLICATION LAG TIME:

ACCEPT WITHOUT REVISION: REJECTION RATE:
ACCEPT WITH REVISION:

THEMATIC ISSUES USED:

CIRCULATION

NUMBER: FREQUENCY:

CURRENT RATES (INDIVIDUAL): **$60**
(INSTITUTIONAL): **$160**   (ASSOCIATE/STUDENT):

ANNUAL INDEX AVAILABILITY: COST:
SPECIAL SUPPLEMENTS: COST:
SUBSCRIPTION ADDRESS: **Lawrence Erlbaum Associates, Inc.**
Journal Sub. Dept.
365 Broadway
Hillsdale, NJ 07642

STYLE/SUBMISSION REQUIREMENTS

STYLE: **APA**   STYLE SHEET:
REVIEW CHARGE: COST:
NUMBER OF COPIES: **3**   PAGE LIMIT:
RESPONSE TO QUERY LETTERS:

GENERAL INFORMATION

JOURNAL TITLE: **JOURNAL OF PERSONALITY AND SOCIAL PSYCHOLOGY**

MANUSCRIPT ADDRESS:

TYPE OF ARTICLES: **Specialized theoretical, methodological, and review papers**

MAJOR CONTENT AREAS: **Attitudes and social cognition; interpersonal relations and group processes; personality processes and individual differences**

TOPICS PREFERRED: **Empirical reports**

REVIEW PERIOD: EARLY PUB OPTION:
PUBLICATION LAG TIME:

ACCEPT WITHOUT REVISION: REJECTION RATE:
ACCEPT WITH REVISION:

THEMATIC ISSUES USED:

CIRCULATION

NUMBER: FREQUENCY: **Monthly**
CURRENT RATES (INDIVIDUAL): **$240**
(INSTITUTIONAL): **$400**   (ASSOCIATE/STUDENT): **$120**

ANNUAL INDEX AVAILABILITY: COST:
SPECIAL SUPPLEMENTS: COST:
SUBSCRIPTION ADDRESS: **APA, Inc.**
1400 North Uhle St.
Arlington, VA 22201

STYLE/SUBMISSION REQUIREMENTS

STYLE: STYLE SHEET:
REVIEW CHARGE: COST:
NUMBER OF COPIES: **4**   PAGE LIMIT:
RESPONSE TO QUERY LETTERS:

GENERAL INFORMATION

JOURNAL TITLE: **JOURNAL OF PSYCHOLOGY AND HUMAN SEXUALITY**

MANUSCRIPT ADDRESS: **Eli Coleman, PhD**
Program in Human Sexuality
1300 South 2nd Street
Minneapolis, MN 55454-1092

TYPE OF ARTICLES: **Research; reviews; theoretical; case studies; commentaries**

MAJOR CONTENT AREAS: **Human sexuality**

TOPICS PREFERRED: **Broad spectrum**

REVIEW PERIOD: **<2 mo**   EARLY PUB OPTION: **No**
PUBLICATION LAG TIME: **6 mo or more**

ACCEPT WITHOUT REVISION: **10%**   REJECTION RATE: **50%**
ACCEPT WITH REVISION: **40%**

THEMATIC ISSUES USED: **Yes**

CIRCULATION

NUMBER: **<1000**   FREQUENCY: **Quarterly**

CURRENT RATES (INDIVIDUAL): **$24**
(INSTITUTIONAL): **$35**   (ASSOCIATE/STUDENT):

ANNUAL INDEX AVAILABILITY: **No**   COST:
SPECIAL SUPPLEMENTS: **No**   COST:
SUBSCRIPTION ADDRESS: **The Haworth Press, Inc.**
10 Alice Street
Binghamton, NY 13904-1580

STYLE/SUBMISSION REQUIREMENTS

STYLE: **APA**   STYLE SHEET: **Yes**
REVIEW CHARGE: **No**   COST:
NUMBER OF COPIES: **4 + diskette**   PAGE LIMIT: **25**
RESPONSE TO QUERY LETTERS: **Yes**

GENERAL INFORMATION

JOURNAL TITLE: **JOURNAL OF READING**

MANUSCRIPT ADDRESS: **P.O. Box 8139**
Newark, DE 19714-8139

TYPE OF ARTICLES: **Currently theory, research, and practice**

MAJOR CONTENT AREAS:

TOPICS PREFERRED:

REVIEW PERIOD: EARLY PUB OPTION:
PUBLICATION LAG TIME:

ACCEPT WITHOUT REVISION: REJECTION RATE:
ACCEPT WITH REVISION:

THEMATIC ISSUES USED:

CIRCULATION

NUMBER: FREQUENCY: **8 X year**

CURRENT RATES (INDIVIDUAL):
(INSTITUTIONAL):   (ASSOCIATE/STUDENT):

ANNUAL INDEX AVAILABILITY: **Yes**   COST:
SPECIAL SUPPLEMENTS: COST:
SUBSCRIPTION ADDRESS: **IRA**
800 Barksdale Rd.
Newark, DE 19714-8139

STYLE/SUBMISSION REQUIREMENTS

STYLE: STYLE SHEET:
REVIEW CHARGE: COST:
NUMBER OF COPIES: **4**   PAGE LIMIT:
RESPONSE TO QUERY LETTERS:

GENERAL INFORMATION

JOURNAL TITLE: **THE JOURNAL OF RELIGION IN PSYCHOTHERAPY**
MANUSCRIPT ADDRESS: **William M. Clements, Ph.D.**
1325 N. College Ave.
Claremont, CA 91711-3199

TYPE OF ARTICLES: **Research; reviews; theoretical; commentaries; book reviews; case studies**
MAJOR CONTENT AREAS: **Intersections formed between religion (broadly conceived), psychotherapy and a disciplinary orientation such as psychiatry, psychology, marriage**
TOPICS PREFERRED: **and family therapy, pastoral counseling**

REVIEW PERIOD: **3-5 mo**   EARLY PUB OPTION: **Yes**
PUBLICATION LAG TIME: **3-5 mo**

ACCEPT WITHOUT REVISION: REJECTION RATE:
ACCEPT WITH REVISION:

THEMATIC ISSUES USED: **Yes**

CIRCULATION

NUMBER: FREQUENCY: **Quarterly**

CURRENT RATES (INDIVIDUAL): **$24**
(INSTITUTIONAL): **$32**   (ASSOCIATE/STUDENT):

ANNUAL INDEX AVAILABILITY: **No**   COST:
SPECIAL SUPPLEMENTS: COST:
SUBSCRIPTION ADDRESS: **The Haworth Press, Inc.**
10 Alice St.
Binghamton, NY 13904-1580

STYLE/SUBMISSION REQUIREMENTS

STYLE: **APA**   STYLE SHEET: **Yes**
REVIEW CHARGE: **No**   COST:
NUMBER OF COPIES: **3**   PAGE LIMIT: **~25**
RESPONSE TO QUERY LETTERS: **Telephone queries**

GENERAL INFORMATION

JOURNAL TITLE: **THE JOURNAL OF RELIGIOUS GERONTOLOGY**

MANUSCRIPT ADDRESS: **William M. Clements, Ph.D.**
1325 N. College Ave.
Claremont, CA 91711-3199

TYPE OF ARTICLES: **Research; reviews; theoretical; commentaries; book reviews**

MAJOR CONTENT AREAS: **Intersections formed between religion and human aging and another discipline such as history, marriage and family, and sociology**

TOPICS PREFERRED:

REVIEW PERIOD: **3-5 mo**   EARLY PUB OPTION: **Yes**
PUBLICATION LAG TIME: **>6 mo**

ACCEPT WITHOUT REVISION: **10%**   REJECTION RATE: **10%**
ACCEPT WITH REVISION: **80%**

THEMATIC ISSUES USED: **Yes**

CIRCULATION

NUMBER: FREQUENCY: **Quarterly**

CURRENT RATES (INDIVIDUAL): **$32**
(INSTITUTIONAL): **$40**   (ASSOCIATE/STUDENT):

ANNUAL INDEX AVAILABILITY: **No**   COST:
SPECIAL SUPPLEMENTS: **No**   COST:
SUBSCRIPTION ADDRESS: **The Haworth Press, Inc.**
10 Alice St.
Binghamton, NY 13904-1580

STYLE/SUBMISSION REQUIREMENTS

STYLE: **Chicago**   STYLE SHEET: **Yes**
REVIEW CHARGE: **No**   COST:
NUMBER OF COPIES: **3**   LIMIT: **~25**
RESPONSE TO QUERY LETTERS: **Telephone queries**

GENERAL INFORMATION

JOURNAL TITLE: **JOURNAL OF RESEARCH IN CHILDHOOD EDUCATION**

MANUSCRIPT ADDRESS: **Dr. John R. Cryan, Editor**
2801 W. Bancroft St.
College of Education and Allied Prof.
Toledo, OH 43606

TYPE OF ARTICLES: **Research; theoretical; case studies**

MAJOR CONTENT AREAS: **Any content area that impacts the education of children, birth through early adolescense**

TOPICS PREFERRED:

REVIEW PERIOD: **3-5 mo**   EARLY PUB OPTION: **Yes**
PUBLICATION LAG TIME: **6 mo or more**

ACCEPT WITHOUT REVISION: **0%**   REJECTION RATE: **82%**
ACCEPT WITH REVISION: **18%**

THEMATIC ISSUES USED: **No**

CIRCULATION

NUMBER: **4000**   FREQUENCY: **2 X yr**

CURRENT RATES (INDIVIDUAL): **$20**
(INSTITUTIONAL): **$60**   (ASSOCIATE/STUDENT):
ANNUAL INDEX AVAILABILITY: **Yes**   COST:
SPECIAL SUPPLEMENTS: **No**   COST:
SUBSCRIPTION ADDRESS: **ACEI**
11141 Georgia Ave.
Suite 200
Wheaton, MD 20902

STYLE/SUBMISSION REQUIREMENTS

STYLE: **APA**   STYLE SHEET: **Yes**
REVIEW CHARGE: **No**   COST:
NUMBER OF COPIES: **4 or 1+disk**   PAGE LIMIT: **30**
RESPONSE TO QUERY LETTERS: **Yes**

GENERAL INFORMATION

JOURNAL TITLE: **JOURNAL OF RESEARCH IN CRIME AND DELINQUENCY**

MANUSCRIPT ADDRESS: **Jeffrey Fagan**
School of Criminal Justice
Rutgers University
15 Washington St.
Newark, NJ 07012

TYPE OF ARTICLES: **Research; theoretical; reviews**

MAJOR CONTENT AREAS: **Crime; delinquency; criminal justice; juvenile justice; sociological theories of deviance; substance use/abuse**

TOPICS PREFERRED: **Same**

REVIEW PERIOD: **3-5 mo**   EARLY PUB OPTION: **No**
PUBLICATION LAG TIME: **>6 mo**

ACCEPT WITHOUT REVISION: **2%**   REJECTION RATE: **85%**
ACCEPT WITH REVISION: **10-12%**

THEMATIC ISSUES USED: **Yes**

CIRCULATION

NUMBER: **1200**   FREQUENCY: **Quarterly**

CURRENT RATES (INDIVIDUAL): **$36**
(INSTITUTIONAL): **$95**   (ASSOCIATE/STUDENT):

ANNUAL INDEX AVAILABILITY: COST:
SPECIAL SUPPLEMENTS: COST:
SUBSCRIPTION ADDRESS: **Sage Publications, Inc.**
2455 Teller Rd.
Newbury Park, CA 91320

STYLE/SUBMISSION REQUIREMENTS

STYLE: **Chicago**   STYLE SHEET: **Yes**
REVIEW CHARGE: **No**   COST:
NUMBER OF COPIES: **4**   PAGE LIMIT: **20-30**
RESPONSE TO QUERY LETTERS: **Yes**

GENERAL INFORMATION

JOURNAL TITLE: **JOURNAL OF SCHOOL HEALTH**

MANUSCRIPT ADDRESS: **American School Health Association**
P.O. Box 708
Kent, OH 44240-0708

TYPE OF ARTICLES: **Research; reviews; theoretical; commentaries; case studies; book reviews**
MAJOR CONTENT AREAS: **Health promotion in school settings with relevance to administrators, educators, nurses, physicians, dentists, psychologists, etc.**
TOPICS PREFERRED: **Health of children and adolescents; health of employees in public and private pre-schools and child care centers, kindergartens, etc.**
REVIEW PERIOD: **3-5 mo**　　EARLY PUB OPTION: **No**
PUBLICATION LAG TIME: **3-5 mo**

ACCEPT WITHOUT REVISION: **5%**　　REJECTION RATE: **70%**
ACCEPT WITH REVISION: **25%**

THEMATIC ISSUES USED: **Yes**

CIRCULATION

NUMBER: **8000**　　FREQUENCY: **Monthly**

CURRENT RATES (INDIVIDUAL): **$70**
(INSTITUTIONAL): **$80**　　(ASSOCIATE/STUDENT): **$25**

ANNUAL INDEX AVAILABILITY: **Yes**　　COST: **None**
SPECIAL SUPPLEMENTS: **No**　　COST:
SUBSCRIPTION ADDRESS: **American School Health Association**
P.O. Box 708
Kent, OH 44240-0708

STYLE/SUBMISSION REQUIREMENTS

STYLE: **AMA**　　STYLE SHEET: **Yes**
REVIEW CHARGE: **No**　　COST:
NUMBER OF COPIES: **Orig+ 5 copies**　　PAGE LIMIT: **14**
RESPONSE TO QUERY LETTERS: **Yes**

GENERAL INFORMATION

JOURNAL TITLE: **JOURNAL OF SEX AND MARITAL THERAPY**

MANUSCRIPT ADDRESS: **Editors**
Journal of Sex and Marital Therapy
65 East 76th St., Suite 1A
New York, NY 10021

TYPE OF ARTICLES:

MAJOR CONTENT AREAS: **New therapeutic techniques; research on outcomes; special clinical problems; theoretical parameters of sexual functioning**

TOPICS PREFERRED:

REVIEW PERIOD: EARLY PUB OPTION:
PUBLICATION LAG TIME:

ACCEPT WITHOUT REVISION: REJECTION RATE:
ACCEPT WITH REVISION:

THEMATIC ISSUES USED:

CIRCULATION

NUMBER: FREQUENCY: **Quarterly**

CURRENT RATES (INDIVIDUAL): **$34**
(INSTITUTIONAL): **$65**   (ASSOCIATE/STUDENT):

ANNUAL INDEX AVAILABILITY: COST:
SPECIAL SUPPLEMENTS: COST:
SUBSCRIPTION ADDRESS: **Subscriptions Department of Brunner/Mazel**
19 Union Square West
New York, NY 10003

STYLE/SUBMISSION REQUIREMENTS

STYLE: STYLE SHEET: **Yes**
REVIEW CHARGE: COST:
NUMBER OF COPIES: PAGE LIMIT:
RESPONSE TO QUERY LETTERS:

GENERAL INFORMATION

JOURNAL TITLE: **JOURNAL OF SOCIAL HISTORY**

MANUSCRIPT ADDRESS: **Carnegie Mellon University**
Pittsburg, PA 15213

TYPE OF ARTICLES: **Research; theoretical; reviews; commentaries;**
case studies; book reviews
MAJOR CONTENT AREAS: **Social history-all aspects**

TOPICS PREFERRED:

REVIEW PERIOD: **<2 mo**   EARLY PUB OPTION: **No**
PUBLICATION LAG TIME: **>6 mo**

ACCEPT WITHOUT REVISION: **5%**   REJECTION RATE:
ACCEPT WITH REVISION: **15%**

THEMATIC ISSUES USED: **Yes, rarely**

CIRCULATION

NUMBER: **1500**   FREQUENCY: **Quarterly**

CURRENT RATES (INDIVIDUAL): **$25**
(INSTITUTIONAL): **$51**   (ASSOCIATE/STUDENT): **$17**

ANNUAL INDEX AVAILABILITY: **Yes**   COST: **Free**
SPECIAL SUPPLEMENTS: **No**   COST:
SUBSCRIPTION ADDRESS: **As above**

STYLE/SUBMISSION REQUIREMENTS

STYLE: **Chicago**   STYLE SHEET: **No**
REVIEW CHARGE: **No**   COST:
NUMBER OF COPIES: **2**   PAGE LIMIT: **None**
RESPONSE TO QUERY LETTERS: **Yes**

GENERAL INFORMATION

JOURNAL TITLE: **JOURNAL OF SOCIAL ISSUES**

MANUSCRIPT ADDRESS: **Stuart Oskamp, Editor**
Faculty in Psychology
Claremont Graduate School
Claremont, CA 91711

TYPE OF ARTICLES: **Research; does not accept unsolicited manuscripts**

MAJOR CONTENT AREAS: **Psychological aspects of social issues**

TOPICS PREFERRED: **No unsolicited manuscripts or book reviews; welcome ideas and proposals for thematic issues**

REVIEW PERIOD: EARLY PUB OPTION:
PUBLICATION LAG TIME:

ACCEPT WITHOUT REVISION: REJECTION RATE:
ACCEPT WITH REVISION:

THEMATIC ISSUES USED: **Yes**

CIRCULATION

NUMBER: FREQUENCY: **Quarterly**

CURRENT RATES (INDIVIDUAL): **$35**
(INSTITUTIONAL): **$140**   (ASSOCIATE/STUDENT):

ANNUAL INDEX AVAILABILITY: COST:
SPECIAL SUPPLEMENTS: COST:
SUBSCRIPTION ADDRESS: **Plenum Publishing**
233 Spring St.
New York, NY 10013

STYLE/SUBMISSION REQUIREMENTS

STYLE: STYLE SHEET:
REVIEW CHARGE: COST:
NUMBER OF COPIES: PAGE LIMIT:
RESPONSE TO QUERY LETTERS:

GENERAL INFORMATION

JOURNAL TITLE: **JOURNAL OF SOCIAL POLICY**

MANUSCRIPT ADDRESS: **The Editor
Journal of Social Policy
University of Leeds
Department of Social Policy
and Sociology
Leeds L52 9JT, U.K.**

TYPE OF ARTICLES: **Review; articles**

MAJOR CONTENT AREAS:

TOPICS PREFERRED:

REVIEW PERIOD: EARLY PUB OPTION:
PUBLICATION LAG TIME:

ACCEPT WITHOUT REVISION: REJECTION RATE:
ACCEPT WITH REVISION:

THEMATIC ISSUES USED:

CIRCULATION

NUMBER: FREQUENCY: **Quarterly**

CURRENT RATES (INDIVIDUAL):
(INSTITUTIONAL): **$116**   (ASSOCIATE/STUDENT):

ANNUAL INDEX AVAILABILITY: COST:
SPECIAL SUPPLEMENTS: COST:
SUBSCRIPTION ADDRESS: **Cambridge University Press
Journals Department
40 West 20th St.
New York, NY 10011**

STYLE/SUBMISSION REQUIREMENTS

STYLE: **Harvard System**   STYLE SHEET: **Yes**
REVIEW CHARGE: COST:
NUMBER OF COPIES: **2**   PAGE LIMIT: **8000 wrds**
RESPONSE TO QUERY LETTERS:

GENERAL INFORMATION

JOURNAL TITLE: **JOURNAL OF SOCIAL PSYCHOLOGY**

MANUSCRIPT ADDRESS: **Heldref Publications**
4000 Albermarle St., N.W.
Washington, DC 20016

TYPE OF ARTICLES: **Research**

MAJOR CONTENT AREAS: **Social psychology**

TOPICS PREFERRED: **Experimental, empirical, and field studies of groups; cultural effects; cross-national problems; language; ethnicity**

REVIEW PERIOD: **<2 mo**   EARLY PUB OPTION: **no**
PUBLICATION LAG TIME: **6 mo or more**

ACCEPT WITHOUT REVISION: REJECTION RATE: **60%**
ACCEPT WITH REVISION:

THEMATIC ISSUES USED: **No**

CIRCULATION

NUMBER: FREQUENCY:

CURRENT RATES (INDIVIDUAL):
(INSTITUTIONAL):   (ASSOCIATE/STUDENT):

ANNUAL INDEX AVAILABILITY: COST:
SPECIAL SUPPLEMENTS: COST:
SUBSCRIPTION ADDRESS:

STYLE/SUBMISSION REQUIREMENTS

STYLE: STYLE SHEET:
REVIEW CHARGE: COST:
NUMBER OF COPIES: PAGE LIMIT:
RESPONSE TO QUERY LETTERS:

GENERAL INFORMATION

JOURNAL TITLE: **JOURNAL OF STUDIES ON ALCOHOL**

MANUSCRIPT ADDRESS: **Editors, Drs. Jack H. Mendelson and
Nancy K. Mello
Alcohol and Drug Abuse Research Center
McLean Hospital
Harvard Medical School
115 Mill St.
Belmont, MA 02178**

TYPE OF ARTICLES:

MAJOR CONTENT AREAS:

TOPICS PREFERRED: **Original research reports**

REVIEW PERIOD: EARLY PUB OPTION:
PUBLICATION LAG TIME:

ACCEPT WITHOUT REVISION: REJECTION RATE:
ACCEPT WITH REVISION:

THEMATIC ISSUES USED:

CIRCULATION

NUMBER: FREQUENCY: **Bimonthly**

CURRENT RATES (INDIVIDUAL): **$110**
(INSTITUTIONAL):   (ASSOCIATE/STUDENT):

ANNUAL INDEX AVAILABILITY: COST:
SPECIAL SUPPLEMENTS: COST:
SUBSCRIPTION ADDRESS: **Peggy Markham
Rutgers University
PO Box 969
Piscataway, NJ 08855-0969**

STYLE/SUBMISSION REQUIREMENTS

STYLE: STYLE SHEET:
REVIEW CHARGE: COST:
NUMBER OF COPIES: PAGE LIMIT:
RESPONSE TO QUERY LETTERS:

GENERAL INFORMATION

JOURNAL TITLE: **JOURNAL FOR THE THEORY OF SOCIAL BEHAVIOR**

MANUSCRIPT ADDRESS: **Charles W. Smith**
Sociology
Queen's College
CUNY
Flushing, NY 11367

TYPE OF ARTICLES: **Research; theoretical; case studies**

MAJOR CONTENT AREAS: **Eclectic orientation toward theoretical contributions toward understnading social behavior**

TOPICS PREFERRED:

REVIEW PERIOD: **3-5 mo**   EARLY PUB OPTION: **No**
PUBLICATION LAG TIME: **3-5 mo**

ACCEPT WITHOUT REVISION: **1%**   REJECTION RATE: **25-50%**
ACCEPT WITH REVISION: **25%**

THEMATIC ISSUES USED: **Yes**

CIRCULATION

NUMBER: **1000**   FREQUENCY: **Quarterly**

CURRENT RATES (INDIVIDUAL):
(INSTITUTIONAL):   (ASSOCIATE/STUDENT):

ANNUAL INDEX AVAILABILITY: **Yes**   COST:
SPECIAL SUPPLEMENTS: **No**   COST:
SUBSCRIPTION ADDRESS: **Basil Blackwell**
108 Cowley Rd.
Oxford

STYLE/SUBMISSION REQUIREMENTS

STYLE: **APA**   STYLE SHEET: **No**
REVIEW CHARGE: **No**   COST:
NUMBER OF COPIES: **5**   PAGE LIMIT: **10,000 words**
RESPONSE TO QUERY LETTERS: **Yes**

GENERAL INFORMATION

JOURNAL TITLE: **JOURNAL OF WOMEN AND AGING**

MANUSCRIPT ADDRESS: **J. Dianne Garner, DSW, Editor**
Journal of Women and Aging
Department of Social Work
Washburn University
Topeka, KS 66621

TYPE OF ARTICLES: **Research; theoretical; case studies; book reviews**

MAJOR CONTENT AREAS: **Health; mental health; family; programs and services; policy and social conditions**

TOPICS PREFERRED: **All topics should focus on older women. Target audience is professionals who provide services to older women**

REVIEW PERIOD: **<2 mo**   EARLY PUB OPTION: **No**
PUBLICATION LAG TIME: **>6 mo**

ACCEPT WITHOUT REVISION: **10%**   REJECTION RATE: **40%**
ACCEPT WITH REVISION: **50%**

THEMATIC ISSUES USED: **Yes**

CIRCULATION

NUMBER: FREQUENCY: **Quarterly**

CURRENT RATES (INDIVIDUAL): **$28**
(INSTITUTIONAL): **$38**   (ASSOCIATE/STUDENT): **$28**

ANNUAL INDEX AVAILABILITY: **No**   COST:
SPECIAL SUPPLEMENTS: **No**   COST:
SUBSCRIPTION ADDRESS: **The Haworth Press, Inc.**
10 Alice St.
Binghamton, NY 13904-1580

STYLE/SUBMISSION REQUIREMENTS

STYLE: **APA**   STYLE SHEET: **Yes**
REVIEW CHARGE: **No**   COST:
NUMBER OF COPIES: **3 + diskette**   PAGE LIMIT: **20**
RESPONSE TO QUERY LETTERS: **Yes**

GENERAL INFORMATION

JOURNAL TITLE: **LOSS, GRIEF & CARE: A JOURNAL OF PROFESSIONAL PRACTICE**

MANUSCRIPT ADDRESS: **Dr. Austin H. Kutscher, Editor**
The Foundation of Thanatology
630 West 168th St.
New York, NY 10031

TYPE OF ARTICLES: **Articles of interest to anyone whose professional practice focuses on loss, grief, and caregiving**

MAJOR CONTENT AREAS:

TOPICS PREFERRED:

REVIEW PERIOD: EARLY PUB OPTION:
PUBLICATION LAG TIME:

ACCEPT WITHOUT REVISION: REJECTION RATE:
ACCEPT WITH REVISION:

THEMATIC ISSUES USED:

CIRCULATION

NUMBER: FREQUENCY: **Quarterly**

CURRENT RATES (INDIVIDUAL): **$32**
(INSTITUTIONAL): **$45**   (ASSOCIATE/STUDENT):

ANNUAL INDEX AVAILABILITY: COST:
SPECIAL SUPPLEMENTS: COST:
SUBSCRIPTION ADDRESS: **The Haworth Press, Inc.**
10 Alice St.
Binghamton, NY 13904-1580

STYLE/SUBMISSION REQUIREMENTS

STYLE: STYLE SHEET:
REVIEW CHARGE: **No**   COST:
NUMBER OF COPIES: PAGE LIMIT: **20**
RESPONSE TO QUERY LETTERS:

GENERAL INFORMATION

JOURNAL TITLE:　**MARRIAGE ENCOUNTER**

MANUSCRIPT ADDRESS:　**Marriage Encounter**
955 Lake Dr.
St. Paul, MN 55120

TYPE OF ARTICLES:　**Research; theoretical; case studies;**
commentaries; book reviews; personal
experiences

MAJOR CONTENT AREAS:　**Personal growth; relationship skills;**
communication skills

TOPICS PREFERRED:　**Growth and relationship**

REVIEW PERIOD:　**3-5 mo**　　EARLY PUB OPTION:　**Yes**
PUBLICATION LAG TIME:　**>6 mo**

ACCEPT WITHOUT REVISION:　**20%**　　REJECTION RATE:　**60%**
ACCEPT WITH REVISION:　**20%**

THEMATIC ISSUES USED:　**Yes**

CIRCULATION

NUMBER:　**6000**　　FREQUENCY:　**9 X yr**

CURRENT RATES (INDIVIDUAL):　**$15**
(INSTITUTIONAL):　　(ASSOCIATE/STUDENT):

ANNUAL INDEX AVAILABILITY:　**No**　　COST:
SPECIAL SUPPLEMENTS:　**Yes**　　COST:　**Varies**
SUBSCRIPTION ADDRESS:　**Marriage Encounter**
955 Lake Dr.
St. Paul, MN 55120

STYLE/SUBMISSION REQUIREMENTS

STYLE:　　STYLE SHEET:　**No**
REVIEW CHARGE:　**No**　　COST:
NUMBER OF COPIES:　**1**　　PAGE LIMIT:　**Varies**
RESPONSE TO QUERY LETTERS:　**In limited cases**

GENERAL INFORMATION

JOURNAL TITLE: **MARRIAGE AND FAMILY REVIEW**

MANUSCRIPT ADDRESS: **Marvin B. Sussman, Ph.D.**
Professor of Human Behavior
Dept. of Individual and Family
Studies
University of Delaware
Newark, DE 19716

TYPE OF ARTICLES: **Articles that discuss new research and theory**
and evaluate the meaning and importance of
research. Publication of thematic issues only

MAJOR CONTENT AREAS: **Multidisciplinary; of practical value to both**
socially-oriented and clinically-oriented
marriage and family specialists

TOPICS PREFERRED: **Topics related to the study of the family unit**
and the comple issues affecting today's families;
contact the editor for a list of thematic issues in
progress

REVIEW PERIOD: **3 mo**   EARLY PUB OPTION: **No**
PUBLICATION LAG TIME: **10 mo**
ACCEPT WITHOUT REVISION: **5%**   REJECTION RATE:
ACCEPT WITH REVISION: **95%**
THEMATIC ISSUES USED: **Yes**

CIRCULATION

NUMBER: **850**   FREQUENCY: **Quarterly**
CURRENT RATES (INDIVIDUAL): **$40**
(INSTITUTIONAL): **$90**   (ASSOCIATE/STUDENT):

ANNUAL INDEX AVAILABILITY: **None**   COST:
SPECIAL SUPPLEMENTS: **None**   COST:
SUBSCRIPTION ADDRESS: **The Haworth Press, Inc.**
10 Alice St.
Binghamton, NY 13904-1580

STYLE/SUBMISSION REQUIREMENTS

STYLE: **APA**   STYLE SHEET: **Yes**
REVIEW CHARGE: **No**   COST:
NUMBER OF COPIES: **Orig, 2 copies**   PAGE LIMIT: **25**
+ diskette
RESPONSE TO QUERY LETTERS: **Yes; suggestions for**
thematic issues invited

GENERAL INFORMATION

JOURNAL TITLE: **MEASUREMENT AND EVALUATION IN COUNSELING AND DEVELOPMENT**
MANUSCRIPT ADDRESS: **William D. Schafer, Editor**
EDMS, College of Education
University of Maryland
College Park, MD 20742-1115

TYPE OF ARTICLES: **Research; reviews; theoretical; case studies; commentaries; test reviews; software reviews**
MAJOR CONTENT AREAS: **Theoretical and other problems of the measurement specialist; articles directing administrators, counselors, personnel workers**
TPPICS PREFERRED: **Clearly described implications for practitioners in measurement and evaluation**

REVIEW PERIOD: **3-5 mo**   EARLY PUB OPTION: **No**
PUBLICATION LAG TIME: **> 6 mo**

ACCEPT WITHOUT REVISION: **1%**   REJECTION RATE: **69%**
ACCEPT WITH REVISION: **30%**

THEMATIC ISSUES USED: **Yes**

CIRCULATION

NUMBER: **2615**   FREQUENCY: **Quarterly**

CURRENT RATES (INDIVIDUAL): **$19**
(INSTITUTIONAL): **$23**   (ASSOCIATE/STUDENT): **$14**

ANNUAL INDEX AVAILABILITY: **No**   COST:
SPECIAL SUPPLEMENTS: **No**   COST:
SUBSCRIPTION ADDRESS: **Subscription Dept. AACD**
5999 Stevenson Avenue
Alexandria, VA 22304

STYLE/SUBMISSION REQUIREMENTS

STYLE: **APA**   STYLE SHEET: **No**
REVIEW CHARGE: **No**   COST:
NUMBER OF COPIES: **4**   PAGE LIMIT: **None**
RESPONSE TO QUERY LETTERS: **Yes**

GENERAL INFORMATION

JOURNAL TITLE: **MCN**

MANUSCRIPT ADDRESS: **(Same as below)**
Barbara E. Bishop R.N., Editor

TYPE OF ARTICLES:

MAJOR CONTENT AREAS:

TOPICS PREFERRED:

REVIEW PERIOD: EARLY PUB OPTION:
PUBLICATION LAG TIME:

ACCEPT WITHOUT REVISION: REJECTION RATE:
ACCEPT WITH REVISION:

THEMATIC ISSUES USED:

CIRCULATION

NUMBER: FREQUENCY: **Bimonthly**

CURRENT RATES (INDIVIDUAL): **$20**
(INSTITUTIONAL): **$30**   (ASSOCIATE/STUDENT):

ANNUAL INDEX AVAILABILITY: COST:
SPECIAL SUPPLEMENTS: COST:
SUBSCRIPTION ADDRESS: **American Journal of Nursing Co.**
555 W. 57th St.
New York, NY 100019-2961

STYLE/SUBMISSION REQUIREMENTS

STYLE: STYLE SHEET: **On**
REVIEW CHARGE: COST: **Reqst**
NUMBER OF COPIES: **3**   PAGE LIMIT: **15**
RESPONSE TO QUERY LETTERS:

GENERAL INFORMATION

JOURNAL TITLE: **MEDIATION QUARTERLY**

MANUSCRIPT ADDRESS: **Peter R. Maida, Ph.D.**
Institute of Criminal Justice and
** Criminology**
2220 G. LeFrak
University of Maryland
College Park, MD 20742

TYPE OF ARTICLES: **Research; reviews; theoretical; case studies;**
commentaries; book reviews

MAJOR CONTENT AREAS: **Mediation, primarily in family, community,**
education, and courts

TOPICS PREFERRED: **Any, as long as they address mediation**

REVIEW PERIOD: **3-5 mo**   EARLY PUB OPTION: **No**
PUBLICATION LAG TIME: **3-5 mo**

ACCEPT WITHOUT REVISION: **0%**   REJECTION RATE: **50%**
ACCEPT WITH REVISION: **50%**

THEMATIC ISSUES USED: **Yes**

CIRCULATION

NUMBER: **2000**   FREQUENCY: **Quarterly**

CURRENT RATES (INDIVIDUAL): **$45**
(INSTITUTIONAL): **$72**   (ASSOCIATE/STUDENT):

ANNUAL INDEX AVAILABILITY: **No**   COST:
SPECIAL SUPPLEMENTS: **No**   COST:
SUBSCRIPTION ADDRESS: **Jossey-Bass, Inc.**
350 Sansome St.
San Francisco, CA 94104

STYLE/SUBMISSION REQUIREMENTS

STYLE: STYLE SHEET: **Yes**
REVIEW CHARGE: **No**   COST:
NUMBER OF COPIES: **3**   PAGE LIMIT: **20**
RESPONSE TO QUERY LETTERS: **Yes**

GENERAL INFORMATION

JOURNAL TITLE: **MEDICAL ANTHROPOLOGY QUATERLY**

MANUSCRIPT ADDRESS: **The Editors**
Medical Anthropology Quarterly
Department of Anthropology
University of Massachusettes
Boston, MA 02125

TYPE OF ARTICLES:

MAJOR CONTENT AREAS:

TOPICS PREFERRED:

REVIEW PERIOD: EARLY PUB OPTION:
PUBLICATION LAG TIME:

ACCEPT WITHOUT REVISION: REJECTION RATE:
ACCEPT WITH REVISION:

THEMATIC ISSUES USED:

CIRCULATION

NUMBER: FREQUENCY: **Quarterly**

CURRENT RATES (INDIVIDUAL): **$60**
(INSTITUTIONAL):   (ASSOCIATE/STUDENT):

ANNUAL INDEX AVAILABILITY: COST:
SPECIAL SUPPLEMENTS: COST:
SUBSCRIPTION ADDRESS: **American Anthropology Association**
1703 New Hampshir Ave., NW
Washington, DC 20009

STYLE/SUBMISSION REQUIREMENTS

STYLE: **MAQ**   STYLE SHEET: **Yes**
REVIEW CHARGE: COST:
NUMBER OF COPIES: **3**   PAGE LIMIT:
RESPONSE TO QUERY LETTERS:

GENERAL INFORMATION

JOURNAL TITLE: **MEMORY AND COGNITION**

MANUSCRIPT ADDRESS: **Margaret Jean Intons-Peterson, Editor**
Department of Psychology
Indiana University
Bloomington, IN 47405

TYPE OF ARTICLES:

MAJOR CONTENT AREAS: **Broad range of topics in human experimental**
psychology

TOPICS PREFERRED:

REVIEW PERIOD: EARLY PUB OPTION:
PUBLICATION LAG TIME:

ACCEPT WITHOUT REVISION: REJECTION RATE:
ACCEPT WITH REVISION:

THEMATIC ISSUES USED:

CIRCULATION

NUMBER: FREQUENCY: **Bimonthly**

CURRENT RATES (INDIVIDUAL): **$35**
(INSTITUTIONAL): **$84**   (ASSOCIATE/STUDENT):

ANNUAL INDEX AVAILABILITY: COST:
SPECIAL SUPPLEMENTS: COST:
SUBSCRIPTION ADDRESS: **Psychonomic Society Publications**
1710 Fortview Rd.
Austin, TX 78704

STYLE/SUBMISSION REQUIREMENTS

STYLE: **APA**   STYLE SHEET:
REVIEW CHARGE: COST:
NUMBER OF COPIES: **5**   PAGE LIMIT:
RESPONSE TO QUERY LETTERS:

GENERAL INFORMATION

JOURNAL TITLE: **MONOGRAPHS OF THE SOCIETY FOR RESEARCH IN CHILD DEVELOPMENT**

MANUSCRIPT ADDRESS: **W.C. Bransom**
Institute of Human Development
Tolman Hall
University of California
Berkley, CA 94720

TYPE OF ARTICLES: **Major reports from programatic studies; integrated collections of individual reports**

MAJOR CONTENT AREAS: **Any aspect of infant through adolescent development and factors that shape it**

TOPICS PREFERRED:

REVIEW PERIOD: **< 2 mo**   EARLY PUB OPTION: **No**
PUBLICATION LAG TIME: **> 6 mo**

ACCEPT WITHOUT REVISION: **0%**   REJECTION RATE: **60%**
ACCEPT WITH REVISION: **40%**

THEMATIC ISSUES USED:

CIRCULATION

NUMBER: FREQUENCY:

CURRENT RATES (INDIVIDUAL):
(INSTITUTIONAL):   (ASSOCIATE/STUDENT):

ANNUAL INDEX AVAILABILITY: COST:
SPECIAL SUPPLEMENTS: COST:
SUBSCRIPTION ADDRESS:

STYLE/SUBMISSION REQUIREMENTS

STYLE: STYLE SHEET:
REVIEW CHARGE: COST:
NUMBER OF COPIES: PAGE LIMIT:
RESPONSE TO QUERY LETTERS:

GENERAL INFORMATION

JOURNAL TITLE: **MULTIVARIATE BEHAVIORAL RESEARCH**

MANUSCRIPT ADDRESS: **Dr. Stanley A. Mulaik, Editor MBR**
School of Psychology
Georgia Institute of Technology
Atlanta, GA 30332

TYPE OF ARTICLES: **Research; theoretical; commentaries;**
methodological

MAJOR CONTENT AREAS: **Multivariate statistics and their application**

TOPICS PREFERRED: **Theoretical articles; paradigmatic examples of**
applications of more recently developed
multivariate statistical methods

REVIEW PERIOD: **3-5 mo**   EARLY PUB OPTION: **No**

PUBLICATION LAG TIME: **>6 mo**

ACCEPT WITHOUT REVISION: **10%**   REJECTION RATE: **60%**

ACCEPT WITH REVISION: **30%**

THEMATIC ISSUES USED: **Yes**

CIRCULATION

NUMBER: **1800**   FREQUENCY: **Quarterly**

CURRENT RATES (INDIVIDUAL): **$35**

(INSTITUTIONAL): **$75**   (ASSOCIATE/STUDENT):

ANNUAL INDEX AVAILABILITY: **No**   COST:

SPECIAL SUPPLEMENTS: **No**   COST:

SUBSCRIPTION ADDRESS: **Lawrence Erlbaum Associates, Inc.**
365 Broadway
Hillsdale, NJ 07642

STYLE/SUBMISSION REQUIREMENTS

STYLE: **APA**   STYLE SHEET: **No**

REVIEW CHARGE: **No**   COST:

NUMBER OF COPIES: **4**   PAGE LIMIT: **40**

RESPONSE TO QUERY LETTERS: **In limited cases**

GENERAL INFORMATION

JOURNAL TITLE: **NEWSLETTER OF THE ASSOCIATION OF GAY AND LESBIAN PSYCHIATRISTS**
MANUSCRIPT ADDRESS: **1439 Pineville Rd.**
New Hope, PA 18938

TYPE OF ARTICLES: **Commentaries; book reviews; news**

MAJOR CONTENT AREAS: **News about the Association of Gay and Lesbian Psychiatrists**

TOPICS PREFERRED: **As above**

REVIEW PERIOD: **<2 mo**   EARLY PUB OPTION: **No**
PUBLICATION LAG TIME: **3-5 mo**

ACCEPT WITHOUT REVISION: **70%**   REJECTION RATE:
ACCEPT WITH REVISION:

THEMATIC ISSUES USED: **No**

CIRCULATION

NUMBER: **400**   FREQUENCY: **Quarterly**

CURRENT RATES (INDIVIDUAL): **$15**
(INSTITUTIONAL): **$15**   (ASSOCIATE/STUDENT): **$15**

ANNUAL INDEX AVAILABILITY: **No**   COST:
SPECIAL SUPPLEMENTS: **No**   COST:
SUBSCRIPTION ADDRESS: **1439 Pineville Rd.**
New Hope, PA 18938

STYLE/SUBMISSION REQUIREMENTS

STYLE: **None**   STYLE SHEET: **No**
REVIEW CHARGE: **No**   COST:
NUMBER OF COPIES: **1**   PAGE LIMIT: **5**
RESPONSE TO QUERY LETTERS: **No**

GENERAL INFORMATION

JOURNAL TITLE: **NURSING RESEARCH**

MANUSCRIPT ADDRESS: **Florence S. Downs, Ed.D, FAAN Editor
Associate Dean, School of Nursing
University of Pennsylvania
420 Guardian Dr., S2,
Philadelphia, PA 19104**

TYPE OF ARTICLES:

MAJOR CONTENT AREAS: **Research, research methods, instrument
development, theory**

TOPICS PREFERRED: **Those relevant to nursing**

REVIEW PERIOD: **2 mo**   EARLY PUB OPTION: **Yes**
PUBLICATION LAG TIME: **7-8 mo**

ACCEPT WITHOUT REVISION: **1 %**   REJECTION RATE: **86%**
ACCEPT WITH REVISION: **13%**

THEMATIC ISSUES USED: **Rarely**

CIRCULATION

NUMBER: **12,000**   FREQUENCY: **Bimonthly**

CURRENT RATES (INDIVIDUAL): **$23**
(INSTITUTIONAL): **$35**   (ASSOCIATE/STUDENT): **$15.00**

ANNUAL INDEX AVAILABILITY: **No**   COST:
SPECIAL SUPPLEMENTS: **No**   COST:
SUBSCRIPTION ADDRESS: **Nursing Research
555 W. 57th St.
NY, NY 10019-2961**

STYLE/SUBMISSION REQUIREMENTS

STYLE: **Am. Psy. Asoc.**   STYLE SHEET:
REVIEW CHARGE: COST:
NUMBER OF COPIES: PAGE LIMIT:
RESPONSE TO QUERY LETTERS:

GENERAL INFORMATION

JOURNAL TITLE: **OMEGA**

MANUSCRIPT ADDRESS: **Dr. Robert Kastenbaum**
Department of Communication
Arizona State University
Tempe, AZ 85287-1205

TYPE OF ARTICLES:

MAJOR CONTENT AREAS:

TOPICS PREFERRED:
REVIEW PERIOD: EARLY PUB OPTION:
PUBLICATION LAG TIME:

ACCEPT WITHOUT REVISION: REJECTION RATE:
ACCEPT WITH REVISION:

THEMATIC ISSUES USED:

CIRCULATION

NUMBER: FREQUENCY: **8 X yr**

CURRENT RATES (INDIVIDUAL): **$54**
(INSTITUTIONAL): **$145**   (ASSOCIATE/STUDENT):

ANNUAL INDEX AVAILABILITY: COST:
SPECIAL SUPPLEMENTS: COST:
SUBSCRIPTION ADDRESS: **Baywood Publishing Company, Inc.**
26 Austin Ave. P.O. Box 337
Amityville, NY 11701

STYLE/SUBMISSION REQUIREMENTS

STYLE: STYLE SHEET: **Yes**
REVIEW CHARGE: COST:
NUMBER OF COPIES: **3**   PAGE LIMIT:
RESPONSE TO QUERY LETTERS:

GENERAL INFORMATION

JOURNAL TITLE: **PERSONALITY AND SOCIAL PSYCHOLOGY BULLETIN**

MANUSCRIPT ADDRESS: **Richard E. Petty**
Dept. of Psychology
Ohio State University
404 C West 17th Ave.
Columbus, OH 43210

TYPE OF ARTICLES: **Relatively brief empirical, theoretical, and review papers in all areas of personality and social psychology**

MAJOR CONTENT AREAS:

TOPICS PREFERRED: **Articles on the interface of personality & social psychology**

REVIEW PERIOD: EARLY PUB OPTION:
PUBLICATION LAG TIME:

ACCEPT WITHOUT REVISION: REJECTION RATE:
ACCEPT WITH REVISION:

THEMATIC ISSUES USED:

CIRCULATION

NUMBER: FREQUENCY: **Quarterly**

CURRENT RATES (INDIVIDUAL): **$40**
(INSTITUTIONAL): **$110**   (ASSOCIATE/STUDENT):

ANNUAL INDEX AVAILABILITY: COST:
SPECIAL SUPPLEMENTS: COST:
SUBSCRIPTION ADDRESS: **Sage Publications, Inc.**
2455 Teller Rd.
Newbury Park, CA 91320

STYLE/SUBMISSION REQUIREMENTS

STYLE: **APA**   STYLE SHEET:
REVIEW CHARGE: **$30**   COST:
NUMBER OF COPIES: **4**   PAGE LIMIT: **12-18**
RESPONSE TO QUERY LETTERS:

GENERAL INFORMATION

JOURNAL TITLE: **PERSONNEL PSYCHOLOGY**

MANUSCRIPT ADDRESS: **Professor Michael A. Campion**
Graduate School of Management
Krannert Building
Purdue University
West Lafayette, IN 47907

TYPE OF ARTICLES: **Research; reviews; book reviews**

MAJOR CONTENT AREAS: **Employee selection; training and development;**
job analysis; productivity; improvement
programs; work attitudes; labor-management
TOPICS PREFERRED: **Relations; compensation**

REVIEW PERIOD: **<2 mo**   EARLY PUB OPTION: **No**
PUBLICATION LAG TIME: **3 mo**

ACCEPT WITHOUT REVISION: **0%**   REJECTION RATE: **75%**
ACCEPT WITH REVISION: **25%**

THEMATIC ISSUES USED: **No**

CIRCULATION

NUMBER: **3441**   FREQUENCY: **Quarterly**

CURRENT RATES (INDIVIDUAL): **$50**
(INSTITUTIONAL): **$50**   (ASSOCIATE/STUDENT): **$32**

ANNUAL INDEX AVAILABILITY: **Yes**   COST: **NA**
SPECIAL SUPPLEMENTS: **No**   COST:
SUBSCRIPTION ADDRESS: **9660 Hillcroft, Suite 337**
Houston, TX 77096

STYLE/SUBMISSION REQUIREMENTS

STYLE: **APA**   STYLE SHEET: **No**
REVIEW CHARGE: **No**   COST:
NUMBER OF COPIES: **4**   PAGE LIMIT: **None**
RESPONSE TO QUERY LETTERS: **In limited cases**

GENERAL INFORMATION

JOURNAL TITLE: **POLICY STUDIES JOURNAL**

MANUSCRIPT ADDRESS: **Mel Dubnick**
Public Administration Dept.
University of Kansas
Lawrence, KS 66045

TYPE OF ARTICLES: **Research; reviews; theoretical; case studies;**
commentaries; book reviews
MAJOR CONTENT AREAS: **Policy studies and American government**

TOPICS PREFERRED:

REVIEW PERIOD: **<2 mo**   EARLY PUB OPTION: **No**
PUBLICATION LAG TIME: **3-5 mo**

ACCEPT WITHOUT REVISION: **5%**   REJECTION RATE: **85%**
ACCEPT WITH REVISION: **10%**

THEMATIC ISSUES USED: **Yes**

CIRCULATION

NUMBER: **2300**   FREQUENCY: **Quarterly**

CURRENT RATES (INDIVIDUAL): **$18**
(INSTITUTIONAL): **$60**   (ASSOCIATE/STUDENT):

ANNUAL INDEX AVAILABILITY: **Yes**   COST:
SPECIAL SUPPLEMENTS: COST:
SUBSCRIPTION ADDRESS: **Policy Studies Organization**
361 Lincoln Hall
702 South Wright
University of Illinois
Urbana, Il 61801

STYLE/SUBMISSION REQUIREMENTS

STYLE: **MLA**   STYLE SHEET: **Yes**
REVIEW CHARGE: **No**   COST:
NUMBER OF COPIES: **4+1 to co-ed.**   PAGE LIMIT: **15-25**
RESPONSE TO QUERY LETTERS: **Yes**

GENERAL INFORMATION

JOURNAL TITLE: **POLICY STUDIES REVIEW**

MANUSCRIPT ADDRESS: **Dennis Palumbo and Michael Musheno
Co-Editors
School of Justice Studies
Arizona State University
Tempe, AZ 85287**

TYPE OF ARTICLES: **Research; reviews; theoretical; commentaries;
case studies; book reviews**
MAJOR CONTENT AREAS: **Policy studies as well as theoretical and
methodological pieces**

TOPICS PREFERRED: **Policy processes and outcomes of particular
policies**

REVIEW PERIOD: **<2 mo**   EARLY PUB OPTION: **No**
PUBLICATION LAG TIME:

ACCEPT WITHOUT REVISION: **5%**   REJECTION RATE: **85%**
ACCEPT WITH REVISION: **10%**

THEMATIC ISSUES USED: **Yes**

CIRCULATION

NUMBER: **2300**   FREQUENCY: **Quarterly**

CURRENT RATES (INDIVIDUAL): **$18**
(INSTITUTIONAL): **$58**   (ASSOCIATE/STUDENT): **$12**

ANNUAL INDEX AVAILABILITY: **Yes**   COST:
SPECIAL SUPPLEMENTS: COST:
SUBSCRIPTION ADDRESS: **Policy Studies Organization
361 Lincoln Hall
702 South Wright
University of Illinois
Urbana, IL 61801**

STYLE/SUBMISSION REQUIREMENTS

STYLE: **APA**   STYLE SHEET: **Yes**
REVIEW CHARGE: **No**   COST:
NUMBER OF COPIES: **4**   PAGE LIMIT: **30**
RESPONSE TO QUERY LETTERS: **Yes**

GENERAL INFORMATION

JOURNAL TITLE: **PREVENTION IN HUMAN SERVICES**

MANUSCRIPT ADDRESS: **Robert E. Hess, Chief**
Bureau of Mental Health
450 West State
Boise, ID 83720

TYPE OF ARTICLES:

MAJOR CONTENT AREAS:

TOPICS PREFERRED:

REVIEW PERIOD: EARLY PUB OPTION:
PUBLICATION LAG TIME:

ACCEPT WITHOUT REVISION: REJECTION RATE:
ACCEPT WITH REVISION:

THEMATIC ISSUES USED:

CIRCULATION

NUMBER: FREQUENCY: **Biannual**

CURRENT RATES (INDIVIDUAL): **$36**
(INSTITUTIONAL): **$95**   (ASSOCIATE/STUDENT):

ANNUAL INDEX AVAILABILITY: COST:
SPECIAL SUPPLEMENTS: COST:
SUBSCRIPTION ADDRESS: **The Haworth Press, Inc.**
10 Alice St.
Binghamton, NY 13904-1580

STYLE/SUBMISSION REQUIREMENTS

STYLE: STYLE SHEET:
REVIEW CHARGE: **No**   COST:
NUMBER OF COPIES: **3 + diskette**   PAGE LIMIT: **20**
RESPONSE TO QUERY LETTERS:

GENERAL INFORMATION

JOURNAL TITLE: **PSYCHIATRY**

MANUSCRIPT ADDRESS: **David M. Reiss, M.D.**
Division of Research
Department of Psychiatry and
Behaviorial Sciences
George Washington Univ. Medical Cntr.
2300 Eye St. Washignton, DC 20037

TYPE OF ARTICLES:

MAJOR CONTENT AREAS: **Multidisciplinary**

TOPICS PREFERRED: **Contributions that foster a thoughtful**
integration of biological and interpersonal
reasoning

REVIEW PERIOD: EARLY PUB OPTION:
PUBLICATION LAG TIME:

ACCEPT WITHOUT REVISION: REJECTION RATE:
ACCEPT WITH REVISION:

THEMATIC ISSUES USED:

CIRCULATION

NUMBER: FREQUENCY: **Quarterly**

CURRENT RATES (INDIVIDUAL): **$27.50**
(INSTITUTIONAL): **$75** (ASSOCIATE/STUDENT):

ANNUAL INDEX AVAILABILITY: COST:
SPECIAL SUPPLEMENTS: COST:
SUBSCRIPTION ADDRESS: **The Guilford Press**
72 Spring St.
New York, NY 10012

STYLE/SUBMISSION REQUIREMENTS

STYLE: STYLE SHEET:
REVIEW CHARGE: COST:
NUMBER OF COPIES: **4** PAGE LIMIT:
RESPONSE TO QUERY LETTERS:

GENERAL INFORMATION

JOURNAL TITLE: **PSYCHOANALYTIC QUARTERLY**

MANUSCRIPT ADDRESS: **Editor**
Room 210
175 Fifth Avenue
New York, NY 10010

TYPE OF ARTICLES:

MAJOR CONTENT AREAS:

TOPICS PREFERRED:

REVIEW PERIOD: EARLY PUB OPTION:
PUBLICATION LAG TIME:

ACCEPT WITHOUT REVISION: REJECTION RATE:
ACCEPT WITH REVISION:

THEMATIC ISSUES USED:

CIRCULATION

NUMBER: FREQUENCY: **Quarterly**

CURRENT RATES (INDIVIDUAL): **request**
(INSTITUTIONAL):   (ASSOCIATE/STUDENT):

ANNUAL INDEX AVAILABILITY: COST:
SPECIAL SUPPLEMENTS: COST:
SUBSCRIPTION ADDRESS: **Psychoanalytic Quarterly**
175 Fifth Avenue
New York, NY 10010

STYLE/SUBMISSION REQUIREMENTS

STYLE: STYLE SHEET: **Yes**
REVIEW CHARGE: COST:
NUMBER OF COPIES: **3**   PAGE LIMIT:
RESPONSE TO QUERY LETTERS:

GENERAL INFORMATION

JOURNAL TITLE: **PSYCHOLOGICAL BULLETIN**

MANUSCRIPT ADDRESS: **John C. Masters**
1334 Wesley Hall
Vanderbilt University
Nashville, Tn 37240-0009

TYPE OF ARTICLES: **Reviews; interpretations of critical substantive**
and methodological issues
MAJOR CONTENT AREAS: **Practical problems from all the diverse areas of**
psychology

TOPICS PREFERRED:

REVIEW PERIOD: **5 mo**   EARLY PUB OPTION:
PUBLICATION LAG TIME:

ACCEPT WITHOUT REVISION: REJECTION RATE: **83%**
ACCEPT WITH REVISION: **17%**

THEMATIC ISSUES USED:

CIRCULATION

NUMBER: **7600**   FREQUENCY: **Bimonthly**

CURRENT RATES (INDIVIDUAL): **$100 non-mem/$50 mem**
(INSTITUTIONAL): **$200**   (ASSOCIATE/STUDENT):

ANNUAL INDEX AVAILABILITY: COST:
SPECIAL SUPPLEMENTS: COST:
SUBSCRIPTION ADDRESS: **American Psychological Association**
1200 17th St., NW
Washington, DC 20036

STYLE/SUBMISSION REQUIREMENTS

STYLE: **APA**   STYLE SHEET: **Yes**
REVIEW CHARGE: COST:
NUMBER OF COPIES: **4**   PAGE LIMIT:
RESPONSE TO QUERY LETTERS:

GENERAL INFORMATION

JOURNAL TITLE: **PSYCHOLOGICAL REPORTS**

MANUSCRIPT ADDRESS: **Editor**
Box 9229
Missoula, MT 59807

TYPE OF ARTICLES: **Experimental, theoretical, speculative articles, comments, special reviews, listing of new books**

MAJOR CONTENT AREAS:

TOPICS PREFERRED:

REVIEW PERIOD: EARLY PUB OPTION:
PUBLICATION LAG TIME:

ACCEPT WITHOUT REVISION: REJECTION RATE:
ACCEPT WITH REVISION:

THEMATIC ISSUES USED:

CIRCULATION

NUMBER: FREQUENCY: **Bimonthly**

CURRENT RATES (INDIVIDUAL): **192.50**
(INSTITUTIONAL):   (ASSOCIATE/STUDENT):

ANNUAL INDEX AVAILABILITY: COST:
SPECIAL SUPPLEMENTS: COST:
SUBSCRIPTION ADDRESS:

STYLE/SUBMISSION REQUIREMENTS

STYLE: **APA**   STYLE SHEET:
REVIEW CHARGE: COST:
NUMBER OF COPIES: **2**   PAGE LIMIT:
RESPONSE TO QUERY LETTERS:

GENERAL INFORMATION

JOURNAL TITLE: **PSYCHOLOGY AND AGING**

MANUSCRIPT ADDRESS: **M. Powell Lawten, Editor**
Philadelphi Geriatric Center
5301 Old York Rd
Philadelphia, PA 19141

TYPE OF ARTICLES: **Adult development and aging**

MAJOR CONTENT AREAS: **Original research, theoretical analysis, practical**
clinical problems, policy, critical reviews of
content areas, clinical case studies

TOPICS PREFERRED: **Original research investigations**

REVIEW PERIOD: EARLY PUB OPTION:
PUBLICATION LAG TIME:

ACCEPT WITHOUT REVISION: REJECTION RATE:
ACCEPT WITH REVISION:

THEMATIC ISSUES USED:

CIRCULATION

NUMBER: FREQUENCY: **Quarterly**

CURRENT RATES (INDIVIDUAL): **$60**
(INSTITUTIONAL): **$120**   (ASSOCIATE/STUDENT):

ANNUAL INDEX AVAILABILITY: COST:
SPECIAL SUPPLEMENTS: COST:
SUBSCRIPTION ADDRESS: **American Psychological Assoc., Inc.**
1400 North Uhle St.
Arlington, VA 22201

STYLE/SUBMISSION REQUIREMENTS

STYLE: **APA**   STYLE SHEET:
REVIEW CHARGE: COST:
NUMBER OF COPIES: **4**   PAGE LIMIT:
RESPONSE TO QUERY LETTERS:

GENERAL INFORMATION

JOURNAL TITLE: **PSYCHOLOGY AND HEALTH**

MANUSCRIPT ADDRESS: **Dr. Lydia Temoshok**
Henry M. Jackson Foundation
Building 1
Walter Reed Army Medical Center
Washington, DC 20307

TYPE OF ARTICLES: **Original studies; reviews; brief reports**

MAJOR CONTENT AREAS: **Psychological aspects of physical illnesses,**
treatment processes and recovery; psychosocial
factors; health attitudes and behavior
TOPICS PREFERRED: **Prevention; individual-health care system**
interface; communication; pyschologically based
interventions

REVIEW PERIOD: EARLY PUB OPTION:
PUBLICATION LAG TIME:

ACCEPT WITHOUT REVISION: REJECTION RATE:
ACCEPT WITH REVISION:

THEMATIC ISSUES USED:

CIRCULATION

NUMBER: FREQUENCY: **Quarterly**

CURRENT RATES (INDIVIDUAL): **(on request)**
(INSTITUTIONAL):   (ASSOCIATE/STUDENT):

ANNUAL INDEX AVAILABILITY: COST:
SPECIAL SUPPLEMENTS: COST:
SUBSCRIPTION ADDRESS: **STBS, Ltd.**
P.O. Box 197
London WC2E 9PX, U.K.

STYLE/SUBMISSION REQUIREMENTS

STYLE: STYLE SHEET: **Yes**
REVIEW CHARGE: COST:
NUMBER OF COPIES: **3**   PAGE LIMIT:
RESPONSE TO QUERY LETTERS:

GENERAL INFORMATION

JOURNAL TITLE: **PSYCHOLOGY IN THE SCHOOLS**

MANUSCRIPT ADDRESS: **Gerald B. Fuller, Editor**
P.O. Box 4150
Traverse City, MI 49685

TYPE OF ARTICLES: **Research, opinion, practice**

MAJOR CONTENT AREAS:

TOPICS PREFERRED: **Clearly describe implications for practitioners in schools**

REVIEW PERIOD: EARLY PUB OPTION:
PUBLICATION LAG TIME:

ACCEPT WITHOUT REVISION: REJECTION RATE:
ACCEPT WITH REVISION:

THEMATIC ISSUES USED:

CIRCULATION

NUMBER: FREQUENCY: **Quarterly**

CURRENT RATES (INDIVIDUAL): **$30**
(INSTITUTIONAL): **$90**   (ASSOCIATE/STUDENT):

ANNUAL INDEX AVAILABILITY: COST:
SPECIAL SUPPLEMENTS: COST:
SUBSCRIPTION ADDRESS: **4 Conant Square**
Brandon, VT 05733

STYLE/SUBMISSION REQUIREMENTS

STYLE: **APA**   STYLE SHEET:
REVIEW CHARGE: COST:
NUMBER OF COPIES: **3**   PAGE LIMIT:
RESPONSE TO QUERY LETTERS:

GENERAL INFORMATION

JOURNAL TITLE: **PSYCHOTHERAPY**

MANUSCRIPT ADDRESS: **Donald K. Freedhelm, Ph.D., Editor**
Dept of Psychology
Case Western Reserve University
Cleveland, OH 44106

TYPE OF ARTICLES: **Research; theoretical; case studies; practice articles**

MAJOR CONTENT AREAS:

TOPICS PREFERRED: **Family therapy; group therapy; theoretical issues**

REVIEW PERIOD: **2-3 mo**   EARLY PUB OPTION: **No**
PUBLICATION LAG TIME:

ACCEPT WITHOUT REVISION: **1%**   REJECTION RATE: **75%**
ACCEPT WITH REVISION: **24%**

THEMATIC ISSUES USED: **Yes**

CIRCULATION

NUMBER: **7000**   FREQUENCY: **Quarterly**

CURRENT RATES (INDIVIDUAL): **$60**
(INSTITUTIONAL): **$75**   (ASSOCIATE/STUDENT): **$35**

ANNUAL INDEX AVAILABILITY: **Yes**   COST: **$10**
SPECIAL SUPPLEMENTS: **Yes**   COST: **$20**
SUBSCRIPTION ADDRESS: **Division of Psychotherapy**
3875 N. 44th St., Ste.102
Phoenix, AZ 85018

STYLE/SUBMISSION REQUIREMENTS

STYLE: **APA**   STYLE SHEET: **No**
REVIEW CHARGE: **No**   COST:
NUMBER OF COPIES: **4**   PAGE LIMIT: **30**
RESPONSE TO QUERY LETTERS: **Yes**

GENERAL INFORMATION

JOURNAL TITLE: **REHABILITATION COUNSELING BULLETIN**

MANUSCRIPT ADDRESS: **Norman L. Berven,**
Rehab. Psych. and Special Ed.
University of Wisconsin-Madison
432 N. Murray St.
Madison, WI 53706

TYPE OF ARTICLES: **Research; reviews; theoretical**

MAJOR CONTENT AREAS: **Topics related to disability and the provision of**
rehab services to people with disabilities
(physical, developmental, and psychiatric)
TOPICS PREFERRED:

REVIEW PERIOD: **<2mo**   EARLY PUB OPTION: **No**
PUBLICATION LAG TIME: **6 mo or more**

ACCEPT WITHOUT REVISION: **0%**   REJECTION RATE: **40%**
ACCEPT WITH REVISION: **60%, with resubmissions 65%**

THEMATIC ISSUES USED: **Yes**

CIRCULATION

NUMBER: **3700**   FREQUENCY: **Quarterly**

CURRENT RATES (INDIVIDUAL): **$18**
(INSTITUTIONAL): **$18**   (ASSOCIATE/STUDENT): **$18**

ANNUAL INDEX AVAILABILITY: **No**   COST:
SPECIAL SUPPLEMENTS: **No**   COST:
SUBSCRIPTION ADDRESS: **American Assn. for counseling**
and Development
5999 Stevenson Ave.
Alexandria, VA 22304

STYLE/SUBMISSION REQUIREMENTS

STYLE: **APA**   STYLE SHEET: **No**
REVIEW CHARGE: **No**   COST:
NUMBER OF COPIES: **4**   PAGE LIMIT: **None**
RESPONSE TO QUERY LETTERS: **Yes**

GENERAL INFORMATION

JOURNAL TITLE: **REHABILITATION DIGEST**

MANUSCRIPT ADDRESS: **45 Sheppard Ave. East,**
Suite 801
Toronto, Ont M2N 5W9
Canada

TYPE OF ARTICLES: **Research; commentaries; book reviews**

MAJOR CONTENT AREAS: **Physical disability; rehabilitation; personalities;**
policies and health care issues

TOPICS PREFERRED:

REVIEW PERIOD:	**<2 mo**	EARLY PUB OPTION:	**No**
PUBLICATION LAG TIME:	**3-5 mo**		
ACCEPT WITHOUT REVISION:	**10%**	REJECTION RATE:	**60%**
ACCEPT WITH REVISION:	**30%**		
THEMATIC ISSUES USED:	**Yes**		

CIRCULATION

NUMBER:	**2200**	FREQUENCY:	**Quarterly**
CURRENT RATES (INDIVIDUAL):	**$19/$22 U.S.**		
(INSTITUTIONAL):		(ASSOCIATE/STUDENT):	
ANNUAL INDEX AVAILABILITY:	**No**	COST:	
SPECIAL SUPPLEMENTS:	**No**	COST:	
SUBSCRIPTION ADDRESS:	**Same as above**		

STYLE/SUBMISSION REQUIREMENTS

STYLE:	**N/A**	STYLE SHEET:	**No**
REVIEW CHARGE:	**No**	COST:	
NUMBER OF COPIES:	**2**	PAGE LIMIT:	**10**
RESPONSE TO QUERY LETTERS:	**Yes**		

GENERAL INFORMATION

JOURNAL TITLE: **REHABILITATION PSYCHOLOGY**

MANUSCRIPT ADDRESS: **M. Eisenberg, Editor**
Rehabilitation Psychology
Psychology Service (116B)
VA Medical Center
Hampton, VA 23667

TYPE OF ARTICLES: **Research; review; theoretical; case studies;**
commentaries; book reviews
MAJOR CONTENT AREAS: **Rehabilitation of physically impaired persons**

TOPICS PREFERRED:

REVIEW PERIOD: **3-5 mo**   EARLY PUB OPTION: **No**
PUBLICATION LAG TIME: **>6 mo**

ACCEPT WITHOUT REVISION: **12%**   REJECTION RATE: **78%**
ACCEPT WITH REVISION: **10%**

THEMATIC ISSUES USED: **Yes**

CIRCULATION

NUMBER: **1300**   FREQUENCY: **Quarterly**

CURRENT RATES (INDIVIDUAL): **$28**
(INSTITUTIONAL): **$48**   (ASSOCIATE/STUDENT): **$20**

ANNUAL INDEX AVAILABILITY: **Yes**   COST:
SPECIAL SUPPLEMENTS: **No**   COST:
SUBSCRIPTION ADDRESS: **Springert Publishing Co.**
536 Broadway
New York, NY 10012

STYLE/SUBMISSION REQUIREMENTS

STYLE: **APA**   STYLE SHEET: **Yes**
REVIEW CHARGE: **No**   COST:
NUMBER OF COPIES: **4**   PAGE LIMIT: **25**
RESPONSE TO QUERY LETTERS: **Yes**

GENERAL INFORMATION

JOURNAL TITLE: **RESEARCH ON AGING**

MANUSCRIPT ADDRESS: **Research on Aging: Institute of Gerontology**
71 C East Ferry
Detroit, MI 48202

TYPE OF ARTICLES: **Research**

MAJOR CONTENT AREAS: **Aging related issues concerning economics, health care, work, retirement, and family**

TOPICS PREFERRED: **Topics that have national relevance**

REVIEW PERIOD: **3-5 mo**   EARLY PUB OPTION: **No**
PUBLICATION LAG TIME: **3-5 mo**

ACCEPT WITHOUT REVISION: **3%**   REJECTION RATE: **66%**
ACCEPT WITH REVISION: **31%**

THEMATIC ISSUES USED: **Yes**

CIRCULATION

NUMBER: **750**   FREQUENCY: **Quarterly**

CURRENT RATES (INDIVIDUAL): **$39**
(INSTITUTIONAL): **$110**   (ASSOCIATE/STUDENT):

ANNUAL INDEX AVAILABILITY: **Yes**   COST:
SPECIAL SUPPLEMENTS: **No**   COST:
SUBSCRIPTION ADDRESS:

STYLE/SUBMISSION REQUIREMENTS

STYLE: STYLE SHEET: **No**
REVIEW CHARGE: **No**   COST:
NUMBER OF COPIES: **3**   PAGE LIMIT:
RESPONSE TO QUERY LETTERS: **In limited cases**

GENERAL INFORMATION

JOURNAL TITLE: **REVIEW OF RELIGIOUS RESEARCH**

MANUSCRIPT ADDRESS: **D. Paul Johnson, Editor**
Department of Sociology
Texas Tech University
Lubbock, TX 79409

TYPE OF ARTICLES: **Research; reviews; theoretical; commentaries; book reviews; case studies**
MAJOR CONTENT AREAS: **Sociological and/or social scientific study of religion**

TOPICS PREFERRED: **Within the general area of social scientific study of religion with particular interest in applied research**
REVIEW PERIOD: **3-5 mo**   EARLY PUB OPTION: **No**
PUBLICATION LAG TIME: **>6 mo**

ACCEPT WITHOUT REVISION: **5%**   REJECTION RATE: **55%**
ACCEPT WITH REVISION: **40%**

THEMATIC ISSUES USED: **Yes**

CIRCULATION

NUMBER: **1300**   FREQUENCY: **Quarterly**

CURRENT RATES (INDIVIDUAL): **$22**
(INSTITUTIONAL): **$30**   (ASSOCIATE/STUDENT):

ANNUAL INDEX AVAILABILITY: COST:
SPECIAL SUPPLEMENTS: COST:
SUBSCRIPTION ADDRESS: **Review of Religious Research**
108 Marist Hall
Catholic University of America
Washington, DC 20064

STYLE/SUBMISSION REQUIREMENTS

STYLE: **Chicago**   STYLE SHEET: **Yes**
REVIEW CHARGE: **If not member**   COST: **$15**
NUMBER OF COPIES: **4**   PAGE LIMIT:
RESPONSE TO QUERY LETTERS: **Yes**

GENERAL INFORMATION

JOURNAL TITLE: **RURAL SOCIOLOGY**

MANUSCRIPT ADDRESS: **Steve M. Murdock**
Dept. of Rural Sociology
Texas A & M University
College Station, TX 77843-2125

TYPE OF ARTICLES: **Research reports; book reviews; review essays; commentary on research methodology and theory**

MAJOR CONTENT AREAS: **Contributions to the methodological and theoretical base of rural sociology within the larger discipline of sociology**

TOPICS PREFERRED: **Topics related to research, teaching, and extension agendas relative to rural issues and to policy**

REVIEW PERIOD: **3-5 mo**   EARLY PUB OPTION: **No**
PUBLICATION LAG TIME: **3-5 mo**

ACCEPT WITHOUT REVISION: **<3%**   REJECTION RATE: **85%**
ACCEPT WITH REVISION: **12%**

THEMATIC ISSUES USED: **Yes, but infrequently**

CIRCULATION

NUMBER: **4000**   FREQUENCY: **Quarterly**

CURRENT RATES (INDIVIDUAL): **$40**
(INSTITUTIONAL): **$63**   (ASSOCIATE/STUDENT): **$20**

ANNUAL INDEX AVAILABILITY: **No**   COST:
SPECIAL SUPPLEMENTS: **No**   COST:
SUBSCRIPTION ADDRESS: **Patrick C. Jobes, Treasurer**
Rural Sociological Society
Dept. of Sociology, Wilson Hall
Montana State University
Bozeman, MT, 59715

STYLE/SUBMISSION REQUIREMENTS

STYLE: **ASR**   STYLE SHEET: **Yes**
REVIEW CHARGE: **No**   COST:
NUMBER OF COPIES: **4**   PAGE LIMIT: **30**
RESPONSE TO QUERY LETTERS: **Yes**

GENERAL INFORMATION

JOURNAL TITLE: **SAGE**

MANUSCRIPT ADDRESS: **P.O. Box 42721**
Atlanta, GA   30311-0741

TYPE OF ARTICLES: **Articles, critical essays, interviews, book/film**
reviews, exhibit reviews, research reports,
essays, resource listings, documents &
announcements focusing on the lives & cultures
of black women everywhere

MAJOR CONTENT AREAS:

TOPICS PREFERRED:
REVIEW PERIOD: EARLY PUB OPTION:
PUBLICATION LAG TIME:

ACCEPT WITHOUT REVISION: REJECTION RATE:
ACCEPT WITH REVISION:

THEMATIC ISSUES USED: **Yes**

CIRCULATION

NUMBER: FREQUENCY: **2 X yr**

CURRENT RATES (INDIVIDUAL): **$15**
(INSTITUTIONAL): **$25**   (ASSOCIATE/STUDENT):

ANNUAL INDEX AVAILABILITY: COST:
SPECIAL SUPPLEMENTS: COST:
SUBSCRIPTION ADDRESS: **Same as above**

STYLE/SUBMISSION REQUIREMENTS

STYLE: **MCA & APA**   STYLE SHEET:
REVIEW CHARGE: COST:
NUMBER OF COPIES: **3**   PAGE LIMIT: **20**
RESPONSE TO QUERY LETTERS:

GENERAL INFORMATION

JOURNAL TITLE: **SEX ROLES**

MANUSCRIPT ADDRESS: **Phyllis A. Katz**
Institute for Research on Social
Problems
520 Pearl St.
Boulder, CO 80302

TYPE OF ARTICLES: **Research; critical reviews; book reviews**

MAJOR CONTENT AREAS: **Cross-disciplinary; basic processes underlying gender role socialization in children; consequences**

TOPICS PREFERRED: **Sex-role sterotypes; childrearing practices; gender roles and political socialization**

REVIEW PERIOD: EARLY PUB OPTION:
PUBLICATION LAG TIME:

ACCEPT WITHOUT REVISION: REJECTION RATE:
ACCEPT WITH REVISION:

THEMATIC ISSUES USED:

CIRCULATION

NUMBER: FREQUENCY: **Monthly**

CURRENT RATES (INDIVIDUAL): **$29.50**
(INSTITUTIONAL): **$187.50**   (ASSOCIATE/STUDENT):

ANNUAL INDEX AVAILABILITY: COST:
SPECIAL SUPPLEMENTS: COST:
SUBSCRIPTION ADDRESS: **Plenum Publishing**
233 Spring St.
New York, NY 10013

STYLE/SUBMISSION REQUIREMENTS

STYLE: **APA**   STYLE SHEET:
REVIEW CHARGE: COST:
NUMBER OF COPIES: **3**   PAGE LIMIT:
RESPONSE TO QUERY LETTERS:

GENERAL INFORMATION

JOURNAL TITLE: **SEXUALITY AND DISABILITY**

MANUSCRIPT ADDRESS: **Dr. Arnold Melman, Editor**
Department of Urology
Beth Israel Medical Center
First Avenue and 16th St.
New York, NY 10003

TYPE OF ARTICLES:

MAJOR CONTENT AREAS: **Normal and abnormal sexual function**

TOPICS PREFERRED: **New knowledge; technique and available**
modalities

REVIEW PERIOD: **6 wk**   EARLY PUB OPTION:
PUBLICATION LAG TIME:

ACCEPT WITHOUT REVISION: REJECTION RATE:
ACCEPT WITH REVISION:

THEMATIC ISSUES USED:

CIRCULATION

NUMBER: FREQUENCY: **Quarterly**

CURRENT RATES (INDIVIDUAL): **$36**
(INSTITUTIONAL): **$95**   (ASSOCIATE/STUDENT):

ANNUAL INDEX AVAILABILITY: COST:
SPECIAL SUPPLEMENTS: COST:
SUBSCRIPTION ADDRESS: **Human Sciences Press**
233 Spring St.
New York, NY 10013-1578

STYLE/SUBMISSION REQUIREMENTS

STYLE: STYLE SHEET:
REVIEW CHARGE: COST:
NUMBER OF COPIES: **3**   PAGE LIMIT:
RESPONSE TO QUERY LETTERS:

GENERAL INFORMATION

JOURNAL TITLE: **SIGNS: JOURNAL OF WOMEN IN CULTURE AND SOCIETY**

MANUSCRIPT ADDRESS: **Editors,** *Signs*
Center for Advanced Feminist Studies
495 Ford Hall
University of Minnesota
Minneapolis, MN 55455

TYPE OF ARTICLES:

MAJOR CONTENT AREAS: **Interdisciplinary scholarship on women**

TOPICS PREFERRED:

REVIEW PERIOD: **≥ 10 wk**   EARLY PUB OPTION:
PUBLICATION LAG TIME:

ACCEPT WITHOUT REVISION: REJECTION RATE:
ACCEPT WITH REVISION:

THEMATIC ISSUES USED:

CIRCULATION

NUMBER: FREQUENCY: **Quarterly**

CURRENT RATES (INDIVIDUAL): **$29**
(INSTITUTIONAL): **$62**   (ASSOCIATE/STUDENT): **$21**

ANNUAL INDEX AVAILABILITY: COST:
SPECIAL SUPPLEMENTS: COST:
SUBSCRIPTION ADDRESS:

STYLE/SUBMISSION REQUIREMENTS

STYLE: **Chicago**   STYLE SHEET:
REVIEW CHARGE: COST:
NUMBER OF COPIES: **3**   PAGE LIMIT: **35**
RESPONSE TO QUERY LETTERS:

GENERAL INFORMATION

JOURNAL TITLE: **SMITH COLLEGE STUDIES IN SOCIAL WORK**

MANUSCRIPT ADDRESS: **Joan Laird**
Smith College Studies in Social Work
Lilly Hall-Smith College
Northampton, MA 01063

TYPE OF ARTICLES: **Research; reviews; theoretical; case studies; commentaries; book reviews**

MAJOR CONTENT AREAS: **Clinical social work focus; individual family, marital, group therapy; policy practice**

TOPICS PREFERRED:

REVIEW PERIOD: **<2 mo**   EARLY PUB OPTION: **No**
PUBLICATION LAG TIME: **3-5 mo**

ACCEPT WITHOUT REVISION: **5%**   REJECTION RATE: **50%**
ACCEPT WITH REVISION: **45%**

THEMATIC ISSUES USED: **Yes**

CIRCULATION

NUMBER: **1200**   FREQUENCY: **3 X yr**

CURRENT RATES (INDIVIDUAL):
(INSTITUTIONAL):   (ASSOCIATE/STUDENT):

ANNUAL INDEX AVAILABILITY: **No**   COST:
SPECIAL SUPPLEMENTS: **No**   COST:
SUBSCRIPTION ADDRESS: **Attn: Nancy Merchant**
Smith College School for Social Work
Lilly Hall
Northampton, MA 01063

STYLE/SUBMISSION REQUIREMENTS

STYLE: **APA**   STYLE SHEET: **No**
REVIEW CHARGE: **No**   COST:
NUMBER OF COPIES: **3**   PAGE LIMIT: **18-23**
RESPONSE TO QUERY LETTERS: **Yes**

GENERAL INFORMATION

JOURNAL TITLE: **SOCIAL BIOLOGY**

MANUSCRIPT ADDRESS: **Richard H. Osborne, Editor**
P.O. Box 2349
Port Angeles, WA 98362

TYPE OF ARTICLES:

MAJOR CONTENT AREAS:

TOPICS PREFERRED:

REVIEW PERIOD: EARLY PUB OPTION:
PUBLICATION LAG TIME:

ACCEPT WITHOUT REVISION: REJECTION RATE:
ACCEPT WITH REVISION:

THEMATIC ISSUES USED:

CIRCULATION

NUMBER: FREQUENCY: **2 X yr**

CURRENT RATES (INDIVIDUAL):
(INSTITUTIONAL): **$65**   (ASSOCIATE/STUDENT):

ANNUAL INDEX AVAILABILITY: **Yes**   COST:
SPECIAL SUPPLEMENTS: COST:
SUBSCRIPTION ADDRESS: **Same as above**

STYLE/SUBMISSION REQUIREMENTS

STYLE: STYLE SHEET:
REVIEW CHARGE: COST:
NUMBER OF COPIES: PAGE LIMIT:
RESPONSE TO QUERY LETTERS:

GENERAL INFORMATION

JOURNAL TITLE: **SOCIAL COGNITION**

MANUSCRIPT ADDRESS: **David J. Schneider**
Department of Psychology
Rice University
P.O. Box 1892
Houston, TX 77251

TYPE OF ARTICLES: **Reports of empirical research, conceptual**
analysis, critical reviews on role of cognitive
processes in study of personality, development,
and social behavior

MAJOR CONTENT AREAS:

TOPICS PREFERRED:

REVIEW PERIOD: EARLY PUB OPTION:
PUBLICATION LAG TIME:

ACCEPT WITHOUT REVISION: REJECTION RATE:
ACCEPT WITH REVISION:

THEMATIC ISSUES USED:

CIRCULATION

NUMBER: FREQUENCY: **Quarterly**

CURRENT RATES (INDIVIDUAL): **$25**
(INSTITUTIONAL): **$70**   (ASSOCIATE/STUDENT):

ANNUAL INDEX AVAILABILITY: COST:
SPECIAL SUPPLEMENTS: COST:
SUBSCRIPTION ADDRESS: **Guilford Publications, Inc.**
72 Spring St.
New York, NY 10012

STYLE/SUBMISSION REQUIREMENTS

STYLE: **APA**   STYLE SHEET:
REVIEW CHARGE: COST:
NUMBER OF COPIES: **4**   PAGE LIMIT:
RESPONSE TO QUERY LETTERS:

GENERAL INFORMATION

JOURNAL TITLE: **SOCIAL FORCES**

MANUSCRIPT ADDRESS: **Department of Sociology**
University of North Carolina
Chapel Hill, NC 27599-3210

TYPE OF ARTICLES: **Research; theoretical; case studies**

MAJOR CONTENT AREAS: **Entire discipline of sociology**

TOPICS PREFERRED: **Anything sociology**

REVIEW PERIOD: **<2 mo**   EARLY PUB OPTION: **No**
PUBLICATION LAG TIME: **6 mo or more**

ACCEPT WITHOUT REVISION: **2%**   REJECTION RATE: **85%**
ACCEPT WITH REVISION: **13%**

THEMATIC ISSUES USED: **No**

CIRCULATION

NUMBER: **4400**   FREQUENCY: **Quarterly**

CURRENT RATES (INDIVIDUAL): **$25 or $21 for Am. Soc. Assn. members**
(INSTITUTIONAL): **$42**   (ASSOCIATE/STUDENT): **$10**

ANNUAL INDEX AVAILABILITY: **Yes**   COST: **$10**
SPECIAL SUPPLEMENTS: **No**   COST:
SUBSCRIPTION ADDRESS: **University of North Carolina**
Box 2288
Chapel Hill, NC 27515

STYLE/SUBMISSION REQUIREMENTS

STYLE: **ASA**   STYLE SHEET: **Yes**
REVIEW CHARGE: **Yes**   COST: **$10**
NUMBER OF COPIES: **5**   PAGE LIMIT: **None**
RESPONSE TO QUERY LETTERS: **Yes**

GENERAL INFORMATION

JOURNAL TITLE: **SOCIAL INDICATORS RESEARCH**

MANUSCRIPT ADDRESS: **Alex C. Michalos, Editor**
Department of Philosophy
University of Guelph
Guelph, Ontario
Canada N1G 2W1

TYPE OF ARTICLES: **Scholarly; technical**

MAJOR CONTENT AREAS: **Any area related to quality of life research**

TOPICS PREFERRED:

REVIEW PERIOD: **5 mo**   EARLY PUB OPTION:
PUBLICATION LAG TIME: **1 yr**

ACCEPT WITHOUT REVISION: REJECTION RATE: **70%**
ACCEPT WITH REVISION:

THEMATIC ISSUES USED: **No**

CIRCULATION

NUMBER: **800**   FREQUENCY: **8 X yr**

CURRENT RATES (INDIVIDUAL): **$42**
(INSTITUTIONAL): **$113**   (ASSOCIATE/STUDENT):

ANNUAL INDEX AVAILABILITY: **No**   COST:
SPECIAL SUPPLEMENTS: **No**   COST:
SUBSCRIPTION ADDRESS: **Kluwer Academic Publishers**
P.O. Box 358
Accord Station
Hingham, MA 02018-0358

STYLE/SUBMISSION REQUIREMENTS

STYLE: **APA**   STYLE SHEET: **None**
REVIEW CHARGE: **None**   COST: **None**
NUMBER OF COPIES: **2**   PAGE LIMIT: **None**
RESPONSE TO QUERY LETTERS:

GENERAL INFORMATION

JOURNAL TITLE: **SOCIAL POLICY**

MANUSCRIPT ADDRESS: **25 West 43rd St.**
Room 620
New York, NY 10036

TYPE OF ARTICLES: **Research; theoretical; case studies;**
commentaries; book reviews

MAJOR CONTENT AREAS: **Social policy; education; economics; self-help;**
community action; human service; housing

TOPICS PREFERRED: **Topics that relate to the above**

REVIEW PERIOD: **<2 mo**   EARLY PUB OPTION: **No**
PUBLICATION LAG TIME: **2-5 mo**

ACCEPT WITHOUT REVISION: **10%**   REJECTION RATE: **40%**
ACCEPT WITH REVISION: **50%**

THEMATIC ISSUES USED: **Yes**

CIRCULATION

NUMBER: **3000**   FREQUENCY: **Quarterly**

CURRENT RATES (INDIVIDUAL): **$20**
(INSTITUTIONAL): **$35**   (ASSOCIATE/STUDENT): **$12**

ANNUAL INDEX AVAILABILITY: **No**   COST:
SPECIAL SUPPLEMENTS: **No**   COST:
SUBSCRIPTION ADDRESS: **Same as above**

STYLE/SUBMISSION REQUIREMENTS

STYLE: **Chicago**   STYLE SHEET: **No**
REVIEW CHARGE: **No**   COST:
NUMBER OF COPIES: **2**   PAGE LIMIT: **~6-20**
RESPONSE TO QUERY LETTERS: **Yes**

GENERAL INFORMATION

JOURNAL TITLE: **SOCIAL PROBLEMS**

MANUSCRIPT ADDRESS: **Merry Morash, Professor**
School of Criminal Justice
Michigan State University
East Lansing, MI 48824

TYPE OF ARTICLES: **Research; theoretical**

MAJOR CONTENT AREAS: **Community; crime and delinquency; drinking**
and drugs; education; environment and
technology; family; health; policy; sexual
behavior; etc.
TOPICS PREFERRED: **Primary emphasis on contributions to theory**
and research as they pertain to social problems

REVIEW PERIOD: **3-5 mo**   EARLY PUB OPTION: **No**
PUBLICATION LAG TIME: **3-4 mo**

ACCEPT WITHOUT REVISION: **5%**   REJECTION RATE: **85%**
ACCEPT WITH REVISION: **10%**

THEMATIC ISSUES USED: **Yes**

CIRCULATION

NUMBER: **3953**   FREQUENCY: **Quarterly**

CURRENT RATES (INDIVIDUAL): **$66, but is included in dues for SSBP**
(INSTITUTIONAL): **$66**   (ASSOCIATE/STUDENT):

ANNUAL INDEX AVAILABILITY: **Yes**   COST:
SPECIAL SUPPLEMENTS: **No**   COST:
SUBSCRIPTION ADDRESS: **Journals Department**
University of California Press
2120 Berkeley Way
Berkeley, CA 94720

STYLE/SUBMISSION REQUIREMENTS

STYLE: **Chicago**   STYLE SHEET: **Yes**
REVIEW CHARGE: **No**   COST: **$50/pub**
NUMBER OF COPIES: **5**   PAGE LIMIT: **35**
RESPONSE TO QUERY LETTERS: **Yes**

GENERAL INFORMATION

JOURNAL TITLE: **SOCIAL SCIENCE JOURNAL**

MANUSCRIPT ADDRESS: **Michael J. Katovich**
Department of Sociology
Texas Christian University
Fort Worth, TX 76129

TYPE OF ARTICLES: **Research; reviews; theoretical; case studies;**
commentaries; book reviews;
MAJOR CONTENT AREAS: **Sociology; economics; political science**

TOPICS PREFERRED: **Authors are encouraged to submit manuscripts**
that deal with topics that have interdisciplinary
and multidisciplinary relevance
REVIEW PERIOD: **2-3 mo** EARLY PUB OPTION: **No**
PUBLICATION LAG TIME: **3-5 mo**

ACCEPT WITHOUT REVISION: **<1%** REJECTION RATE: **60%**
ACCEPT WITH REVISION: **12.5%**

THEMATIC ISSUES USED: **Yes**

CIRCULATION

NUMBER: **1000** FREQUENCY: **Quarterly**

CURRENT RATES (INDIVIDUAL): **$25**
(INSTITUTIONAL): **$80** (ASSOCIATE/STUDENT):

ANNUAL INDEX AVAILABILITY: **Yes** COST: **None**
SPECIAL SUPPLEMENTS: **No** COST:
SUBSCRIPTION ADDRESS: **Professor William Rug**
Western Social Science Assoc.
Department of Sociology
Texas Christian University
Fort Worth, TX 76129

STYLE/SUBMISSION REQUIREMENTS

STYLE: **Chicago** STYLE SHEET: **No**
REVIEW CHARGE: **No** COST:
NUMBER OF COPIES: **4** PAGE LIMIT: **30**
RESPONSE TO QUERY LETTERS: **Yes**

GENERAL INFORMATION

JOURNAL TITLE: **SOCIAL SCIENCE AND MEDICINE**

MANUSCRIPT ADDRESS: **Peter J. McEwan**
Glengarden
Ballater
Aberdeenshire
AB35 5UB, U.K.

TYPE OF ARTICLES: **Research; reviews; theoretical; commentaries; book reviews**

MAJOR CONTENT AREAS: **All social sciences in relation to medicine and medical services**

TOPICS PREFERRED: **No discrimination**

REVIEW PERIOD: **<2 mo**   EARLY PUB OPTION: **Yes**
PUBLICATION LAG TIME: **3-5 mo**

ACCEPT WITHOUT REVISION: **5%**   REJECTION RATE: **70%**
ACCEPT WITH REVISION: **25%**

THEMATIC ISSUES USED: **Yes**

CIRCULATION

NUMBER: FREQUENCY: **2 wk**

CURRENT RATES (INDIVIDUAL):
(INSTITUTIONAL): **2140 DM** (ASSOCIATE/STUDENT):

ANNUAL INDEX AVAILABILITY: **Yes**   COST:
SPECIAL SUPPLEMENTS: **No**   COST:
SUBSCRIPTION ADDRESS: **Pergammon Press Plc.**
Headington Hill Hall
Oxford OX3 0BW, U.K.

STYLE/SUBMISSION REQUIREMENTS

STYLE: **Special**   STYLE SHEET: **No**
REVIEW CHARGE: **No**   COST:
NUMBER OF COPIES: **3**   PAGE LIMIT: **None**
RESPONSE TO QUERY LETTERS: **Yes**

GENERAL INFORMATION

JOURNAL TITLE: **SOCIAL SCIENCE QUARTERLY**

MANUSCRIPT ADDRESS: **Social Science Quarterly**
Charles M. Bonjean, Editor
W.C. Hogg Building
U. of Texas at Austin
Austin, TX 78713

TYPE OF ARTICLES:

MAJOR CONTENT AREAS: **Race, gender, American politics and other topics**
of interest to a heterogenous readership

TOPICS PREFERRED: **Those of interest to readers in more than one**
social science discipline

REVIEW PERIOD: **6-10 wk**   EARLY PUB OPTION: **No**
PUBLICATION LAG TIME: **8-11 mo**

ACCEPT WITHOUT REVISION: REJECTION RATE: **88%**
ACCEPT WITH REVISION:

THEMATIC ISSUES USED:

CIRCULATION

NUMBER: FREQUENCY: **Quarterly**

CURRENT RATES (INDIVIDUAL): **$25**
(INSTITUTIONAL): **$45**   (ASSOCIATE/STUDENT):

ANNUAL INDEX AVAILABILITY: **Yes**   COST:
SPECIAL SUPPLEMENTS: COST:
SUBSCRIPTION ADDRESS: **The U. of Texas Press**
2100 Comal
Austin, TX 78722

STYLE/SUBMISSION REQUIREMENTS

STYLE: **Own**   STYLE SHEET: **Yes**
REVIEW CHARGE: **None**   COST: **None**
NUMBER OF COPIES: **4**   PAGE LIMIT: **30**
RESPONSE TO QUERY LETTERS: **Yes**

GENERAL INFORMATION

JOURNAL TITLE: **SOCIAL SERVICE REVIEW**

MANUSCRIPT ADDRESS: **Social Service Review**
969 E. 60th St
Chicago, IL 60637

TYPE OF ARTICLES: **Research; reviews; theoretical; case studies;**
book reviews; history of social welfare
MAJOR CONTENT AREAS: **Social welfare research; practice; policy;**
history; stress research-based articles

TOPICS PREFERRED:

REVIEW PERIOD: **3-5 mo**   EARLY PUB OPTION: **No**
PUBLICATION LAG TIME: **>6 mo**

ACCEPT WITHOUT REVISION: **30%**   REJECTION RATE: **65%**
ACCEPT WITH REVISION: **5%**

THEMATIC ISSUES USED: **No**

CIRCULATION

NUMBER: **2000**   FREQUENCY: **Quarterly**

CURRENT RATES (INDIVIDUAL): **$28**
(INSTITUTIONAL): **$44**   (ASSOCIATE/STUDENT): **$20**

ANNUAL INDEX AVAILABILITY: **Yes**   COST: **Dec. iss.**
SPECIAL SUPPLEMENTS: **No**   COST:
SUBSCRIPTION ADDRESS: **University of Chicago Press-**
Journals Division
P.O. Box 37005
Chicago, IL 60637

STYLE/SUBMISSION REQUIREMENTS

STYLE: **Chicago**   STYLE SHEET: **Yes**
REVIEW CHARGE: **No**   COST:
NUMBER OF COPIES: **4**   PAGE LIMIT: **None**
RESPONSE TO QUERY LETTERS: **No**

GENERAL INFORMATION

JOURNAL TITLE: **SOCIAL WELFARE**

MANUSCRIPT ADDRESS: **Samaj Kalyan Bhawan
B-12 Institutional Area
South of I.I.T.
New Delhi-110 016, India**

TYPE OF ARTICLES: **Research; commentaries; reviews; book reviews; theoretical case studies; short stories; program articles**

MAJOR CONTENT AREAS: **Entire spectrum of welfare and development work in with special emphasis on women and children, their education, rural development**

TOPICS PREFERRED: **Achievements of individuals and institutions; burning social problems; efforts made to tackle these problems**

REVIEW PERIOD: **<2 mo**   EARLY PUB OPTION: **Yes**
PUBLICATION LAG TIME:

ACCEPT WITHOUT REVISION: **5%**   REJECTION RATE: **70%**
ACCEPT WITH REVISION: **25%**

THEMATIC ISSUES USED: **Yes**

CIRCULATION

NUMBER: **4000**   FREQUENCY: **Monthly**

CURRENT RATES (INDIVIDUAL): **$20 by sea Mail and $30 by Air Mail**
(INSTITUTIONAL):   (ASSOCIATE/STUDENT):

ANNUAL INDEX AVAILABILITY: COST:
SPECIAL SUPPLEMENTS: **No**   COST:
SUBSCRIPTION ADDRESS: **Pay and Accounts Officer
B-12, Institutional Area
South of I.I.T.
New Delhi-110 016, India**

STYLE/SUBMISSION REQUIREMENTS

STYLE: **For layman**   STYLE SHEET: **If req**
REVIEW CHARGE: **No**   COST:
NUMBER OF COPIES: **1**   PAGE LIMIT: **6**
RESPONSE TO QUERY LETTERS: **Yes**

GENERAL INFORMATION

JOURNAL TITLE: **SOCIAL WORK**

MANUSCRIPT ADDRESS: **NASW**
7981 Easkin Avenue
Silver Spring, MD 20910

TYPE OF ARTICLES: **Research; reviews; theoretical; case studies;**
commentaries; book reviews
MAJOR CONTENT AREAS: **Social work; anything that will be of interest**
and/or utility to professional social work

TOPICS PREFERRED:

REVIEW PERIOD: **3-5 mo**   EARLY PUB OPTION: **No**
PUBLICATION LAG TIME: **>6 mo**

ACCEPT WITHOUT REVISION: **5%**   REJECTION RATE: **80%**
ACCEPT WITH REVISION: **15%**

THEMATIC ISSUES USED: **Yes**

CIRCULATION

NUMBER: **135,000**   FREQUENCY: **Bimonthly**

CURRENT RATES (INDIVIDUAL): **$51**
(INSTITUTIONAL): **$64**   (ASSOCIATE/STUDENT):

ANNUAL INDEX AVAILABILITY: **Yes**   COST: **Nov. issue**
SPECIAL SUPPLEMENTS: **No**   COST:
SUBSCRIPTION ADDRESS: **NASW**
P.O. Box 92180
Washington, DC 20090-2180

STYLE/SUBMISSION REQUIREMENTS

STYLE: **APA**   STYLE SHEET: **Yes**
REVIEW CHARGE: **No**   COST:
NUMBER OF COPIES: **4**   PAGE LIMIT: **18**
RESPONSE TO QUERY LETTERS: **Form letter only**

GENERAL INFORMATION

JOURNAL TITLE: **SOCIAL WORK IN HEALTH CARE**

MANUSCRIPT ADDRESS: **Gary Rosenberg Ph.D., Editor**
Director, Dept. of Social Work
The Mount Sinai School of Medicine
One Gustave L. Levy Place
Box 1246
New York, NY 10029

TYPE OF ARTICLES: **Research; reviews; theoretical; case studies;**
book reviews

MAJOR CONTENT AREAS: **Range of issues relating to the practice,**
research, and education in social work
operations in health care settings
TOPICS PREFERRED: **Medicine and social work; prevention/primary**
care/wellness; nursing and social work; women's
health care; collaboration; family
REVIEW PERIOD: **3-5 mo**   EARLY PUB OPTION: **No**
PUBLICATION LAG TIME: **6-9 mo**

ACCEPT WITHOUT REVISION: **1%**   REJECTION RATE: **51%**
ACCEPT WITH REVISION: **48%**

THEMATIC ISSUES USED: **Yes**

CIRCULATION

NUMBER: **2100**   FREQUENCY: **Quarterly**

CURRENT RATES (INDIVIDUAL): **$36**
(INSTITUTIONAL): **$85**   (ASSOCIATE/STUDENT):

ANNUAL INDEX AVAILABILITY: **No**   COST:
SPECIAL SUPPLEMENTS: **No**   COST:
SUBSCRIPTION ADDRESS: **The Haworth Press, Inc.**
10 Alice Street
Binghamton, NY 13904-1580

STYLE/SUBMISSION REQUIREMENTS

STYLE: **APA**   STYLE SHEET: **Yes**
REVIEW CHARGE: **No**   COST:
NUMBER OF COPIES: **3 + diskette**   PAGE LIMIT: **20**
RESPONSE TO QUERY LETTERS: **Yes**

GENERAL INFORMATION

JOURNAL TITLE: **SOCIOLOGICAL FORUM**

MANUSCRIPT ADDRESS: **Robin M. Williams, Jr., Editor**
C/O Barbara Cain
352 Uris Hall
Cornell University
Ithaca, NY 14853-7601

TYPE OF ARTICLES:

MAJOR CONTENT AREAS: **Integrative articles that link sub-fields of**
sociology or relate sociological research to other
disciplines
TOPICS PREFERRED: **Innovative articles that develop topics or areas**
in new ways or directions

REVIEW PERIOD: EARLY PUB OPTION:
PUBLICATION LAG TIME:

ACCEPT WITHOUT REVISION: REJECTION RATE:
ACCEPT WITH REVISION:

THEMATIC ISSUES USED:

CIRCULATION

NUMBER: FREQUENCY: **Quarterly**

CURRENT RATES (INDIVIDUAL): **$38**
(INSTITUTIONAL): **$75**   (ASSOCIATE/STUDENT):

ANNUAL INDEX AVAILABILITY: COST:
SPECIAL SUPPLEMENTS: COST:
SUBSCRIPTION ADDRESS: **Plenum Publishing**
233 Spring St.
New York, NY 10013

STYLE/SUBMISSION REQUIREMENTS

STYLE: STYLE SHEET:
REVIEW CHARGE: **Yes**   COST: **$10**
NUMBER OF COPIES: **4**   PAGE LIMIT:
RESPONSE TO QUERY LETTERS:

GENERAL INFORMATION

JOURNAL TITLE: **SOCIOLOGICAL INQUIRY**

MANUSCRIPT ADDRESS: **Dr. Dennis L. Peck, Editor**
The University of Alabama
Box 0219
Tuscaloosa, AL 35487-0219

TYPE OF ARTICLES: **Research; reviews; theoretical; case studies;**
commentaries; book reviews; special essay
MAJOR CONTENT AREAS: **General sociology**

TOPICS PREFERRED: **All topics related to sociological inquiry**

REVIEW PERIOD: **<2 mo**   EARLY PUB OPTION: **No**
PUBLICATION LAG TIME: **>6 mo**

ACCEPT WITHOUT REVISION: REJECTION RATE: **90-95%**
ACCEPT WITH REVISION:

THEMATIC ISSUES USED: **Yes**

CIRCULATION

NUMBER: **>3000**   FREQUENCY: **Quarterly**

CURRENT RATES (INDIVIDUAL): **$18**
(INSTITUTIONAL): **$30**   (ASSOCIATE/STUDENT):

ANNUAL INDEX AVAILABILITY: **Yes**   COST: **None**
SPECIAL SUPPLEMENTS: **No**   COST:
SUBSCRIPTION ADDRESS: **The University of Texas Press**
Box 7819
Austin, TX 78713

STYLE/SUBMISSION REQUIREMENTS

STYLE: **ASA**   STYLE SHEET: **Yes**
REVIEW CHARGE: **No**   COST:
NUMBER OF COPIES: **4**   PAGE LIMIT: **30-35**
RESPONSE TO QUERY LETTERS: **Yes**

GENERAL INFORMATION

JOURNAL TITLE: **SOCIOLOGICAL METHODS AND RESEARCH**

MANUSCRIPT ADDRESS: **J. Scott Long**
Department of Sociology
Ballantine 744, Indiana University
Bloomington, IN 47405

TYPE OF ARTICLES:

MAJOR CONTENT AREAS:

TOPICS PREFERRED: **Articles that advance the understanding of the field through systematic presentations that clarify methodological problems and assist in ordering the known facts in an area**

REVIEW PERIOD: EARLY PUB OPTION:
PUBLICATION LAG TIME:

ACCEPT WITHOUT REVISION: REJECTION RATE:
ACCEPT WITH REVISION:

THEMATIC ISSUES USED:

CIRCULATION

NUMBER: FREQUENCY: **Quarterly**

CURRENT RATES (INDIVIDUAL): **$36**
(INSTITUTIONAL): **$99**   (ASSOCIATE/STUDENT):

ANNUAL INDEX AVAILABILITY: COST:
SPECIAL SUPPLEMENTS: COST:
SUBSCRIPTION ADDRESS: **Sage Publications, Inc.**
2455 Teller Rd.
Newbury Park, CA 91320

STYLE/SUBMISSION REQUIREMENTS

STYLE: STYLE SHEET: **Yes**
REVIEW CHARGE: COST:
NUMBER OF COPIES: **4**   PAGE LIMIT:
RESPONSE TO QUERY LETTERS:

GENERAL INFORMATION

JOURNAL TITLE: **SOCIOLOGICAL PERSPECTIVES**

MANUSCRIPT ADDRESS: **John C. Pock, Editor**
Dept. of Sociology
Reed College
Portland, OR 97202-8199

TYPE OF ARTICLES: **Articles considered for publication are selected**
from papers presented at the annual meeting of
the Pacific Sociological Association and
submitted manuscripts

MAJOR CONTENT AREAS: **Any area of sociological inquiry**

TOPICS PREFERRED:

REVIEW PERIOD: EARLY PUB OPTION:
PUBLICATION LAG TIME:

ACCEPT WITHOUT REVISION: REJECTION RATE:
ACCEPT WITH REVISION:

THEMATIC ISSUES USED:

CIRCULATION

NUMBER: FREQUENCY: **Quarterly**

CURRENT RATES (INDIVIDUAL): **Included in $20 PSA membership fee**
(INSTITUTIONAL):   (ASSOCIATE/STUDENT):

ANNUAL INDEX AVAILABILITY: COST:
SPECIAL SUPPLEMENTS: COST:
SUBSCRIPTION ADDRESS: **Frederick W. Preston**
Secretary-Treasurer, Pacific
Sociological Association
Dept. of Sociology
University of Nevada, Las Vegas
Las Vegas, NV 89154

STYLE/SUBMISSION REQUIREMENTS

STYLE: **Chicago**   STYLE SHEET: **Yes**
REVIEW CHARGE: **$10**   COST:
NUMBER OF COPIES: **3**   PAGE LIMIT:
RESPONSE TO QUERY LETTERS:

GENERAL INFORMATION

JOURNAL TITLE: **SOCIOLOGICAL PRACTICE**

MANUSCRIPT ADDRESS: **Dr. Jan Fritz, Editor-in-Chief**
254 Serena Dr.
Palm Desert, CA 92260

TYPE OF ARTICLES: **Research; review; theoretical; case studies;**
commentaries; book reviews; historical pieces
MAJOR CONTENT AREAS: **Each issue is a theme issue**

TOPICS PREFERRED: **Varies**

REVIEW PERIOD: **<2 mo**   EARLY PUB OPTION: **No**
PUBLICATION LAG TIME: **3-5 mo**

ACCEPT WITHOUT REVISION: **Varies**   REJECTION RATE:
ACCEPT WITH REVISION:

THEMATIC ISSUES USED: **Yes**

CIRCULATION

NUMBER: **400+**   FREQUENCY: **Yearly**

CURRENT RATES (INDIVIDUAL): **$18**
(INSTITUTIONAL): **$18**   (ASSOCIATE/STUDENT):

ANNUAL INDEX AVAILABILITY: **No**   COST:
SPECIAL SUPPLEMENTS: **No**   COST:
SUBSCRIPTION ADDRESS: **Michigan State University Press**
1405 Harrison Rd.
25 Manly Miles Bldg.
East Lansing, MI 48823-5202

STYLE/SUBMISSION REQUIREMENTS

STYLE: **Soc. Prac. Ass.**   STYLE SHEET: **Yes**
REVIEW CHARGE: **No**   COST:
NUMBER OF COPIES: **4**   PAGE LIMIT: **Varies**
RESPONSE TO QUERY LETTERS: **Yes**

GENERAL INFORMATION

JOURNAL TITLE: **SOCIOLOGICAL SPECTRUM**

MANUSCRIPT ADDRESS: **P.O. Drawer E**
Missisippi State, MS 39762

TYPE OF ARTICLES: **Research; reviews; theoretical**

MAJOR CONTENT AREAS: **General sociology**

TOPICS PREFERRED: **Wide range**

REVIEW PERIOD: **3-5 mo**   EARLY PUB OPTION: **No**
PUBLICATION LAG TIME: **>6 mo**

ACCEPT WITHOUT REVISION: **5%**   REJECTION RATE: **40%**
ACCEPT WITH REVISION: **55%**

THEMATIC ISSUES USED: **Yes**

CIRCULATION

NUMBER: **500**   FREQUENCY: **Quarterly**

CURRENT RATES (INDIVIDUAL): **$42**
(INSTITUTIONAL): **$85**   (ASSOCIATE/STUDENT):

ANNUAL INDEX AVAILABILITY: **Yes**   COST:
SPECIAL SUPPLEMENTS: **No**   COST:
SUBSCRIPTION ADDRESS: **Hemishpere Publishing**
1900 Frost Rd., Suite 101
Bristol, PA 19007

STYLE/SUBMISSION REQUIREMENTS

STYLE: **APA**   STYLE SHEET: **Yes**
REVIEW CHARGE: **Yes**   COST: **$10**
NUMBER OF COPIES: **Orig + 3**   PAGE LIMIT: **None**
RESPONSE TO QUERY LETTERS: **In limited cases**

GENERAL INFORMATION

JOURNAL TITLE: **SOCIOLOGICAL THEORY**

MANUSCRIPT ADDRESS: **Alan Siza, Editor**
Department of Sociology
Frazer 716
University of Kansas
Lawrence, KS 66045

TYPE OF ARTICLES: **Theoretical**

MAJOR CONTENT AREAS: **Substantive theories; history; metatheory;**
formal theory construction; synthesis of existing
bodies of theories
TOPICS PREFERRED: **All areas of sociological theory**

REVIEW PERIOD: EARLY PUB OPTION:
PUBLICATION LAG TIME:

ACCEPT WITHOUT REVISION: REJECTION RATE:
ACCEPT WITH REVISION:

THEMATIC ISSUES USED:

CIRCULATION

NUMBER: FREQUENCY: **2 X yr**

CURRENT RATES (INDIVIDUAL): **$25**
(INSTITUTIONAL): **$34**   (ASSOCIATE/STUDENT): **$47**

ANNUAL INDEX AVAILABILITY: COST:
SPECIAL SUPPLEMENTS: COST:
SUBSCRIPTION ADDRESS: **American Sociological Association**
1722 N. Street, NW
Washington, DC 20036

STYLE/SUBMISSION REQUIREMENTS

STYLE: **Harvard**   STYLE SHEET:
REVIEW CHARGE: **Yes**   COST: **$15**
NUMBER OF COPIES: **4**   PAGE LIMIT:
RESPONSE TO QUERY LETTERS:

GENERAL INFORMATION

JOURNAL TITLE: **SOCIOLOGY**

MANUSCRIPT ADDRESS: **Larry Ray & Alan Warde**
Department of Sociology
University of Lancaster
Lancaster, LA14YW, U.K.

TYPE OF ARTICLES:

MAJOR CONTENT AREAS:

TOPICS PREFERRED:

REVIEW PERIOD: EARLY PUB OPTION:
PUBLICATION LAG TIME:

ACCEPT WITHOUT REVISION: REJECTION RATE:
ACCEPT WITH REVISION:

THEMATIC ISSUES USED:

CIRCULATION

NUMBER: FREQUENCY:

CURRENT RATES (INDIVIDUAL): **£25.00**
(INSTITUTIONAL): **£53.00**   (ASSOCIATE/STUDENT):

ANNUAL INDEX AVAILABILITY: COST:
SPECIAL SUPPLEMENTS: COST:
SUBSCRIPTION ADDRESS: **Business Manager**
351 Stanton Road
Dorridge, Solihull
W. Midlands B938E4, U.K.

STYLE/SUBMISSION REQUIREMENTS

STYLE: STYLE SHEET:
REVIEW CHARGE: COST:
NUMBER OF COPIES: PAGE LIMIT:
RESPONSE TO QUERY LETTERS:

GENERAL INFORMATION

JOURNAL TITLE: **SOCIOLOGY AND SOCIAL RESEARCH: AN INTERNATIONAL JOURNAL**

MANUSCRIPT ADDRESS: **Office of the Managing Editor**
Sociology and Social Research
University of Southern California
Los Angeles, CA 90089-2539

TYPE OF ARTICLES: **Research-prefer quantitative studies**

MAJOR CONTENT AREAS: **Detailed research on original projects in all areas of sociology**

TOPICS PREFERRED: **Relevant to today's subjects of interest**

REVIEW PERIOD: **<2 mo**   EARLY PUB OPTION: **No**
PUBLICATION LAG TIME: **3-5 mo**

ACCEPT WITHOUT REVISION: **5%**   REJECTION RATE: **75%**
ACCEPT WITH REVISION: **20%**

THEMATIC ISSUES USED: **No**

CIRCULATION

NUMBER: **2500**   FREQUENCY: **Quarterly**

CURRENT RATES (INDIVIDUAL): **$40**
(INSTITUTIONAL): **$60**   (ASSOCIATE/STUDENT):

ANNUAL INDEX AVAILABILITY: **Yes**   COST: **July issue**
SPECIAL SUPPLEMENTS: **No**   COST:
SUBSCRIPTION ADDRESS: **Same as above**

STYLE/SUBMISSION REQUIREMENTS

STYLE: **Computer**   STYLE SHEET: **Yes**
REVIEW CHARGE: **Yes**   COST: **$25**
NUMBER OF COPIES: **2**   PAGE LIMIT: **18-20**
RESPONSE TO QUERY LETTERS:

GENERAL INFORMATION

JOURNAL TITLE: **SYMBOLIC INTERACTION**

MANUSCRIPT ADDRESS: **David Maines**
Department of Sociology
Pennsylvania State University
University Park, PA 16802

TYPE OF ARTICLES: **Research**

MAJOR CONTENT AREAS: **Study of human behavior; social life**

TOPICS PREFERRED:

REVIEW PERIOD: EARLY PUB OPTION:
PUBLICATION LAG TIME:

ACCEPT WITHOUT REVISION: REJECTION RATE:
ACCEPT WITH REVISION:

THEMATIC ISSUES USED:

CIRCULATION

NUMBER: FREQUENCY:

CURRENT RATES (INDIVIDUAL):
(INSTITUTIONAL):   (ASSOCIATE/STUDENT):

ANNUAL INDEX AVAILABILITY: COST:
SPECIAL SUPPLEMENTS: COST:
SUBSCRIPTION ADDRESS: **JAI Press, Inc.**
55 Old Post Rd.
P.O. Box 1678
Greenwich, CT 06836-1678

STYLE/SUBMISSION REQUIREMENTS

STYLE: **ASA**   STYLE SHEET:
REVIEW CHARGE: **Yes**   COST: **$10**
NUMBER OF COPIES: **5**   PAGE LIMIT:
RESPONSE TO QUERY LETTERS:

GENERAL INFORMATION

JOURNAL TITLE: **THE AMERICAN JOURNAL OF ART THERAPY**

MANUSCRIPT ADDRESS: **Gladys Agell, Editor**
Vermont College of Norwich University
Montpelier, VT 05602

TYPE OF ARTICLES: **Research; reviews; theoretical; commentaries; case studies; book reviews**

MAJOR CONTENT AREAS:

TOPICS PREFERRED: **Art therapy**

REVIEW PERIOD: **3-5 mo** EARLY PUB OPTION: **No**
PUBLICATION LAG TIME: **3-5 mo**

ACCEPT WITHOUT REVISION: **0%** REJECTION RATE: **20%**
ACCEPT WITH REVISION: **80%**

THEMATIC ISSUES USED:

CIRCULATION

NUMBER: **1900** FREQUENCY: **Quarterly**

CURRENT RATES (INDIVIDUAL): **$27**
(INSTITUTIONAL): **$48** (ASSOCIATE/STUDENT): **$21**

ANNUAL INDEX AVAILABILITY: **Yes** COST: **NA**
SPECIAL SUPPLEMENTS: **No** COST:
SUBSCRIPTION ADDRESS: **The American Journal of Art Therapy**
Vermont College of Norwich University
Montpelier, VT 05602

STYLE/SUBMISSION REQUIREMENTS

STYLE: **APA** STYLE SHEET: **Yes**
REVIEW CHARGE: **No** COST:
NUMBER OF COPIES: **3** PAGE LIMIT: **None**
RESPONSE TO QUERY LETTERS: **Yes**

GENERAL INFORMATION

JOURNAL TITLE: **THE AMERICAN JOURNAL OF ECONOMICS AND SOCIOLOGY**

MANUSCRIPT ADDRESS: **Frank C. Genovese,**
Editor-in-Chief
Babson College
Babson Park, MA 02157

TYPE OF ARTICLES: **Research; case studies (rarely)**

MAJOR CONTENT AREAS: **Interdisciplinary—seeks constructive synthesis in social thought**

TOPICS PREFERRED: **Solutions to challenges society (especially U.S.A.) faces; philosophical and moral aspects of economics; social & political matters**

REVIEW PERIOD: **3-5 mo**　　EARLY PUB OPTION: **No**

PUBLICATION LAG TIME: **>6 mo**

ACCEPT WITHOUT REVISION: **0%**　　REJECTION RATE: **60%**

ACCEPT WITH REVISION: **30%**

THEMATIC ISSUES USED: **No**

CIRCULATION

NUMBER: **2100-3000**　　FREQUENCY: **Quarterly**

CURRENT RATES (INDIVIDUAL): **$25**

(INSTITUTIONAL): **$30**　　(ASSOCIATE/STUDENT):

ANNUAL INDEX AVAILABILITY: **Yes**　　COST: **Last iss.**

SPECIAL SUPPLEMENTS: **No**　　COST:

SUBSCRIPTION ADDRESS: **The American Journal of Economics and Sociology**
41 East 72nd St.
New York, NY 10021

STYLE/SUBMISSION REQUIREMENTS

STYLE: **MLA**　　STYLE SHEET: **No**

REVIEW CHARGE: **No**　　COST:

NUMBER OF COPIES: **3**　　PAGE LIMIT: **25**

RESPONSE TO QUERY LETTERS: **Yes**

GENERAL INFORMATION

JOURNAL TITLE: **THE AMERICAN JOURNAL OF NURSING**

MANUSCRIPT ADDRESS:

TYPE OF ARTICLES:

MAJOR CONTENT AREAS:

TOPICS PREFERRED:

REVIEW PERIOD: EARLY PUB OPTION:
PUBLICATION LAG TIME:

ACCEPT WITHOUT REVISION: REJECTION RATE:
ACCEPT WITH REVISION:

THEMATIC ISSUES USED:

CIRCULATION

NUMBER: FREQUENCY: **Monthly**

CURRENT RATES (INDIVIDUAL): **$30**
(INSTITUTIONAL): **$35**   (ASSOCIATE/STUDENT):

ANNUAL INDEX AVAILABILITY: COST:
SPECIAL SUPPLEMENTS: COST:
SUBSCRIPTION ADDRESS: **The American Journal of Nursing**
Subscriptions
P.O. Box 1726
Riverton, NJ 08077-7326

STYLE/SUBMISSION REQUIREMENTS

STYLE: STYLE SHEET:
REVIEW CHARGE: COST:
NUMBER OF COPIES: PAGE LIMIT:
RESPONSE TO QUERY LETTERS:

GENERAL INFORMATION

JOURNAL TITLE: **THE AUSTRALIAN AND NEW ZEALAND JOURNAL OF FAMILY THERAPY**
MANUSCRIPT ADDRESS: **P.O. Box 633**
Lane Cove NSW
Australia 2066

TYPE OF ARTICLES: **Research; reviews; theoretical; commentaries; book reviews; case studies**
MAJOR CONTENT AREAS: **Therapy using a family-oriented systems theory**

TOPICS PREFERRED: **Material related to the above**

REVIEW PERIOD: **<2 mo**   EARLY PUB OPTION: **Yes**
PUBLICATION LAG TIME: **3-5 mo**

ACCEPT WITHOUT REVISION: **10%**   REJECTION RATE: **30%**
ACCEPT WITH REVISION: **60%**

THEMATIC ISSUES USED: **No**

CIRCULATION

NUMBER: **1500**   FREQUENCY: **Quarterly**

CURRENT RATES (INDIVIDUAL): **$65**
(INSTITUTIONAL): **$82**   (ASSOCIATE/STUDENT):

ANNUAL INDEX AVAILABILITY: **Yes**   COST: **Nil**
SPECIAL SUPPLEMENTS: **No**   COST:
SUBSCRIPTION ADDRESS: **P.O. Box 633**
Lane Cove NSW
Australia 2066

STYLE/SUBMISSION REQUIREMENTS

STYLE: **Specific**   STYLE SHEET: **Yes**
REVIEW CHARGE: **No**   COST:
NUMBER OF COPIES: **3**   PAGE LIMIT: **No**
RESPONSE TO QUERY LETTERS: **Yes**

GENERAL INFORMATION

JOURNAL TITLE: **THE BRITISH JOURNAL OF SOCIOLOGY**

MANUSCRIPT ADDRESS: **Editor**
The London School of Economics
Houghton Street, Aldwych,
London WC2A 2AE, U.K.

TYPE OF ARTICLES: **Wide range of sociological topics rooted in**
theory and scholarly in presentation

MAJOR CONTENT AREAS:

TOPICS PREFERRED:

REVIEW PERIOD: EARLY PUB OPTION:
PUBLICATION LAG TIME:

ACCEPT WITHOUT REVISION: REJECTION RATE: **75%**
ACCEPT WITH REVISION:

THEMATIC ISSUES USED: **Occasionally**

CIRCULATION

NUMBER: FREQUENCY: **Quarterly**

CURRENT RATES (INDIVIDUAL): **$66**
(INSTITUTIONAL): **$88** (ASSOCIATE/STUDENT):

ANNUAL INDEX AVAILABILITY: COST:
SPECIAL SUPPLEMENTS: COST:
SUBSCRIPTION ADDRESS: **Routledge**
11 Newfetter Lane
London EC4P 4EE, U.K.

STYLE/SUBMISSION REQUIREMENTS

STYLE: **JS** STYLE SHEET: **In each issue**
REVIEW CHARGE: COST:
NUMBER OF COPIES: **3** PAGE LIMIT: **7500 words**
RESPONSE TO QUERY LETTERS: **Immediate**

GENERAL INFORMATION

JOURNAL TITLE: **THE COUNSELING PSYCHOLOGIST**

MANUSCRIPT ADDRESS: **Bruce R. Fretz, Editor**
Dept. of Psychology
University of Maryland
College Park, MD 20742

TYPE OF ARTICLES: **Major articles or set of articles in a specific theme of importance to the theory, research, and practice of counseling psychology**

MAJOR CONTENT AREAS:

TOPICS PREFERRED:

REVIEW PERIOD: EARLY PUB OPTION:
PUBLICATION LAG TIME:

ACCEPT WITHOUT REVISION: REJECTION RATE:
ACCEPT WITH REVISION:

THEMATIC ISSUES USED: **Yes**

CIRCULATION

NUMBER: FREQUENCY: **Quarterly**

CURRENT RATES (INDIVIDUAL): **$35**
(INSTITUTIONAL): **$98**   (ASSOCIATE/STUDENT):

ANNUAL INDEX AVAILABILITY: COST:
SPECIAL SUPPLEMENTS: COST:
SUBSCRIPTION ADDRESS: Sage Publications Inc.
2455 Teller Rd.
Newbury Park, CA 91320

STYLE/SUBMISSION REQUIREMENTS

STYLE: **APA**   STYLE SHEET:
REVIEW CHARGE: COST:
NUMBER OF COPIES: **4**   PAGE LIMIT:
RESPONSE TO QUERY LETTERS:

GENERAL INFORMATION

JOURNAL TITLE: **THE ECONOMIC AND SOCIAL REVIEW**

MANUSCRIPT ADDRESS: **Dr. Patrick Clancy**
Department of Sociology
University College
Belfield, Dublin 4
Ireland

TYPE OF ARTICLES: **Theoretical; research; applied**

MAJOR CONTENT AREAS: **All areas of social science**

TOPICS PREFERRED:

REVIEW PERIOD: EARLY PUB OPTION:
PUBLICATION LAG TIME:

ACCEPT WITHOUT REVISION: REJECTION RATE:
ACCEPT WITH REVISION:

THEMATIC ISSUES USED:

CIRCULATION

NUMBER: FREQUENCY: **Quarterly**

CURRENT RATES (INDIVIDUAL): **$35**
(INSTITUTIONAL): **$50**   (ASSOCIATE/STUDENT):

ANNUAL INDEX AVAILABILITY: **Yes**   COST: **None**
SPECIAL SUPPLEMENTS: COST:
SUBSCRIPTION ADDRESS: **Mr. John Roughan, Secretary**
Economic and Social Studies
4 Burlington Rd.
Dublin 4 Ireland

STYLE/SUBMISSION REQUIREMENTS

STYLE: STYLE SHEET:
REVIEW CHARGE: COST:
NUMBER OF COPIES: **3**   PAGE LIMIT: **9000 words**
RESPONSE TO QUERY LETTERS:

GENERAL INFORMATION

JOURNAL TITLE: **THE FAMILY THERAPY NETWORKER**

MANUSCRIPT ADDRESS: **7705 13th St.**
Washington, DC 20012

TYPE OF ARTICLES: **Research; theoretical; reviews; case studies; commentaries; book reviews**

MAJOR CONTENT AREAS: **Each issue has a theme with a main "umbrella" piece and related features and sidebars; fiction; practice**

TOPICS PREFERRED: **Anything family related or pertaining to the field is relevant**

REVIEW PERIOD: **3-5 mo**   EARLY PUB OPTION: **No**
PUBLICATION LAG TIME: **Varies**

ACCEPT WITHOUT REVISION: REJECTION RATE:
ACCEPT WITH REVISION:

THEMATIC ISSUES USED: **Yes**

CIRCULATION

NUMBER: **40,000**   FREQUENCY: **Bimonthly**

CURRENT RATES (INDIVIDUAL): **$20**
(INSTITUTIONAL): **$26**   (ASSOCIATE/STUDENT):

ANNUAL INDEX AVAILABILITY: **No**   COST:
SPECIAL SUPPLEMENTS: **No**   COST:
SUBSCRIPTION ADDRESS: **8528 Bradford Rd.**
Silver Spring, MD 20901

STYLE/SUBMISSION REQUIREMENTS

STYLE: **Chicago**   STYLE SHEET: **No**
REVIEW CHARGE: **No**   COST:
NUMBER OF COPIES: **3**   PAGE LIMIT: **3000 words**
RESPONSE TO QUERY LETTERS: **Yes**

GENERAL INFORMATION

JOURNAL TITLE: **THE GERONTOLOGIST**

MANUSCRIPT ADDRESS: **Rosalie A. Kane, Editor-in-Chief**
School of Public Health
University of Minnesota
420 Delaware St., SE
Box 197
Minneapolis, MN 55455

TYPE OF ARTICLES:

MAJOR CONTENT AREAS: **All areas of multidisciplinary focus pertaining to practice and applied research**

TOPICS PREFERRED: **Practice concepts; program evaluation; training and education; the humanities**

REVIEW PERIOD: EARLY PUB OPTION:
PUBLICATION LAG TIME:

ACCEPT WITHOUT REVISION: REJECTION RATE:
ACCEPT WITH REVISION:

THEMATIC ISSUES USED:

CIRCULATION

NUMBER: FREQUENCY: **Bimonthly**

CURRENT RATES (INDIVIDUAL): **$45**
(INSTITUTIONAL): **$75**   (ASSOCIATE/STUDENT):

ANNUAL INDEX AVAILABILITY: COST:
SPECIAL SUPPLEMENTS: COST:
SUBSCRIPTION ADDRESS: **The Gerontological Society of America**
Department 5018
Washington, DC 20061-5018

STYLE/SUBMISSION REQUIREMENTS

STYLE: **APA**   STYLE SHEET:
REVIEW CHARGE: COST:
NUMBER OF COPIES: **4**   PAGE LIMIT: **10-20**
RESPONSE TO QUERY LETTERS:

GENERAL INFORMATION

JOURNAL TITLE: **THE HOSPICE JOURNAL**

MANUSCRIPT ADDRESS: **Madalon O'Rawe Amenta, RN, DPH, Editor**
Associate Professor of Nursing
5512 Northumberland Street
Pittsburgh, PA 15217

TYPE OF ARTICLES: **Research; reviews; theoretical; case studies;**
book reviews

MAJOR CONTENT AREAS: **Hospice care and its component disciplines;**
spiritual care; family aspects; home care; acute
care; pain control; bereavement; etc.
TOPICS PREFERRED: **Do not discriminate**

REVIEW PERIOD: **3-5 mo**   EARLY PUB OPTION: **No**
PUBLICATION LAG TIME: **6 mo or more**

ACCEPT WITHOUT REVISION: **10%**   REJECTION RATE: **50%**
ACCEPT WITH REVISION: **40%**

THEMATIC ISSUES USED: **Yes**

CIRCULATION

NUMBER: **2619**   FREQUENCY: **Quarterly**

CURRENT RATES (INDIVIDUAL): **$35**
(INSTITUTIONAL): **$60**   (ASSOCIATE/STUDENT):

ANNUAL INDEX AVAILABILITY: **No**   COST:
SPECIAL SUPPLEMENTS: **No**   COST:
SUBSCRIPTION ADDRESS: **The Haworth Press, Inc.**
10 Alice Street
Binghamton, NY 13904-1580

STYLE/SUBMISSION REQUIREMENTS

STYLE: **APA or AMA**   STYLE SHEET: **No**
REVIEW CHARGE: **No**   COST:
NUMBER OF COPIES: **3 + diskette**   PAGE LIMIT: **25**
RESPONSE TO QUERY LETTERS: **Yes**

GENERAL INFORMATION

JOURNAL TITLE: **THE IRISH JOURNAL OF PSYCHOLOGY**

MANUSCRIPT ADDRESS: **Editor, IJP**
Department of psychology
25 Westland Row
Trinity College
Dublin 2, Ireland

TYPE OF ARTICLES: **Research; reviews; theoretical; commentaries;**
book reviews; case studies
MAJOR CONTENT AREAS: **Psychology-all aspects**

TOPICS PREFERRED: **Any**

REVIEW PERIOD: **3-5 mo**   EARLY PUB OPTION: **No**
PUBLICATION LAG TIME: **3-5 mo**

ACCEPT WITHOUT REVISION: **10%**   REJECTION RATE: **30%**
ACCEPT WITH REVISION: **60%**

THEMATIC ISSUES USED: **Yes**

CIRCULATION

NUMBER: **900**   FREQUENCY: **Quarterly**

CURRENT RATES (INDIVIDUAL): **IR£ 40**
(INSTITUTIONAL): **IR£ 40**   (ASSOCIATE/STUDENT):

ANNUAL INDEX AVAILABILITY: **No**   COST:
SPECIAL SUPPLEMENTS: **No**   COST:
SUBSCRIPTION ADDRESS: **Same as above**

STYLE/SUBMISSION REQUIREMENTS

STYLE: **APA**   STYLE SHEET: **No**
REVIEW CHARGE: **No**   COST:
NUMBER OF COPIES: **3**   PAGE LIMIT: **25**
RESPONSE TO QUERY LETTERS: **Yes**

GENERAL INFORMATION

JOURNAL TITLE: **THE JOURNAL OF CONSUMER AFFAIRS**

MANUSCRIPT ADDRESS: **Carole J. Makela**
164 Aylesworth Hall
Colorado State University
Fort Collins, CO 80523

TYPE OF ARTICLES: **Research; review; theoretical; case studies;**
commentaries; book reviews
MAJOR CONTENT AREAS: **Consumer policy; consumer education;**
consumer behavior

TOPICS PREFERRED: **All the above with clearly stated implications for**
the consumer interest

REVIEW PERIOD: **3-5 mo**   EARLY PUB OPTION: **No**
PUBLICATION LAG TIME: **>6 mo**

ACCEPT WITHOUT REVISION: **5%**   REJECTION RATE: **65%**
ACCEPT WITH REVISION: **30%**

THEMATIC ISSUES USED: **No**

CIRCULATION

NUMBER: **1750**   FREQUENCY: **2 X yr**

CURRENT RATES (INDIVIDUAL): **$50**
(INSTITUTIONAL): **$80**   (ASSOCIATE/STUDENT): **$20**

ANNUAL INDEX AVAILABILITY: **No**   COST:
SPECIAL SUPPLEMENTS: **No**   COST:
SUBSCRIPTION ADDRESS: **American Council on Consumer Interests**
240 Stanley Hall
University of Missouri
Columbia, MO 65211

STYLE/SUBMISSION REQUIREMENTS

STYLE: **APA**   STYLE SHEET: **Yes**
REVIEW CHARGE: **Yes**   COST: **$20**
NUMBER OF COPIES: **3**   PAGE LIMIT: **6000 words**
RESPONSE TO QUERY LETTERS: **Yes**

GENERAL INFORMATION

JOURNAL TITLE: **THE JOURNAL OF FAMILY MEDICINE**

MANUSCRIPT ADDRESS: **Department of Family Medicine**
Medical College of Georgia
Augusta, GA 30911

TYPE OF ARTICLES: **Research; review; commentaries; book reviews**

MAJOR CONTENT AREAS: **Clinical medicine; behavioral medicine**

TOPICS PREFERRED: **Relevant to family physicians**

REVIEW PERIOD: **<2 mo**   EARLY PUB OPTION: **No**
PUBLICATION LAG TIME: **3-5 mo**

ACCEPT WITHOUT REVISION: **10%**   REJECTION RATE: **75%**
ACCEPT WITH REVISION: **15%**

THEMATIC ISSUES USED: **No**

CIRCULATION

NUMBER: **78,000**   FREQUENCY: **Monthly**

CURRENT RATES (INDIVIDUAL):
(INSTITUTIONAL):   (ASSOCIATE/STUDENT):

ANNUAL INDEX AVAILABILITY: **Yes/biannual**   COST: **N/A**
SPECIAL SUPPLEMENTS: **Rarely**   COST:
SUBSCRIPTION ADDRESS:

STYLE/SUBMISSION REQUIREMENTS

STYLE: **AMA**   STYLE SHEET: **Yes**
REVIEW CHARGE: **No**   COST:
NUMBER OF COPIES: **3**   PAGE LIMIT: **NA**
RESPONSE TO QUERY LETTERS: **In limited cases**

GENERAL INFORMATION

JOURNAL TITLE: **THE JOURNAL OF RELIGION IN PSYCHOTHERAPY**

MANUSCRIPT ADDRESS: **William M. Clements, Ph.D.**
Professor of Pastoral Care and Counseling
School of Theology at Claremont
1325 N. College Ave.
Claremont, CA 91711-3199

TYPE OF ARTICLES: **Research; reviews; theoretical; commentaries; book reviews; case studies**

MAJOR CONTENT AREAS: **Intersections formed between religion (broadly conceived), psychotherapy and a disciplinary orientation such as psychiatry, psychology, marriage and family therapy, pastoral counseling**

TOPICS PREFERRED:

REVIEW PERIOD: **3-5 mo**   EARLY PUB OPTION: **Yes**
PUBLICATION LAG TIME: **3-5 mo**

ACCEPT WITHOUT REVISION: REJECTION RATE:
ACCEPT WITH REVISION:

THEMATIC ISSUES USED: **Yes**

CIRCULATION

NUMBER: FREQUENCY: **Quarterly**

CURRENT RATES (INDIVIDUAL): **$24**
(INSTITUTIONAL): **$32**   (ASSOCIATE/STUDENT):

ANNUAL INDEX AVAILABILITY: **No**   COST:
SPECIAL SUPPLEMENTS: COST:
SUBSCRIPTION ADDRESS: **The Haworth Press, Inc.**
10 Alice St.
Binghamton, NY 13904-1580

STYLE/SUBMISSION REQUIREMENTS

STYLE: **APA**   STYLE SHEET: **Yes**
REVIEW CHARGE: **No**   COST:
NUMBER OF COPIES: **3 + diskette**   PAGE LIMIT: **25**
RESPONSE TO QUERY LETTERS: **Telephone queries**

GENERAL INFORMATION

JOURNAL TITLE: **THE JOURNAL OF RELIGIOUS GERONTOLOGY**

MANUSCRIPT ADDRESS: **William M. Clements, Ph.D.**
Professor of Pastoral Care and Counseling
School of Theology at Claremont
1325 N. College Ave.
Claremont, CA 91711-3199

TYPE OF ARTICLES: **Research; reviews; theoretical; commentaries; book reviews**

MAJOR CONTENT AREAS: **Intersections formed between religion and human aging and another discipline such as history, marriage and family, and sociology**

TOPICS PREFERRED:

REVIEW PERIOD: **3-5 mo**   EARLY PUB OPTION: **Yes**
PUBLICATION LAG TIME: **>6 mo**

ACCEPT WITHOUT REVISION: **10%**   REJECTION RATE: **10%**
ACCEPT WITH REVISION: **80%**

THEMATIC ISSUES USED: **Yes**

CIRCULATION

NUMBER: FREQUENCY: **Quarterly**

CURRENT RATES (INDIVIDUAL): **$32**
(INSTITUTIONAL): **$40**   (ASSOCIATE/STUDENT):

ANNUAL INDEX AVAILABILITY: **No**   COST:
SPECIAL SUPPLEMENTS: **No**   COST:
SUBSCRIPTION ADDRESS: **The Haworth Press, Inc.**
10 Alice St.
Binghamton, NY 13904-1580

STYLE/SUBMISSION REQUIREMENTS

STYLE: **Chicago**   STYLE SHEET: **Yes**
REVIEW CHARGE: **No**   COST:
NUMBER OF COPIES: **3 + diskette**   PAGE LIMIT: **20**
RESPONSE TO QUERY LETTERS: **Telephone queries**

GENERAL INFORMATION

JOURNAL TITLE: **THE JOURNAL OF SEX RESEARCH**

MANUSCRIPT ADDRESS: **Paul R. Abramson, Ph.D., Editor**
Department of Psychology
UCLA
Los Angeles, CA 90024-1563

TYPE OF ARTICLES: **Research, review, theoretical, case studies**

MAJOR CONTENT AREAS: **Multidisciplinary; all research relevant to human sexual behavior**
TOPICS PREFERRED: **Any relevant to human sexual behavior**

REVIEW PERIOD: **3-5 mo**   EARLY PUB OPTION: **No**
PUBLICATION LAG TIME: **6 mo**

ACCEPT WITHOUT REVISION: **5%**   REJECTION RATE: **80%**
ACCEPT WITH REVISION: **15%**

THEMATIC ISSUES USED: **Occasionally, with formal proposal to editor**

CIRCULATION

NUMBER: **1600**   FREQUENCY: **Quarterly**
CURRENT RATES (INDIVIDUAL): **$47**
(INSTITUTIONAL): **$74**   (ASSOCIATE/STUDENT):

ANNUAL INDEX AVAILABILITY: **No**   COST:
SPECIAL SUPPLEMENTS: **No**   COST:
SUBSCRIPTION ADDRESS: **Society for the Scientific Study of Sex, Inc.**
Box 208
Mt. Vernon, IA 52314

STYLE/SUBMISSION REQUIREMENTS

STYLE: **APA**   STYLE SHEET: **No**
REVIEW CHARGE: **No**   COST:
NUMBER OF COPIES: **4**   PAGE LIMIT: **40**
RESPONSE TO QUERY LETTERS:

GENERAL INFORMATION

JOURNAL TITLE: **THE POLITICAL SCIENCE QUARTERLY**

MANUSCRIPT ADDRESS: **Managing Editor**
475 Riverside Drive, Suite 1274
New York, NY 10115-0012

TYPE OF ARTICLES: **Research**

MAJOR CONTENT AREAS: **Broad political science interest; no theoretical;**
written for the non-specialist

TOPICS PREFERRED:

REVIEW PERIOD: **3-5 mo**   EARLY PUB OPTION: **No**
PUBLICATION LAG TIME: **>6 mo**

ACCEPT WITHOUT REVISION: **<5%**   REJECTION RATE: **85%**
ACCEPT WITH REVISION: **10%**

THEMATIC ISSUES USED: **No**

CIRCULATION

NUMBER: **10,000**   FREQUENCY: **Quarterly**

CURRENT RATES (INDIVIDUAL): **$32**
(INSTITUTIONAL): **$50**   (ASSOCIATE/STUDENT): **$21**

ANNUAL INDEX AVAILABILITY: **Yes**   COST: **None**
SPECIAL SUPPLEMENTS: **No**   COST:
SUBSCRIPTION ADDRESS: **475 Silverside Drive, Suite 1274**
New York, NY 10115-0012

STYLE/SUBMISSION REQUIREMENTS

STYLE: **Chicago**   STYLE SHEET: **Yes**
REVIEW CHARGE: **No**   COST:
NUMBER OF COPIES: **3**   PAGE LIMIT: **40**
RESPONSE TO QUERY LETTERS: **Yes**

GENERAL INFORMATION

JOURNAL TITLE: **THE PSYCHOANALYTIC STUDY OF THE CHILD**

MANUSCRIPT ADDRESS: **Albert J. Solnir, M.D.,Managing Editor**
P.O. Box 3333
New Haven, CT 06510

TYPE OF ARTICLES: **Research; reviews; theoretical; case studies**

MAJOR CONTENT AREAS: **Psychoanalysis; theoretical and clinical, with an emphasis on developmental aspects**

TOPICS PREFERRED:

REVIEW PERIOD: **3-5 mo**   EARLY PUB OPTION: **No**
PUBLICATION LAG TIME: **This is an annual publication**

ACCEPT WITHOUT REVISION: REJECTION RATE: **66%**
ACCEPT WITH REVISION: **All are offered editing suggestions**

THEMATIC ISSUES USED: **Yes**

CIRCULATION

NUMBER: **7500-8500**   FREQUENCY: **Yearly**

CURRENT RATES (INDIVIDUAL): **$55**
(INSTITUTIONAL):   (ASSOCIATE/STUDENT):

ANNUAL INDEX AVAILABILITY: **No**   COST:
SPECIAL SUPPLEMENTS: COST:
SUBSCRIPTION ADDRESS: **Yale University Press**
92A Yale Station
New Haven, CT 06520

STYLE/SUBMISSION REQUIREMENTS

STYLE: **Yale U. Press**   STYLE SHEET: **Yes**
REVIEW CHARGE: **No**   COST:
NUMBER OF COPIES: **7**   PAGE LIMIT: **15-50**
RESPONSE TO QUERY LETTERS: **Yes**

GENERAL INFORMATION

JOURNAL TITLE: **THE PSYCHOLOGICAL RECORD**

MANUSCRIPT ADDRESS: **Kenyon College**
Gambier, OH 43022

TYPE OF ARTICLES: **Research; theoretical; book reviews**

MAJOR CONTENT AREAS: **Psychology topics**

TOPICS PREFERRED: **Research**

REVIEW PERIOD: **<2 mo**   EARLY PUB OPTION: **No**
PUBLICATION LAG TIME: **3-5 mo**

ACCEPT WITHOUT REVISION: **1%**   REJECTION RATE: **50%**
ACCEPT WITH REVISION: **50%**

THEMATIC ISSUES USED: **Yes**

CIRCULATION

NUMBER: **1300**   FREQUENCY: **Quarterly**

CURRENT RATES (INDIVIDUAL): **$15**
(INSTITUTIONAL): **$45**   (ASSOCIATE/STUDENT): **$10**

ANNUAL INDEX AVAILABILITY: **No**   COST:
SPECIAL SUPPLEMENTS: **No**   COST:
SUBSCRIPTION ADDRESS: **Psychological Record**
Kenyon College
Gambier, OH 43022

STYLE/SUBMISSION REQUIREMENTS

STYLE: **APA**   STYLE SHEET: **No**
REVIEW CHARGE: **No**   COST:
NUMBER OF COPIES: **3**   PAGE LIMIT: **Open**
RESPONSE TO QUERY LETTERS: **No**

GENERAL INFORMATION

JOURNAL TITLE: **THE SOCIAL STUDIES**

MANUSCRIPT ADDRESS: **Managing Editor**
The Social Studies
4000 Albemarle St., NW
Washington, DC 20016

TYPE OF ARTICLES:

MAJOR CONTENT AREAS: **Social studies; social sciences; history;**
interdisciplinary studies

TOPICS PREFERRED: **Curriculum; learning; historical; social science**
ideas; perspectives on social studies; topics of
current interest

REVIEW PERIOD: EARLY PUB OPTION:
PUBLICATION LAG TIME:

ACCEPT WITHOUT REVISION: REJECTION RATE:
ACCEPT WITH REVISION:

THEMATIC ISSUES USED:

CIRCULATION

NUMBER: FREQUENCY: **Bimonthly**

CURRENT RATES (INDIVIDUAL): **$39**
(INSTITUTIONAL):   (ASSOCIATE/STUDENT):

ANNUAL INDEX AVAILABILITY: COST:
SPECIAL SUPPLEMENTS: COST:
SUBSCRIPTION ADDRESS: **Heldref Publications**
(Same as above)

STYLE/SUBMISSION REQUIREMENTS

STYLE: **Chicago**   STYLE SHEET:
REVIEW CHARGE: COST:
NUMBER OF COPIES: **2**   PAGE LIMIT: **3000 words**
RESPONSE TO QUERY LETTERS:

GENERAL INFORMATION

JOURNAL TITLE: **THE SOCIOLOGICAL QUARTERLY**

MANUSCRIPT ADDRESS: **George McCall**
Department of Sociology
University of Missouri
St. Louis, MO 63121

TYPE OF ARTICLES: **Articles relevant to the advancement of sociological theory and research**

MAJOR CONTENT AREAS: **Any topic germaine to the field of sociology is a possible publication**

TOPICS PREFERRED:

REVIEW PERIOD: EARLY PUB OPTION:
PUBLICATION LAG TIME:

ACCEPT WITHOUT REVISION: REJECTION RATE:
ACCEPT WITH REVISION:

THEMATIC ISSUES USED:

CIRCULATION

NUMBER: FREQUENCY: **Quarterly**

CURRENT RATES (INDIVIDUAL): **On**
(INSTITUTIONAL): **Request** (ASSOCIATE/STUDENT):

ANNUAL INDEX AVAILABILITY: COST:
SPECIAL SUPPLEMENTS: COST:
SUBSCRIPTION ADDRESS: **JAl Press, Inc.**
55 Old Post Rd- No. 2
P.O. Box 1678
Greenwich, CT 06836-1678

STYLE/SUBMISSION REQUIREMENTS

STYLE: **ASA** STYLE SHEET:
REVIEW CHARGE: **Yes** COST: **$10**
NUMBER OF COPIES: **5** PAGE LIMIT:
RESPONSE TO QUERY LETTERS:

GENERAL INFORMATION

JOURNAL TITLE: **VIOLENCE AND VICTIMS**

MANUSCRIPT ADDRESS: **Dr. Roland Maiuro**
Harborview Mental Health Center
Department of Psychiatry and
Behavioral Sciences
326 Ninth Ave.
Seattle, WA 98104

TYPE OF ARTICLES: **Theoretical; research; policy;**

MAJOR CONTENT AREAS: **Clinical practice with victimization**

TOPICS PREFERRED: **Reports of original research on violence-related**
victimization within and outside family; legal
issues; implications for interven.

REVIEW PERIOD: EARLY PUB OPTION:
PUBLICATION LAG TIME:

ACCEPT WITHOUT REVISION: REJECTION RATE:
ACCEPT WITH REVISION:

THEMATIC ISSUES USED:

CIRCULATION

NUMBER: FREQUENCY: **Quarterly**

CURRENT RATES (INDIVIDUAL): **$34**
(INSTITUTIONAL): **$68**   (ASSOCIATE/STUDENT):

ANNUAL INDEX AVAILABILITY: COST:
SPECIAL SUPPLEMENTS: COST:
SUBSCRIPTION ADDRESS: **Springer Publishing Company**
536 Broadway
New York, NY 10012-3955

STYLE/SUBMISSION REQUIREMENTS

STYLE: **APA**   STYLE SHEET:
REVIEW CHARGE: COST:
NUMBER OF COPIES: **4**   PAGE LIMIT: **30**
RESPONSE TO QUERY LETTERS:

GENERAL INFORMATION

JOURNAL TITLE: **WOMEN & POLITICS**

MANUSCRIPT ADDRESS: **Janet M. Clark, Ph.D., Editor**
Department of Political Science
P.O. Box 3197
University of Wyoming
Laramie, WY 82071

TYPE OF ARTICLES: **Research; reviews; theoretical; case studies;**
book reviews

MAJOR CONTENT AREAS: **Exploration of the impact of gender on power**
relationships within society; the role of women
in politics and political theory
TOPICS PREFERRED: **Theory building regarding women's political**
participation and political and social issues
affecting women
REVIEW PERIOD: **3-5 mo**   EARLY PUB OPTION: **No**
PUBLICATION LAG TIME: **3-5 mo**

ACCEPT WITHOUT REVISION: **2-3%**   REJECTION RATE: **40%**
ACCEPT WITH REVISION: **50-60%**

THEMATIC ISSUES USED: **Yes**

CIRCULATION

NUMBER: **650**   FREQUENCY: **Quarterly**

CURRENT RATES (INDIVIDUAL): **$32**
(INSTITUTIONAL): **$90**   (ASSOCIATE/STUDENT):

ANNUAL INDEX AVAILABILITY: **No**   COST:
SPECIAL SUPPLEMENTS: **Yes**   COST:
SUBSCRIPTION ADDRESS: **The Haworth Press, Inc.**
10 Alice St.
Binghamton, NY 13904-1580

STYLE/SUBMISSION REQUIREMENTS

STYLE: **AmerPolSciRev**   STYLE SHEET: **No**
REVIEW CHARGE: **No**   COST:
NUMBER OF COPIES: **4 + diskette**   PAGE LIMIT: **20**
RESPONSE TO QUERY LETTERS: **Yes**

GENERAL INFORMATION

JOURNAL TITLE: **WOMEN AND THERAPY**

MANUSCRIPT ADDRESS: **Esther D. Rothblum, PhD, Co-Editor**
Department of Psychology
John Dewey Hall
University of Vermont
Burlington, VT 05405

TYPE OF ARTICLES: **Research; theoretical; case studies;**
commentaries

MAJOR CONTENT AREAS: **Women in therapy; women's mental health**

TOPICS PREFERRED:

REVIEW PERIOD: **3-5 mo**   EARLY PUB OPTION: **No**
PUBLICATION LAG TIME: **>6 mo**

ACCEPT WITHOUT REVISION: **2%**   REJECTION RATE: **60%**
ACCEPT WITH REVISION: **38%**

THEMATIC ISSUES USED: **Yes**

CIRCULATION

NUMBER: **1000**   FREQUENCY: **Quarterly**

CURRENT RATES (INDIVIDUAL): **$36**
(INSTITUTIONAL): **$75**   (ASSOCIATE/STUDENT):

ANNUAL INDEX AVAILABILITY: **No**   COST:
SPECIAL SUPPLEMENTS: **No**   COST:
SUBSCRIPTION ADDRESS: **The Haworth Press, Inc.**
10 Alice St.
Binghamton, NY 13905-1580

STYLE/SUBMISSION REQUIREMENTS

STYLE: **APA**   STYLE SHEET: **Yes**
REVIEW CHARGE: **No**   COST:
NUMBER OF COPIES: **3 + diskette**   PAGE LIMIT: **12-20**
RESPONSE TO QUERY LETTERS: **Yes**

GENERAL INFORMATION

JOURNAL TITLE: **WOMEN'S STUDIES**

MANUSCRIPT ADDRESS: **Wendy Martin, Editor**
Dept. of English
Queen's College
CUNY
Flushing, NY 11367

TYPE OF ARTICLES:

MAJOR CONTENT AREAS: **Scholarly discussion about women in the fields of literature, art, sociology, law, anthropology, political science, economics, and the sciences**

TOPICS PREFERRED: **Scholarly papers, poetry, short fiction, film and book reviews**

REVIEW PERIOD: EARLY PUB OPTION:
PUBLICATION LAG TIME:

ACCEPT WITHOUT REVISION: REJECTION RATE:
ACCEPT WITH REVISION:

THEMATIC ISSUES USED:

CIRCULATION

NUMBER: FREQUENCY: **4 X yr**

CURRENT RATES (INDIVIDUAL): **$55**
(INSTITUTIONAL): **$138**   (ASSOCIATE/STUDENT):

ANNUAL INDEX AVAILABILITY: COST:
SPECIAL SUPPLEMENTS: COST:
SUBSCRIPTION ADDRESS: **Gordon & Breach**
c/o STBS Ltd.
1 Bedford St.
London WC2E 9PP, England, U.K.

STYLE/SUBMISSION REQUIREMENTS

STYLE: **MLA**   STYLE SHEET: **Yes**
REVIEW CHARGE: COST:
NUMBER OF COPIES: **3**   PAGE LIMIT: **60**
RESPONSE TO QUERY LETTERS:

GENERAL INFORMATION

JOURNAL TITLE: **WOMEN'S STUDIES QUARTERLY**

MANUSCRIPT ADDRESS: **WSQ/The Feminist Press**
311 E. 94th St.
New York, NY 10128

TYPE OF ARTICLES: **Research; reviews; theoretical; case studies;**
commentaries; book reviews
MAJOR CONTENT AREAS: **Feminist pedagogy and different areas of**
women's studies; generally, issues are thematic

TOPICS PREFERRED: **Intersections of race & class**

REVIEW PERIOD: **3-5 mo**   EARLY PUB OPTION: **No**
PUBLICATION LAG TIME: **3-5 mo**

ACCEPT WITHOUT REVISION: REJECTION RATE:
ACCEPT WITH REVISION:

THEMATIC ISSUES USED: **Yes**

CIRCULATION

NUMBER: **2500**   FREQUENCY: **2 X yr**

CURRENT RATES (INDIVIDUAL): **$25**
(INSTITUTIONAL): **$35**   (ASSOCIATE/STUDENT):

ANNUAL INDEX AVAILABILITY: **No**   COST:
SPECIAL SUPPLEMENTS: **No**   COST:
SUBSCRIPTION ADDRESS: **Same as above**

STYLE/SUBMISSION REQUIREMENTS

STYLE: **Chicago**   STYLE SHEET: **No**
REVIEW CHARGE: **No**   COST:
NUMBER OF COPIES: **1**   PAGE LIMIT: **9-20**
RESPONSE TO QUERY LETTERS: **Yes**

GENERAL INFORMATION

JOURNAL TITLE: **WORK AND OCCUPATIONS**

MANUSCRIPT ADDRESS: **Curt Tausky, Editor**
Department of Sociology
University of Massachuesetts
Amherst, MA 01003

TYPE OF ARTICLES:

MAJOR CONTENT AREAS: **Disciplines that provide insight and theoretical advances around the issue of work and occupation**

TOPICS PREFERRED:

REVIEW PERIOD: EARLY PUB OPTION:
PUBLICATION LAG TIME:

ACCEPT WITHOUT REVISION: REJECTION RATE:
ACCEPT WITH REVISION:

THEMATIC ISSUES USED:

CIRCULATION

NUMBER: FREQUENCY: **Quarterly**

CURRENT RATES (INDIVIDUAL): **$34**
(INSTITUTIONAL): **$90**   (ASSOCIATE/STUDENT):

ANNUAL INDEX AVAILABILITY: **Yes**   COST:
SPECIAL SUPPLEMENTS: COST:
SUBSCRIPTION ADDRESS: **Sage Publications, Inc.**
2455 Teller Rd.
Newbury Park, CA 91320

STYLE/SUBMISSION REQUIREMENTS

STYLE: **APA**   STYLE SHEET:
REVIEW CHARGE: COST:
NUMBER OF COPIES: **3**   PAGE LIMIT:
RESPONSE TO QUERY LETTERS:

GENERAL INFORMATION

JOURNAL TITLE: **YOUTH AND SOCIETY**

MANUSCRIPT ADDRESS: **Dr. David Gottlieb, Editor
Department of Sociology
University of Houston
Houston, TX 77004**

TYPE OF ARTICLES:

MAJOR CONTENT AREAS:

TOPICS PREFERRED: **Point out implications and
consequences of findings for social
policy; program development;
institutional functioning**

REVIEW PERIOD: EARLY PUB OPTION:
PUBLICATION LAG TIME:

ACCEPT WITHOUT REVISION: REJECTION RATE:
ACCEPT WITH REVISION:

THEMATIC ISSUES USED:

CIRCULATION

NUMBER: FREQUENCY: **Quarterly**

CURRENT RATES (INDIVIDUAL): **$36**
(INSTITUTIONAL): **$106**   (ASSOCIATE/STUDENT):

ANNUAL INDEX AVAILABILITY: COST:
SPECIAL SUPPLEMENTS: COST:
SUBSCRIPTION ADDRESS: **Sage Publications, Inc.
2455 Teller Rd.
Newbury Park, CA 91320**

STYLE/SUBMISSION REQUIREMENTS

STYLE: **APA**   STYLE SHEET:
REVIEW CHARGE: COST:
NUMBER OF COPIES: **3**   PAGE LIMIT:
RESPONSE TO QUERY LETTERS:

For Product Safety Concerns and Information please contact our EU
representative GPSR@taylorandfrancis.com
Taylor & Francis Verlag GmbH, Kaufingerstraße 24, 80331 München, Germany

www.ingramcontent.com/pod-product-compliance
Lightning Source LLC
Chambersburg PA
CBHW070352270326
41926CB00014B/2510

9 780367 426859